WORTH THEIR SALT

Notable but Often
Unnoted Women of Utah

T0290698

WORTH THEIR SALT

Notable but Often
Unnoted Women of Utah

Edited by Colleen Whitley

UTAH STATE UNIVERSITY PRESS
Logan, Utah
1996

Utah State University Press
Logan, Utah 84322-7800

All royalties from the sale of this book will be donated to support publications and collections of the Utah State Historical Society.

Typeset in TEX from WordPerfect files by The Bartlett Press, Inc.

Library of Congress Cataloging-in Publication Data

Worth their salt: notable but often unnoted women of Utah / edited by Colleen
Whitley.
    p. cm.
    Includes bibliographical references (p.).
    ISBN 0-87421-212-X (hbk.) ISBN 0-87421-206-5 (pbk.)
    1. Women–Utah–Biography. 2. Utah—Biography. I. Whitley, Colleen,
1940– .
CT3260.W68 1996
920.72'09792—dc20
[B]   96-25260
                                                                 CIP

Contents

Preface

This book is a labor of love and curiosity and outrage and humor. It began with a conversation among volunteers for the Utah State Historical Society who discovered that each had identified a woman in Utah history who had been overlooked, neglected, or misrepresented in the past. These present-day Utah women recognized the value of their research and their concern for Utah women from the past and asked me if I would edit their collection of biographies. I have coordinated the project, but from the outset it has been a group effort to take note of women who have too often gone unnoticed.

At an initial meeting of a dozen interested writers, we listed the women each had chosen to study. Then we listed writers and subjects that might also be included in such a venture. As we contacted other writers, we were delighted that they responded not only by sending their own essays, but also by telling others about our book. Consequently, word of this project spread like a web, netting writers we would never have found by ourselves. I was happily surprised, for example, to receive telephone calls from David Pace and Rachelle Castor, asking if we had room for biographies of Maud May Babcock and Maude Adams, two significant forces in American theater. One came to Utah and helped determine the development of theater here while the other grew up in Utah and took her talents out into the world.

All of our acquisitions were not quite so serendipitous, however. It became evident early in the project that we had subjects representing a fairly broad cross-section of wealth, ethnic groups, and time span, but we recognized that some groups were not represented, so we attempted to find authors who might want to investigate those areas. For example, we contacted several authors who had written about Jane James, one of the earliest Black women pioneers in the state, and each gave us the same reply: they had based their research on Henry Wolfinger's monograph. It became evident that Wolfinger was the person to write about James. With the aid of Jeffrey O. Johnson of the Utah State Archives we were able to locate Wolfinger, who graciously updated his biography of Jane James for inclusion in this collection.

Wolfinger's essay developed from his extensive research into nineteenth-century documents and it is a splendid example of research using primary sources. Other writers, however, have used other approaches, determined by their own styles and the materials available. Cheryl Livingston looked for documentary evidence about Rachel Urban, one of Park City's most famous madams and, in the process, assembled a collection of folk tales commonly heard about her. Helen Papanikolas used oral histories and interviews to reconstruct the life of Georgia Lathouris Mageras, "Magerou," the midwife, demonstrating that she was important not only to her own Greek community, but to several other minority communities as well. Carol Van Wagoner introduces us to Elizabeth McCune by providing a tour of her magnificent mansion overlooking Salt Lake City. Donna Smart presents Patty Bartlett Sessions's life with the enormous admiration she has developed for this remarkable pioneer midwife while editing Patty's diaries. Patricia Scott demonstrates that Eliza Kirtley Royle's commitment to the Ladies Literary Club was much more than a hobby or a social gathering; the club helped many women gain influence in public by providing both an education and a platform.

Some authors have studied their subjects for years. Judy Dykman has considered a biography of Susanna Bransford Engalitcheff since she first heard about her several years ago. Judy realized that Susanna—with her four husbands, extensive travel, and flamboyant behavior—was an interesting specimen of the Gilded Age. Some authors have lifetime acquaintances with their subjects. Haruko Moriyasu's account of her mother's career as the publisher of a Japanese language newspaper is presented through both a scholar's eye and a daughter's heart.

Other writers chose to reprint or revise works on women they had identified years earlier as important to the state, and, in many cases, to the nation. Miriam Murphy's discussion of Sarah Elizabeth Carmichael outlines the life and analyzes the work of one of Utah's earliest poets. Harriet Arrington pays tribute to her grandmother, Alice Merrill Horne, who as a teacher, legislator, and patron expanded the availability of fine art to all the citizens of the state. Martha Bradley analyzes the life and work of Mary Teasdel, one of the state's early artists.

While most of the women in this book are virtually unknown to general readers, some may be familiar to one generation or segment of the community but not to others. Stanford J. Layton, Miriam Murphy, and Robert Goldberg present—to a general audience—Ivy Baker Priest, Helen Papanikolas, and Esther Landa, respectively.

Whatever approach the authors have used, our fundamental qualification for inclusion in this work is the same: all of the women presented here lived in and affected Utah. Mother Augusta (Anderson) of the Sisters of the Holy Cross, whose life is outlined by Sister Georgia (Costin), was in Utah for only a few years and only because someone assigned her to come; yet in those few years, she established institutions that still serve citizens of the state. Susan Lyman Whitney's Chipeta, "Queen" of the Utes, did not want to come to Utah at all but was forced onto a reservation here. Whatever their length of residence or their sphere of influence, however, each of these women had an impact on the state and affected the way we live now.

Varied as it is, this collection is by no means exhaustive. We tried to pick women who had relatively little written about them and discovered that there are many such women. We can only mention in passing such important women as civic activists Ada Miller, Janie Montoya, Ada Duhigg, and Ione Bennion; philanthropists Sarah Daft, Jennie Judge Kearns, and Annie Clark Tanner; religious reformers Lucretia Heywood Kimball and Henrietta Young; educator Mary Jane Dillworth; historian Juanita Brooks; and volunteers Marion Clegg and Laura Wells. A few of them have had biographical attention, while others have been wholly neglected. Perhaps another volume will some day give all of them the additional notice they are due. Several truly significant Utah women, from Emmeline Wells to Esther Peterson to May Swenson, are not included, but generally they are better known or have been written about to some extent. Nevertheless, all of these women, and many more, certainly could have been included if space allowed and biographers were available, but no collection could possibly mention all of the significant women who aided Utah's growth in the arts, sciences, and civic works.

What we have, then, is a highly eclectic set of snapshots—brief views of some fascinating lives, each written by someone who cares about her or his subject. Since the defining factor of this work is the emotional as well as the intellectual commitment of the writers, each essay is prefaced with an introduction to the author and a statement explaining why he or she chose to write about a specific individual.

The biographies are arranged chronologically, beginning with the oldest and ending with the youngest. This arrangement in many ways demonstrates the growth of the state. The notes are, in John Livingston Lowes's charming phrase, "securely kenneled in the rear,"[1] arranged by chapters, followed by a bibliography.

I am deeply indebted to many people for helping to bring this book together: first, of course, to that core group of volunteers; most particularly, credit goes to Judy Dykman, who spearheaded the original effort, suggested subjects to be included, and helped to contact authors. Her husband, Jim, offered considerable support, including obtaining most of the photographs used here. Another volunteer, Floralee Millsaps, provided guidance and information for individual authors and recommendations for the book as a whole. Second, the authors themselves deserve great credit. All have provided careful research and thoughtful consideration of their subjects and each wrote for the love of the task at his or her own expense, since we agreed at the outset that any profits would be assigned to the Utah State Historical Society. My husband, Tom, a prime example of user-friendly liveware, assisted greatly in the electronic aspects of production, moving files from Mac to IBM, solving format problems, and correcting the inevitable glitches. Thank you also to Judy Dykman, Marion McCardle, Ann Best, Linda Keith, and Donna Falkenborg for proofreading. Finally, this book would never have come to publication without the support of John Alley of the USU Press, whose boundless patience and excellent advice helped all of us through the process of acknowledging these significant Utah women.

Patty Bartlett Sessions in old age, possibly near the time of her death.
Photo courtesy of the Utah State Historical Society.

Patty Bartlett Sessions
Pioneer Midwife

Donna Toland Smart

Donna Toland Smart received her B.A. from the University of Wyoming and her M.A. from the University of Utah. She taught high school English in Wyoming and Utah. She worked as a technical writer with Dr. Aziz and Lola Aitya at the University of Utah in the preparation and publication of the seven-volume Coptic Encyclopedia. With her husband, William B. Smart, she has traveled extensively. They are the parents of five children and grandparents of twelve.

Smart is currently editing the complete diaries of Patty Bartlett Sessions, a 42-year daily record, beginning in 1846. Though some earlier diaries detailing her life in Maine, the family's travels to join the body of the LDS Church, and their persecutions in Missouri and Nauvoo have been lost, those that remain present the personality of a fascinating woman. Despite the difficulties in reading faded handwriting—inscribed with a pen dipped in homemade ink and covering every inch of most pages—and determining spellings of names and identities of persons, Smart describes her endeavors as follows: "The rewards of her diaries overshadowed her lists of wearisome daily rituals and I have enjoyed an intimate encounter with this remarkable woman. As I traveled the pioneer trail from Nauvoo through her words and through her eyes, I sympathized with the challenges and frustrations of all our emigrant foremothers. And, as I saw the building of the Salt Lake Valley through her eyes, I became more aware of the process that still goes on today."

I have strong opinions about Patty Sessions formed during the tedious process of reading and editing her diaries. As forty-two years of her writing flowed by and words multiplied, predominant character traits emerged, habits and activities created recurring patterns, concealed emotions added color to the portrait, and a more-or-less accurate panorama evolved. At times, I felt intrusive, even found the process painful, but at last became convinced that if Patty possessed enough ego and drive to write with such regularity and intensity, she must have sensed her significance and would condone my reading and analysis of her life. This account offers only a tantalizing glimpse into the life of a complicated, yet straightforward woman.

From the beginning, Patty Bartlett most assuredly saw her life as significant. Born amidst the splendid hardwood forests, the hills, and the rocks of Maine's wilderness, she was the first of nine children her father, Enoch Bartlett, had with his second wife, Anna Hall. What she knew of "readin', writin', and 'rithmetic," she learned in a school in her father's shoemaking shop. Her remarkable work ethics she learned from her father and from her mother, whose weaving skills Patty also picked up and used extensively throughout the near-century she lived.[1]

In 1812, when she was only seventeen, Patty married twenty-two-year-old David Sessions, against her parents' wishes. Enoch and Anna vowed that she would not receive any inheritance from them, a promise they kept, Patty later reported with a hint of bitterness. Yet, though separated by miles and beliefs, she always kept in touch with her family; her diaries make note of family letters she wrote or received and refer especially often to her mother, who lived to be more than one hundred years old.

After her marriage, Patty immediately took upon herself the care of her ailing mother-in-law, Rachel Stevens Sessions. She did not spend time or have time to doubt her ability to leap hurdles. As one example, her husband's midwife mother needed Patty's arm to lean upon when she was summoned to deliver a baby. Setting out afoot, their pathway threaded through the rural, overgrown countryside, and when a breathless runner caught up with them to warn that the birth was imminent, Patty left her feeble mother-in-law and hurried ahead to perform the first of a reputed three thousand and more deliveries.[2]

Thrifty and hard working, the young Patty and David Sessions overcame obstacles of poverty and naiveté, purchased land, and established a comfortable farm in Maine, where Patty bore seven children and buried four of them. When David Sr. and Rachel, David's parents, who were living with them, died, she also helped bury them.

Then, in 1833, missionaries of the Church of Jesus Christ of Latter-day Saints, also known as Mormons, came calling. Patty, inclined to be religious, had joined the Methodist Church in 1816, because as she read the Bible, she believed its injunction regarding baptism. She felt ready, therefore, to accept the message of Mormonism at once, but waited until 1834 for baptism, hoping her husband would also be baptized. She withstood months of taunts and persecution from her neighbors and some of her family members as she was the only Mormon around. It was not until September 1835 that other members of her family were baptized.

At a Mormon Church conference held at the Sessions home in 1836, Brigham Young, along with other church authorities, preached on the importance of the gathering of the Saints. Validating their commitment to their new-found faith, the Sessions family—David and Patty, son Perrigrine and his wife, Julia Ann Kilgore, and their baby, Martha Ann; daughter Sylvia and son David Jr.—disposed of their considerable properties and in June 1837 started for Missouri, where many members of the church were gathering. The journey proved to be a trial. Their route required travel by land and water, on rough trails through harsh, unsettled landscapes and on some relatively decent roads. In Kirtland, they felt blessed to hear the Prophet Joseph Smith preach. An attack of measles delayed them several weeks there, setting back their arrival at Far West, Missouri, to early November.

The trip must have been beyond wearisome for Patty, who, pregnant with another daughter, Amanda, gave birth in Missouri on November 14, 1837. At Far West, they again began to build what they believed would be their permanent homestead.[3] But on October 17, 1838, Governor Lilburn W. Boggs issued an "Extermination Order," directing the Missouri militia to drive the Mormons from the state or exterminate them.[4] Following those orders, mobs forced the Sessions family to escape from Far West in February 1839, leading to another difficult journey. Patty and Perrigrine,[5] who also kept a diary on their journey, described that ordeal: the bitter cold of winter, the necessity of tenting along the way, waiting for river ice to melt and allow passage across by boat, the wearing of shoes to shreds, dealing with severe sickness, which undoubtedly also contributed to the premature death in Nauvoo of Perrigrine's wife, Julia. Carrying her ailing eighteen-month-old daughter, Amanda, Patty walked the entire distance. Amanda died May 15, 1841 and was buried in Nauvoo, Illinois.

After settling in Carthage, Illinois, temporarily, they moved to Nauvoo in May 1840, where they settled again and built another home.[6] Surely they must have thought—once again—that this would be where they would live and die. They did, indeed, participate in raising "Nauvoo the Beautiful" from the swamplands of the Mississippi. Living near their prophet rewarded them for their earlier sacrifices. The series of unsigned biographical sketches in the *Women's Exponent* includes quotations from missing early journals in which Patty talks of close associations with the Prophet Joseph Smith and his family. In a sacred ceremony on March 9, 1842, Patty was sealed, as a plural wife, for "time and all eternity" to Smith.[7] Of course, his martyrdom ended that relationship and foreshadowed yet another desperate dislocation—to Winter Quarters and then to the valley of the Great Salt Lake in the Big Company of 1847.[8] Their hope had to be that the Rocky Mountains would shield all the Saints from a hostile world.

Patty declared as much on Friday, September 24, 1847, when she confided to her diary: "go 14 miles . . . got into the valley it is a beautiful place my heart flows with gratitude to God that we have *got home all safe* [italics added] lost nothing have been blesed with life and health I rejoice all the time Saturday 25 . . . I have drove my waggon all the way but part of the two last mts . . . I broke nothing nor turned over had good luck I have cleaned my waggon and myself and visited friends." She was then fifty-two years old.

However, peace and security were elusive. When a federal army under General Johnston approached Salt Lake City in 1856 to put down a supposed Mormon rebellion, Patty along with family and others willingly packed up their belongings and moved south, half-expecting that their homes would be burned and the valley laid waste by the army or by some few fellow-Saints left behind to assure that the army had nothing to confiscate. Fortunately, that dreaded possibility fizzled, and Patty returned to her home and orchards and took up her work with her usual aplomb.[9]

She changed residences for the last time in 1870 after the Union Pacific Railroad chugged into town and bought her property at the present site of North Temple and Fourth West Streets. In order to live nearer to her children, she built a home in Bountiful, the community founded by her son, Perrigrine, and known at first as Sessions Settlement.[10]

Patty's journey from Maine to Bountiful had been difficult. The rigors of crossing the plains have been well documented, but every individual experience was unique. Patty's was no exception. She drove a team and wagon by herself, or walked beside them, for virtually the whole distance. Of course, she also delivered babies (at least seventy-eight between February 1846 and April 1847). The fact that the wives of church leaders such as Ezra T. Benson, Parley P. Pratt, Newell K. Whitney, and Edward Hunter chose her to "put them to bed" indicates their faith in her as a midwife. She administered medically and spiritually to the sick and dying throughout the migration, most graphically at Winter Quarters. She was a key participant and leader among a select group of women who met to buoy each other up through the practice of spiritual gifts. In her journal entries during the trek from Nauvoo to Winter Quarters, in Winter Quarters, and on the way west, Patty shared the spiritual experiences of the sisters. They prayed together, washed and anointed each other, spoke and interpreted in tongues, and participated in what she perceived as healings.

Patty also acted as a catalyst in keeping her family, their belongings and their spirits in good order. Her services were always offered with positive optimism. But she held one regret that stemmed from the fact that her daughter Sylvia had stayed behind with her family and husband, Windsor P. Lyon, who decided not to move west, but to establish his pharmacy business in Iowa. Patty's son David Junior, who worked for Lyon, chose to remain with them. On May 31, 1846, Patty gave vent to her feelings: "When I think that Sylvia and David and Josephine [Sylvia's daughter] is not coming tears fall from my eyes as fast as the drops of rain from the skies for I can now give vent to my feelings by weeping Oh Lord Comfort my poor wounded heart." Despite her disappointment, her own determination to be with the "Saints" never wavered. And her joy was full some years later, when first David and then Sylvia rejoined the Saints and the Sessions family in Great Salt Lake City. After their July arrival in the valley, the Advance Company laid out the city in ten-acre lots. One block, now known as Pioneer Park, was reserved for a fort to house the emigrants until they were able to build permanent homes. Soon after their arrival in the valley, Perrigrine and his father built in the fort a two-room log cabin of sixteen by twenty-four feet, which was connected to the other dwellings. Typically, though, as soon as possible and practical, Patty and David constructed their own adobe house on land assigned to them at North Temple and Fourth West, where they planted a productive garden and orchards and settled into a more or less normal existence.[11]

On January 13, 1850, Patty showed her lack of joy when she recorded that her husband had taken a third wife, Harriet Teaples [or Teeples] Wixom. David Sessions had earlier married a first plural wife, Rosilla Cowan (or Cowen), before the pioneers left Nauvoo. When most of the residents abandoned Nauvoo, Rosilla stayed behind, joining the wagon train four months later. After Rosilla arrived, Patty slept alone most nights, suffering from chilly weather and the mental and emotional trauma of her perception of David's coldness. She literally grappled with Rosilla in an effort to establish the rights and authority of the first wife. Eventually Rosilla, who steadfastly asserted her independence, gave up on the relationship and on persuading David to go back with her, and returned to Nauvoo alone. Perrigrine visited Rosilla on one of his missionary trips years later and reported in his diary that she had apostatized.[12] As during the time of David's first plural marriage, Patty again confided her anguish to her journal when he married Harriet. Nevertheless, she always expressed a desire to do the "right thing," busying herself with her projects and at the same time giving strength and stability to her own and her husbands' households; often, it appears, she provided the major source of livelihood for all of them. On August 11, 1850, after an illness of about ten days, David died at Patty's home. Whenever help was needed or requested, Patty continued to aid his other widow, Harriet, who bore David's child four months later.

After David's death, Patty fretted about the difficulty of chopping wood for herself, so when John Parry, a Welshman whose wife had died as they were crossing the plains, began to court her, Patty assumed a different tone in her writing. During the courtship, she wrote about chopping wood, "it is very hard" (December 9, 1851). On December 14, 1851, she wryly confided, "I was married to John Parry and I feel to thank the Lord that I have some one to cut my wood for me." Of course, as in an episode from a predictable story about early Mormon life, the inevitable happened: Mr. Parry married another wife—named Harriet (family name unknown)—and soul-searching again dominated Patty's journal. Predictably, she became reconciled once more, as she always accommodated herself to any circumstance that interrupted the tranquility of her life. Patty was so self-sufficient that she readily adjusted to physical and emotional difficulties. In her reminiscences, she recalled that John Parry died on January 13, 1868, and she penned a moving eulogy, in which she expressed her appreciation for his goodness and her loneliness at his passing.

Patty's attitude toward her husbands was respect, devotion, and acceptance of their faults. Although she felt "bad" that she had not been consulted earlier about their taking plural wives—at least before President Brigham Young, whom she called simply "Brigham," was consulted—she dismissed that complaint with merely a mention. It appears that both Mr. Sessions and Mr. Parry showed favor toward their younger wives, but they sought Patty's aid in times of their own sickness or material need, for the birthing of their babies, and for food to eat. Apparently neither of them helped much with the physical labor of pruning and caring for the orchards and gardens—or any of the other heavy work that needed to be done. Where were they when she had to hire men to help with the farming or with fixing up the property? She sometimes hinted at her exasperation, but did not belabor the subject. And she regularly met the needs or requests of her husbands in level-headed and supportive ways in times of ill health and in times of material shortages.

Friction, perhaps, was inevitable in marriage to this independent and successful woman, who knew very well who she was and what she wanted from life, and who worked endlessly and seemingly tirelessly at her multiple endeavors. Patty Bartlett Sessions Parry never wavered from her goals, worldly or spiritually. She kept on course as solidly as the granite clings to the ground in Maine, where she was born. She gave tirelessly of her gifts of birthing and healing. She shared the profits of the work of her hands with her family, her church, and those less fortunate. At the same time, she was a resolute and efficient business woman, who kept careful track of loans and payments, of sales, and of business dealings of every kind. Debts, when paid, were carefully crossed out in her account book. For some others, she wrote: "never paid a cent of it." She was frugal to the point of stinginess, but she worked hard for what she accumulated.

Whatever the prophet asked, Patty did, since she accepted his role as inspired. When opportunity arose, she grasped it. For example, besides her midwifery, she established a thriving business in raising and selling fruits, seedlings, and seeds. On November 5, 1868, she "went and put fifteen hundred Dollars into Zions Co operative Mercantile Institution," and by 1883 owned shares worth $16,000. Few, if any, women of her time would be worth so much. She was a humanitarian, who contributed generously to the Perpetual Emigration Fund and other worthy causes. She paid her tithing faithfully, but did not hesitate to ask for a refund if she felt she had overpaid. Her account book for January of 1866 records, "setled my tithing due me $39 00."

In 1883, after she settled in Bountiful, Patty decided that her grandchildren's opportunity for schooling was inadequate. So she built a schoolhouse in Bountiful called the Patty Sessions Academy, hired a teacher, and offered education to her own grandchildren and to other children whose parents could not afford to pay.[13]

Patty also harbored a deep desire to continue her own learning and took advantage of available opportunities by attending medical meetings and lectures and taking classes in grammar or the Deseret Alphabet, in dancing, or whatever. Her mind was never idle. Her hands and feet were never idle either. One tiny scrap of paper among her diaries gives a list of dates with the words "dancing school" beside the numbers. She earned money by taking in boarders and, rather matter of factly, she accommodated the constant combinations of family and friends who seemed to depend on her and appeared at her doorstep "for a visit." She cooked meals and provided beds for those who stayed overnight, or often even longer. The wonder is that she cared enough and took time enough and tapped reserve energies enough to record their names, sometimes spelled phonetically and usually not spelled the same way twice. With all the coming and going at her house, it is no wonder that washing, ironing, and housework figured prominently in her journals. She actually abhorred idleness and was forever engaged in spinning, weaving, knitting, crocheting, sewing for herself or others. In her last months, she wrote daily of knitting stockings. According to one of her descendants, the socks were so full of dropped stitches and other mistakes that each night family members secretly unravelled them and Patty reknit the same yarn the next day.[14] Or she was preoccupied with planting, harvesting, preserving. Or she was visiting, comforting, blessing, healing. Or she was delivering babies.

Besides working on what she called her "domestic concerns," Patty was active in community affairs. She was a charter member of the Council of Health, which was organized by Willard Richards in 1848. This organization instructed its members in midwifery, care of children, handling of diseases, and other health-related topics. In the Council of Health, Patty acted as first counselor to Phoebe Ann Morton Angell, mother of architect Truman O. Angell. After the death of Sister Angell, Patty became president. She later presided over a society established in 1854, especially to help clothe the Indians, an organization that evolved into a formal Relief Society, many meetings of which were held in her home. According to her daughter-in-law, David's wife, Phebe, Patty had been present at the organizational meeting of the Relief Society on March 16, 1842 in Nauvoo, so its precepts and activities again became a central force in her life.[15] Her doors were open to a variety of meetings, such as a straw braiding school.

Before her pioneering in Utah, Patty Bartlett Sessions had been a partner in forging a successful farm life in the wilds of Maine. She had been the first in her family to accept the demands of the gospel as found in the Church of Jesus Christ of Latter-day Saints. Because of such commitment, she had doggedly piled her belongings into wagons or onto her shoulders and resettled seven different times for seven reasons, most of which were not of her own choosing. As a midwife she reverenced life and she had rejoiced in the births of her own children and continued to nurture them with passion even after they were grown, though she buried five out of eight.

The loss of her beloved children probably enhanced her belief in one Latter-day Saint doctrine, that of eternal life. She even attempted to send a message to her deceased children at the suggestion of a dying woman to whom she was ministering at Winter Quarters.[16] But her belief in eternal life becomes more evident through her diligence in performing temple ordinances for her deceased ancestors and friends during her declining years. More proof surfaces as she described her journey back to Maine between May 13, 1870 and August 7, 1870 to explain her religion to her living relatives and former friends. She kept copious records of the ordinances she performed in the Logan temple, to which her financial contributions had exceeded all others.

Patty delivered many of her own grandchildren and some of her great-grandchildren, as well as some of the children of her husbands' other wives. She employed her children and grandchildren; she loaned them money; she bragged that she could dance with them and enjoy herself at an advanced age. As her actions revealed how much family mattered to her, her records also show that her children especially, and her grandchildren in some measure, returned to her the bread that she had cast upon their waters.

However infrequently, she did from time to time express annoyance, even impatience, with her family and other associates for their lack of performance. Debts were to be paid; work was to be done; laws, especially commandments, were to be kept. So she duly noted her own compliance while frankly remarking when she was not treated fairly by others. She believed in the power of prayers, in gifts of the spirit, in healing. She participated in all three as a recipient and as a participant.

Throughout her long years, thousands of babies breathed their first in her capable hands, including one in fulfillment of prophesy. At the end of her arduous journey, on September 26, 1847, she wrote: ". . . went put Lorenzo Youngs wife Hariet to bed with a son the first male born in this valley it was said to me more than 5 months ago that my hands should be the first to handle the first born son in the place of rest for the saints even the city of our God I have come more than one thousand miles to do it since it was spoken." Yet, to her, birth and death were matter of fact and she did not dwell on particulars, except for noting the names she knew.

I cannot overemphasize her compulsion in keeping records, including the names of persons in her diaries. And those names show that she hobnobbed on a first-name basis with early Mormon Church hierarchy. She delivered their babies and laid out their dead. She socialized intimately with many of their wives, particularly those of Brigham Young and Heber C. Kimball. She belonged to the elite and closely knit group who had been sealed to the Prophet Joseph Smith during his lifetime. The names she chronicles reveal also whom she hired, whom she sold to, who received her donations, who paid for obstetrical services, and all manner of other successful business dealings.

Besides the records she wrote so diligently, Patty has left other concrete clues to her character. In 1811, when she was sixteen, Patty Bartlett began to embroider a sampler, which now is treasured by one of her descendants. She toted it around for thirty-seven years and finally finished it in 1848, when she was fifty-three years old. It is rather large and complicated, filled with the alphabet and numbers of various sizes, styles, and colors. Some of her passions are expressed in the laden fruit trees, flowers, and animals that decorate the center section. She has embroidered the words, "Patty Bartlett is my name and with my needle wrought the same A.D. 1811 . . . 1848 recommence again in this 54th yr of my age. Salt Lake Valley. North America . . . August 22 1848." Those dates do not jibe, or else we read it wrongly. But these few words explain much of her nature and perseverance. The verse in the sampler's lower right-hand corner even more passionately describes her philosophy and, in truth, what made Patty work.

> The mind should be inbred in thought
> The hands in skilful labours taught
> Let time be usefully employed
> And art and nature be enjoyed

Other artifacts add other insights. One of Sylvia's descendants owns a medical book dated 1842, W. Beach's *Family Physician; Reformed System of Medicine.* Most of the medical procedures that Patty mentioned are described in this book, such as what constitutes a "Course in Medicine." The LDS Church Museum of Art owns another 1842 book, her midwife book, filled with information and colored illustrations. Both of these books show that Patty did not depend upon experience alone for her skill in medical matters and in bringing babies into the world. She studied throughout her lifetime. The rather boastful title lets us spy into the mind of this exceptional pioneer woman: *Aristotle's Works: Containing the Master-piece, Direction for Midwives, and Counsel and Advice to Child-Bearing Women.* Her well worn, broken down spinning wheel, also owned by the Church Museum, adds further testimony to her diligence in providing for life's necessities. Her diaries explain how she lived and interacted with people. A large portrait at the Daughters of the Utah Pioneers Museum captures Patty's "likeness," as she put it, and other photos preserve the images of her children and grandchildren, of her academy, even of her home. Those who should know say that the plum attributed to Patty's horticultural abilities is still grown and sold in Utah. Her influence still permeates the Sessions family, as I have discovered, through their encouragement and support during the preparation of her diaries.

We might ask what sense of destiny or importance or urgency drove her. Surely she teaches us some lessons—that life's meaning is found in its dailiness, that small, necessary acts can be creations of art, that the orderliness of routine can be preparation for eternity. However, a single, tattered scrap of webbing pressed between the pages of the 1842 medical book may be the key to Patty's constancy in record keeping (since we all hope for some kind of immortality). Cross-stitched in bold red letters and decorated with forest green squiggles are two simple words: "Remember me."

No problem. Patty Bartlett Sessions, pioneer midwife, has become unforgettable through her diaries.

In this 1897 picture of Utah pioneers gathered on Temple Square to celebrate the fiftieth anniversary of the settlement of Utah, Jane Elizabeth Manning James is in the exact center, six rows from the front, the only Black person present. Photo courtesy of the Utah State Historical Society.

JANE MANNING JAMES
A Test of Faith

Henry J. Wolfinger

Henry J. Wolfinger received a bachelor of arts degree from Claremont-McKenna College in California and went on to graduate school at Princeton, specializing in Utah history. He is currently head of the Civilian Appraisal Branch for the National Archives in Washington, D.C., where he helps determine the historic value of federal records. He first encountered Jane James in the spring of 1968 when he arrived in Utah to do research on the federal government's efforts to suppress polygamy and break the temporal power of the LDS Church prior to statehood. Four years later, when he returned to the state, he began to research James's life in earnest and was staggered by the amount of information he found. At that point, "the focus of the research shifted from a narrow look at Jane Elizabeth James's relationship to the Mormon Church to a broader and richer account of her life within the context of the African American community." An earlier version of this text appeared in Social Accommodation in Utah, *edited by Clark S. Knowlton. That work also contains the full text of several documents referenced in this essay.*

It is well known that three Black slaves—Green Flake, Hark Lay, and Oscar Crosby—accompanied the Mormon vanguard that reached the Salt Lake Valley on July 22, 1847. Little attention, however, has been devoted to those early-day Black settlers who, despite their limited numbers, laid the basis for the development of Utah's Black community. Although the sources for studying the origins of this community are quite limited, sufficient material has appeared to sketch the life and character of Jane Elizabeth Manning James, one of these Black pioneers. An early convert to Mormonism, she remained a faithful Latter-day Saint over the course of her life, despite the challenge posed by the church's racial restrictions in her later years. The first half of this essay provides an outline of her life and her relationship to the Mormon Church. The second half broadens the picture by placing her life within the larger context of the development of Utah's small Black community.[1]

Life and Character

Mrs. James was born Jane Elizabeth Manning, the daughter of Isaac and Phyllis Abbott Manning, about 1820.[2] Her birthplace was Wilton, Connecticut, a rural township with a population of slightly less than 2,000, nestled on the Norwalk River about five miles north of the city of Norwalk. The Manning family, which was free, included at least five children who lived to maturity.[3] Phyllis Manning was an ex-slave who had been born into the household of Ebenezer Abbott II, a prominent resident of Wilton. After being given by Abbott to a daughter on her marriage, and later sold to a Stamford man, Phyllis was freed in 1811 at the age of twenty-five. She returned to Wilton and soon married Isaac Manning, a free Black who in 1816 was employed as a spinner.[4] Isaac died about 1825. Sometime after 1830 Phyllis married Cato Treadwell, an impoverished Black widower who had served in the Revolutionary War and who was twenty-three years older than the former Mrs. Manning.[5]

Due to the death of her natural father, Jane Elizabeth Manning as a young girl was sent to reside in the household of Joseph Fitch, a prosperous White farmer of Wilton.[6] Here she worked as a servant, receiving instruction in Christian principles but little in the way of education or skills. Although she had learned to read by later life, she probably was unable to write, for she often signed her name by a mark in business transactions and dictated her correspondence.[7] And on arrival in Nauvoo she described her abilities in terms of such domestic chores as cooking, washing, and ironing.[8]

Mormonism gained its first firm foothold in southwestern Connecticut through the missionary labors of Charles Wesley Wandell, who had helped to bring the faith to Westchester County, New York, in 1841. From here he and an associate pushed across the border to proselytize in Connecticut, where they received "great encouragement, doors being freely opened to them in many places."[9] In December 1841, the first converts were baptized in Norwalk. Four months later a branch was organized in the community. By the fall of 1842 it had forty-one members, some of whom had already emigrated to Nauvoo. Meanwhile, Wandell continued to preach in such nearby townships as New Canaan, Ridgefield, and Danbury.[10] It was during these tours that Jane Elizabeth Manning probably met him and heard of the Prophet Joseph Smith, the principles of the Mormon faith, and the city that had been established on the Mississippi River. Although a Presbyterian, she quickly converted to the new religion and acquainted her relatives with it, a number of whom adopted it for themselves. Like other early Mormons, she experienced gifts of the spirit, including speaking in tongues and healing the sick.[11]

In other religions conversion might be the final step in a profession of faith, but in nineteenth-century Mormonism it was but an initial step, which was followed by the convert's departure from "Babylon" to "Zion" for the purpose of joining the faithful in the work of establishing the kingdom of God on earth. In a report on his missionary labors, Wandell furnished a reflection on the millennial expectations of the converts in southwestern Connecticut.

> The brethren here are very anxious to emigrate to Illinois; so you may expect to see all of us in Zion this Fall, that can possibly get there. . . . Although at the May Conference, held in New York City, four of our members were ordained to the office of elder, yet we cannot fill the openings that are made. May the Lord raise up laborers and send them forth, that the wheat may be speedily gathered into the Lord's garner, even Zion, that the chaff may be burned up by the brightness of his coming.[12]

Among those making preparations to emigrate to Nauvoo were the

Mannings. The party included Jane, her son Sylvester, her mother Phyllis, two brothers, two sisters, a brother-in-law, and a sister-in-law.[13] Their departure from Connecticut apparently was meant to be permanent, for Jane's mother sold the family homesite in Wilton.[14] In early October 1843, they left with a company of Saints under Wandell's direction. The company traveled to Buffalo by boat via the Erie Canal. The Manning family expected to travel to Columbus, Ohio, with the company, but payment of the fares for the full trip was demanded in Buffalo. Lacking money for the fare, the Manning family left the company and journeyed the remainder of the way on foot, a distance of about 750 miles. The long trek took its toll on footwear and clothing, and they had to walk barefoot amid autumn frosts as they approached Nauvoo. The journey also involved racial perils. Free Negroes were unwelcome in much of the North, and the states of the Old Northwest imposed restrictions on their immigration. Authorities in Peoria, Illinois, temporarily detained the Manning party for lack of "free papers." Although the family experienced, in Mrs. James's words, "all kinds of hardship, trial and rebuff," the journey to Nauvoo reinforced her religious faith. She attributed their safe arrival to the blessing of God, "protecting us from all harm, answering our prayers and healing our feet."[15]

The Prophet Joseph Smith and his wife Emma provided the Manning family with temporary quarters at the "Nauvoo Mansion," which served as both a hotel and a residence for the Smith family. The Mannings soon dispersed and established homes, except for Jane, who had not found a position for herself and was impoverished because the trunk carrying her entire wardrobe had disappeared en route to Nauvoo. Joseph and Emma, on learning of her predicament, allowed her to remain at the "Nauvoo Mansion," provided her with clothing, and employed her as a servant to handle washing and other household chores.[16]

Jane remained a member of Joseph Smith's household until shortly before his death six months later. She admired Joseph greatly and later described him as "the finest man I ever saw on earth." She appreciated the kindness and concern that he showed her. He never passed her, she reported, without shaking hands and offering a greeting. Her experience as a member of his household reinforced her religious convictions, and she later rued refusing on two occasions an offer from Emma Smith to be adopted into the family as a child.[17] Her older brother Isaac worked as a cook at the "Nauvoo Mansion." He also taught dancing at the Masonic Hall and quarried stone for the construction of the Nauvoo Temple.[18]

Meanwhile, controversy over the Mormons continued to rise in west central Illinois. The destruction of the *Expositor*, an anti-Smith newspaper that surfaced briefly in Nauvoo in the spring of 1844, was followed by the arrest of Joseph Smith and his brother Hyrum and their subsequent murder in the Carthage jail. Isaac Manning, as an assistant to the Nauvoo sexton, was one of those who helped to bury the brothers.[19]

The murder of the Smiths brought no permanent peace to the region, and in the winter of 1845–46, following periods of near civil war, the Mormons abandoned Nauvoo and retreated across the Mississippi. They settled at Winter Quarters, Nebraska, where the trek to the Rocky Mountains was organized. Though most of Jane Manning's relatives remained members of the church until the death of Joseph Smith, none joined her in the move to the Rockies.[20] Jane, in the meantime, had married before the abandonment of Nauvoo. Her husband was Isaac James, a free Black who had been born and raised in rural Monmouth County, New Jersey. He had converted to Mormonism as a young man, apparently in 1839 at age nineteen, and was an early emigrant to Nauvoo.[21] Their first child, Silas F. James, was born June 10, 1846, probably at Hog Creek in western Iowa, following their flight from Nauvoo.[22]

After the departure of Brigham Young's vanguard in the spring of 1847, the main body of emigrants, about 1,500 in number, left their Winter Quarters encampment in mid-June. At the Elkhorn River they organized into companies known as "tens," "fifties," and "hundreds." The official departure of the companies, marked by the ringing of the bell saved from the Nauvoo Temple, came on June 22, 1847. The large size of the party soon led to the decision that each company should travel singly, forming its own encampments and herding its own stock. The lead company for most of the journey was the Second Fifty of the First Hundred, whose captain was Ira Eldredge and whose members included Isaac and Jane E. James, together with their sons Sylvester and Silas.

The company encountered a number of hardships in crossing the plains. Forage often proved inadequate for the livestock, leading to a steady weakening of the teams of oxen. Suitable fords for crossing streams were sometimes difficult to locate. Blinding dust storms were apt to strike with little notice. Huge herds of buffalo furnished a source of fresh meat, but the beasts could pass so close to the party that on one occasion they stampeded the livestock. By the time the Second Fifty of the First Hundred got to the Green River, on September 5, the journey had taken a heavy toll among the teams. Several days later Captain Eldredge detached the First and Fifth Tens from his vanguard and directed them to proceed as quickly as possible to the Salt Lake Valley for reinforcements to assist those companies that had fallen behind. This advance force, which may have included the James family as members of the First Ten, reached the valley on September 19, 1847. Fortunately, favorable weather continued to prevail, permitting the remainder of the companies to arrive safely, although the last of them did not reach their destination until the first week of October.²³

The James family's first years in the Salt Lake Valley were marked by periods of privation during which even the necessities of life were unavailable. Mrs. James vividly recollected the destructive effects of a plague of crickets and grasshoppers that devastated their crops and stripped trees of leaves and fruit, "bringing poverty and desolation throughout this beautiful valley."²⁴ The experience of these years attested to the wisdom of pursuing a policy of cooperation and mutual aid, for the more fortunate of one season might be the less fortunate of the next. Although Mrs. James was forced to seek aid from her neighbors on occasion,²⁵ she was able to offer assistance at other times, as the following account of Eliza Lyman, wife of Apostle Amasa M. Lyman, demonstrates.

> April 8th, 1849, we baked the last of our flour today, and have no prospect of getting more till after harvest. April 13th Brother Lyman started on a mission to California with Or[r]in Porter Rockwell and others. May the Lord bless and prosper them and return them in safety. He left us without anything from which to make bread, it not being in his power to get it. Not long after Amasa had gone, Jane James, the colored woman, let me have two pounds of flour, it being half of what she had.²⁶

Like many other emigrants, the James family ventured initially into farming.²⁷ Isaac James also worked for Brigham Young, possibly as a coachman.[28] In 1856 their property holdings, located in the First Ward in the southeast corner of Salt Lake City, included a land claim and improvements, a timepiece, and a few other personal possessions. This small stake probably represented a hand-to-mouth existence, but it seems typical of the families living in the ward at that time.[29]

The family grew rapidly. Between 1848 and 1860 at least six children were born, five of whom survived to adulthood.[30] Despite steadily increasing family responsibilities, the household slowly prospered. By 1860 the family had accumulated an ox, a cow, three hogs, and a cart, in addition to their land claim, dwelling, household furnishings, and other improvements.[31] The following year their oldest son, Sylvester, was listed as a member of the Nauvoo legion, armed with a rifle and ten rounds of ammunition.[32] By 1865 the Jameses had added further to their possessions, now valued at $1,100. They had raised a small flock of sheep on a temporary basis during the early 1860s. Three horses had taken the place of an ox as the family's work animals, and a new vehicle seems to have replaced their aging cart. These assets did not represent wealth, but they do suggest prosperity for a rural family. Only four other households in the First Ward held more property than the Jameses, while thirty-one held less.[33]

This prosperity, however, concealed marital difficulties. The consequences of these difficulties are apparent though the causes are not. In late 1869 or early 1870 Isaac James left the household and sold to his wife most of the family realty, consisting of a one-and-a-quarter acre lot and improvements.[34] The sale of the property for a consideration of $500 indicates that Isaac intended his departure to be permanent and that he and his wife did not separate on friendly terms. He does not seem to have maintained any relations with the family after his departure. Within four years Mrs. James had remarried. This relationship lasted less than two years, and following its dissolution she reverted to the use of her former married name.[35] In 1887, when the estate of one of their sons was being settled, she listed Isaac's whereabouts as "unknown."[36] He reappeared in Portland, Oregon, and later returned to Salt Lake City, probably in 1890, where he resided until his death in November 1891.[37]

There can be no doubt that the breakup of her marriage caused Mrs. James embarrassment and concern. It was part of her past that she failed to mention in her reminiscences. As a conscientious Mormon, marriage was to her a religious as well as a secular relationship which, when solemnized by the church, would extend past death and through eternity. It was with this consideration in mind that she wrote Apostle Joseph F. Smith early in 1890 and requested permission to be "sealed" to Walker Lewis, who she felt was more worthy to spend eternal life with her.[38] However, she and Isaac may have become reconciled following his return to Salt Lake City and his readmission to the church. Not only was his funeral held at her home, but a later renewal of her request for adoption into the family of Joseph Smith included Isaac, an indication that she wished both of them to be members of the same family in the afterlife.[39]

In 1869–70, however, Mrs. James's most pressing concern was the care of the family, for she had assumed financial responsibility for the younger children still living in the household.[40] She soon moved to the Eighth Ward and exchanged her First Ward property for a portion of a lot lying on the east side of Fifth East Street between Fifth and Sixth South Streets.[41] Here she established the residence in which she lived for the remainder of her life, a two-story frame house set back from the street and enclosed by a white picket fence.[42] The farm animals and vehicles that had played a vital part in the family's domestic economy during the 1860s disappeared from the lists of the household's assets following Isaac James's departure.[43] The family economy was now dependent on a continuing cash income, although Mrs. James did raise produce in a small family garden and manufactured some household items such as soap.[44] The prosperity that had characterized her household in the 1860s was absent during the remainder of the century. Her limited assets placed her among the poorer residents of the Eighth Ward. In 1884 she ranked one hundred and thirty-fifth among 148 property holders.[45] For a few years a very small portion of her income came from the lease of a five-acre plot on the East Bench, which she inherited in 1872 following the death of an unmarried son.[46] A much more important source of income was her own labor. In addition to managing her household, which at times included several young grandchildren, she engaged in domestic work.[47] Her youngest son, Jessie, lived at home most of his life and no doubt assisted the family through his earnings as a laborer and porter.[48] Despite the squeeze of finances, the household bustled with the activity of children and grandchildren and the arrival and departure of older relatives.

Mrs. James remained a steadfast member of the Mormon Church throughout her life. She was particularly active in the Woman's Relief Society, a church auxiliary which in the Eighth Ward engaged in much charitable work. Joining the local branch on November 1, 1870, soon after moving into the ward,[49] she not only contributed regularly to its work, but also supported its numerous special drives. She donated to the construction of the St. George, Logan, and Manti Temples. Among other church causes to which she contributed were the "Lamanite" (American Indian) Mission, an Old Folks' Excursion at Liberty Park, a fair in behalf of the Deseret Hospital, and a People's Party banner during the bitterly contested municipal campaign of 1890. In recognition of her services, as well as her limited income, the local branch of the Relief Society regularly designated her family as recipients of a Christmas basket containing packages of meat, dried fruits, sugar, and other staples.[50] The quality of her faith and her reputation as a pioneer extended beyond the boundaries of her local ward. In later life both she and her brother, Isaac L. Manning, enjoyed reserved seats near the front and center of the Salt Lake Tabernacle for Sunday services.[51]

Although culturally a member of the Mormon community and devotedly attached to the Mormon faith, Mrs. James remained racially conscious. It may have reflected her position in a virtually all-White community that she expressed this racial consciousness indirectly rather than directly. Although she revered Joseph Smith for his role as prophet of the faith and for his personal warmth and democratic manner, she also took careful note of his stand on slavery. In her reminiscence she noted, "Things came to pass what he prophesied about the colored race being freed. Things that he said has come to pass. I did not hear that, but I knew of it."[52] Despite earlier statements condoning slavery while the Mormons were resident in Missouri, Joseph Smith ran for president of the United States in 1844 on a platform that included a call for the abolition of slavery through a policy of compensated emancipation. The plank concluded with a ringing endorsement of freedom: "Break off the shackles from the poor Black man, and hire him to labor like other human beings, for 'an hour of virtuous liberty on earth is worth a whole

eternity in bondage.' " His presidential campaign coincided with the period during which Mrs. James was resident in his household, and to a
racially conscious Black Mormon such as she, his stand on slavery may
have been vital to her attitude toward him.[53]
The racial practices of her church were a test of Mrs. James's faith,
at least during her later life, as a series of requests to the presiding authorities for temple ordinances attest. Although the origins of Mormon
racial policies remain obscure, the church's practice of excluding Blacks
from certain temple rites and priesthood ordination was becoming fully
developed by the late nineteenth century. The practice was based on the
assumption of Negro inferiority and justified theologically by the "curse
of Canaan" concept.[54] The response to Mrs. James's requests demonstrated that attitudes were hardening. Requests over a number of years
to obtain her endowments[55] were turned down.[56] Similarly, the church
authorities declined her requests, beginning in 1884, to be adopted as a
child into the family of Joseph Smith, though they finally arranged for
her to be adopted into the family as a servant in a special ceremony in
1902.[57] Even when a request was granted, it was given grudgingly. In
forwarding Mrs. James a temple recommend allowing her to be baptized
and confirmed for her dead kindred, Salt Lake Stake President Angus M.
Cannon pointedly noted, "You must be content with this privelege [sic],
awaiting further instructions from the Lord to his servants."[58]
    A sense of millennial expectation, combined with anxiety for her
future salvation, lay behind Mrs. James's repeated requests for temple
ordinances. To a conscientious Black Mormon such as she, the contemporary era was the "fullness of times" and she was one of the saints of
the latter days. Therefore, suggestions that revelation on some future
occasion would lead to a modification of the church's racial practices did
not meet her spiritual needs. As she noted in one of her requests to the
church authorities: "My race was handed down through the flood & God
promised Abraham that in his seed all the nations of the earth should be
blest & as this is the fullness of all dispensations[,] is there no blessing
for me[?]"[59] Mrs. James was also aware of inconsistencies in past racial
practices, though sufficiently circumspect not to mention them directly.
One should take particular notice of her request in 1890 to be sealed to
Walker Lewis, an African American whose ordination into the priesthood

some forty years before was not a matter of public knowledge. Such inconsistencies in the church's racial practices bred hope among those who were alert to them and may help to explain Mrs. James's continuing correspondence with the church authorities on these subjects.[60]

In a church often noted for its authoritarian character and distrust of dissenters, she undoubtedly recognized the futility of attempting to protest the church's racial policies. She does not appear to have directly objected to the decisions of the presiding authorities denying her requests for temple ordinances. Instead, she patiently renewed her requests, couching them in a respectful tone. The persistence of her correspondence, rather than its tenor, signified the maintenance of her point of view. Her reaction to the first presidency's decision authorizing her adoption into Joseph Smith's household at a special ceremony is significant in this respect. She did not accept being adopted into his household as a servant as a satisfactory fulfillment of her request and continued to press her original request for her endowments.[61] In short, she did not directly challenge the church's racial proscriptions, but she also did not accept them. She managed to maintain cordial relations with the church leadership despite the tensions over this issue. At the time of her death, the church newspaper featured a prominent obituary on its front page, and President Joseph F. Smith, nephew of the Prophet Joseph Smith with whom she stayed in Nauvoo, was one of several church officials who spoke at what was described as a crowded funeral.[62]

Yet another test of her faith was death among the family. Mrs. James outlived all but two of her children, Sylvester and Ellen. Of her seven children who reached maturity, five died before the age of forty, and three of these died before thirty. Two daughters, May Ann and Miriam, died in childbirth, the first in 1871 at the age of twenty-two and the second in 1874 at the age of twenty-four.[63] A third daughter, Vilate, died in 1897 at age thirty-eight. As a young woman Vilate had moved to California, where she married a Methodist minister and later served for six years as a missionary in Liberia.[64] One of Mrs. James's sons, Silas, died at twenty-five in 1872 of "consumption." Another son, Jessie, died in 1894 at thirty-seven.[65] Mortality statistics were equally as grim among her grandchildren. Of fourteen who can be located through local records, six died before reaching the age of four.[66]

Age brought the further trials of increasing infirmity and encroaching poverty. Her eyesight grew dimmer, to a point at which she was no longer able to read, and late in life her ability to walk was similarly impaired.[67] In 1893 her brother Isaac L. Manning, who had joined her in the move to Nauvoo but not to Utah, came to Salt Lake City following the death of his wife and daughter. He rejoined the LDS Church, resided at Mrs. James's home, and gained employment as a part-time laborer, plasterer, and carpet cleaner.[68] Mrs. James also worked at least part-time until a few years before her death.[69] After the turn of the century, however, age and disability worsened their financial plight and made them dependent on outside financial assistance. Mrs. James's daughter Ellen, remarried and living in Nevada, contributed small sums of money at different times, and her son Sylvester furnished produce from the garden of his Mill Creek residence.[70] Small contributions of cash and merchandise also arrived from the Eighth Ward Relief Society at various intervals.[71] Burdened by the infirmities of age and weakened by a severe fall, Jane James died April 16, 1908.

Jane Elizabeth James left few sources for a study of her life, but those that are extant shed light on several features of her character. One of her most noticeable traits was a sense of generosity that frequently appeared in her relations with her children. In 1872, for instance, she gave her married daughter Miriam a piece of her homesite for the establishment of a permanent residence. Miriam died in 1874, and in later years her husband, who was raising their children, lost the home through nonpayment of taxes. Mrs. James then transferred, at no apparent cost, yet another piece of her homesite to the three grandchildren.[72] She exhibited similar generosity toward her daughter Ellen, though it may have been misplaced in this instance. In 1886, under entreaties for financial assistance, Mrs. James transferred the whole of her Eighth Ward homesite to her daughter, who was apparently troubled by serious personal problems. Ellen mortgaged the property as security for a loan and moved to Los Angeles. Unable to repay the loan, she transferred the homesite back to her mother, who was saddled with the difficult task of repaying the mortgage to save her home.[73] These incidents suggest that a strong sense of family ties, despite the breakup of her own marriage, underlay Mrs. James's generosity toward her children.

Another visible aspect of her character was the poise and dignity that she maintained in the face of personal and financial adversity. Poise was apparent in the concern that she took in her appearance.[74] Dignity was manifest in the respect that she received from the church authorities despite differences over the church's racial practices. Underlying both her poise and dignity was a quality of endurance that surfaced in religious terms as a personal philosophy in times of adversity. At the time of her death the *Deseret News* spoke of her "undaunted faith," and her own account of a period of extreme deprivation in early-day Utah expressed this sense of endurance and religious commitment: "Oh how I suffered of cold and hunger and keenest of all was to hear my little ones crying for bread, and I had none to give them; but in all the Lord was with us and gave us grace and faith to stand it all."[75]

Her life was not one which brought financial reward or historical recognition. Rather, her achievements were personal. At a time when the racial attitudes of the larger society and the local community were becoming increasingly rigid, and their practices increasingly discriminatory, she managed the difficult task of maintaining her racial and religious identification without sacrificing a sense of personal dignity. Financial distresses and unsuccessful marriages were aspects of her life, but she did not permit them to overcome a natural generosity and a strong sense of family unity. Although knowledge of these personal achievements has dimmed with the passage of time, she did gain recognition from her contemporaries, as the following account of her funeral services indicates. "Mrs. Jane Manning James, the aged colored woman who died last week, was buried yesterday, the funeral services being held at the Eighth Ward meetinghouse, commencing at 2 o'clock. The house was crowded, many in the congregation being of her own race. Flowers in profusion were contributed by friends who had learned to respect the deceased for her undaunted faith and goodness of heart."[76]

Development of Utah's Black Community

The experience of the James family in certain respects parallels those of other members of the Utah Black community. Mrs. James's own sense of family unity can be compared to a pattern of racial cohesiveness that is one of the most noticeable features of Utah's early-day Black population. Utah Blacks numbered fifty-nine in 1860 and 118 in 1870, forming about one-tenth of one percent of the total population at the time of both censuses. In 1870 fifty-one of the 118 Blacks resided in Salt Lake County. They consisted of nine families living in single and separate households, two men involved in logging operations near the mines of Little Cottonwood Canyon and two women employed as domestics by White families. All nine of the families—except that of Mrs. James—were headed by males.[77] Although but a tiny fraction of the total population and scattered in various parts of the county, six of these nine families lived in pairs, side by side with another Black family.[78]

An examination of property transactions reinforces this indication that racial considerations were a major factor in determining the location of Black residences. In the mid-1870s, for instance, three other Black families had settled on the same section of the Eighth Ward block where Mrs. James lived. One family was that of her son-in-law, but the others were unrelated.[79] A similar tendency can be noted in Union, a rural ward located just south of Salt Lake City. By 1880 at least four Black families had settled in Union, together with several single Black men who resided with them as boarders. All of their lands whose location can be plotted with some precision lay within the same forty-acre quarter section.[80] These cases suggest that a sense of racial identification led Blacks to transfer property among themselves and settle in pairs or small groups in early-day Utah.

Intermarriage within the Black population was another factor that promoted a sense of racial identification.[81] It also produced alliances among certain families. The marriage of Mrs. James's oldest son, Sylvester, to Mary Ann Perkins, was complemented by Mrs. James's brief marriage to Frank Perkins, Mary Ann's father. Another link between these families was forged in 1893, when Sylvester's son William Henry gave his uncle, Sylvester Perkins, a four-acre plot of land in Mill Creek. This land Perkins farmed in conjunction with nearby property owned by his brother-in-law, Sylvester James.[82] The James and Leggroan families formed similar alliances. When Ned Leggroan arrived in Salt Lake City in 1869–70, his initial residence was near the home of Sylvester James.[83]

The Leggroan family later moved, first to South Cottonwood and then to Idaho, but several of the children returned to Salt Lake City, and two of Ned's sons married two of Sylvester's daughters. These descendants settled in Mill Creek near the residence of Sylvester James.[84] The tangled relationships among the James, Perkins, and Leggroan families indicate that group settlement and intermarriage were interrelated factors vital in developing a sense of community within the Black population.

African Americans formed but a minute fraction of Utah's population throughout the late nineteenth century, numbering but 232 in 1880 and 672 in 1900, and forming about one-fifth of one percent of the population in both years. The educational backgrounds of many, if not most, of the earliest settlers verged on illiteracy and professional or white-collar employment was absent as late as 1880. The census schedules for Salt Lake County in that year reveal that only a few Blacks held what could be described as semi-skilled positions. Employment opportunities for Black women were even more severely restricted. Six of the ten who were employed held positions as domestic servants while the remaining four were engaged as laundresses. More than two-thirds of the Black men who were employed, twenty-one of thirty, also held positions that can be characterized as unskilled: nine were listed simply as "laborers," four as farmers, three as domestic servants, and one each as a logger, a miner, a janitor, a porter, and a hostler. Seven of the remaining nine held semi-skilled positions: three as barbers, three as cooks, and one as an express driver. The jobs of only two of the thirty lay outside these unskilled and semi-skilled positions. One was described as an artist and the other was listed as a bathhouse keeper.[85]

Given the lack of a Black professional class in 1880, it is not surprising that the first Black institutions seem to have been established only in the period following 1890. An association of Black Republicans was organized by 1892, and several "colored Republican clubs" were politically active during the 1895 campaign for state offices.[86] *The Broad Ax*, a Black weekly newspaper, was published in Salt Lake City between 1896 and 1899.[87] At least two Black Protestant congregations made their appearance in this decade, and by 1900 two Black churches—the African Methodist Episcopal Church and the Calvary Baptist Church— had been established in Salt Lake City.[88] The founding of such institutions as political associations, churches, and newspapers in the 1890s demonstrated that the cohesiveness apparent in Utah's Black population in earlier decades had matured to the point of community. These institutions not only reflected a sense of racial identification among Blacks, but, perhaps more importantly, they furnished opportunities for the exercise of leadership and the expression of community viewpoints.

This sketch of the origins of Utah's Black community merely touches the surface of what was a lengthy and complex development, aspects of which require further investigation. The degree to which early Black settlers and their descendants advanced economically and occupationally is one such subject that can bear study. None of Mrs. James's sons appear to have risen above the station of their father, yet two of the three did obtain realty.[89] Access to real property was typical of other early Black settlers, despite their occupational status as unskilled and semi-skilled workers. The three neighboring Black families to the James household in the 1870s owned the land on which their homes stood. Similarly, of four rural families residing in Union in 1880, three owned twenty-five or more acres of land.[90] Though these holdings were of modest size and value, the situation in Utah seems to contrast favorably with that prevailing in the South at the same time, where the rural freedman was trapped economically by a system of tenancy and sharecropping. It remains to be determined, however, whether access to property afforded Utah Blacks and their descendants opportunities for social and economic advancement.

The changing composition of Utah's Black population in the late nineteenth century is another subject that merits examination. The number of Utah Blacks multiplied almost sixfold between 1870 and 1900, with proportionately the greatest increase occurring in the 1880s. This population growth resulted in part from the stationing of Black troops — "buffalo soldiers," as they were known — in the territory, but substantial immigration was the major cause of the increase. In contrast to earlier Black settlers, who were about equally divided between men and women, the majority of these later immigrants were men, and by 1890 two-thirds of the Black population was male. The sexual imbalance continued throughout the early twentieth century and may have led to significant changes in family and social structure. Another distinguishing characteristic of the later immigrants was their religious affiliation. While many of the earlier settlers had been attached to the Mormon faith, the later immigrants were largely non-Mormon, and most of them seem to have settled in counties dominated by urban and commercial centers, principally Salt Lake County.[91] Whether these immigrants found property as accessible as earlier Black residents, whether their educational levels, occupation skills, and background were similar to those of prior Black settlers, and whether the two groups associated and intermarried across religious and cultural lines remain intriguing subjects for further study.[92]

Mrs. James's own life indicates that the origins of Utah's Black community are intertwined with the development of the Latter-day Saint Church. Until the arrival of the railroad and the beginnings of a mining boom in the late 1860s, most of Utah's Black settlers seem to have emigrated to the area as members of the church or as slaves within Mormon households, where they were exposed to the religion. What portion of their descendants remained members of the church remains unclear, but limited evidence suggests that it was a minority. Only one of Mrs. James's children can be located within the church at the time of his death.[93] Although the rate of attrition remains to be determined and explained, it may have been affected by the development of Black institutions in late nineteenth century Utah. Major Protestant denominations, such as the Methodists and Baptists, had pursued a policy of racial separation during the century, and this resulted in the establishment of Black congregations, churches, and conventions. These institutions often became focal points of the Black community, and, as noted, two Black churches had been founded in Salt Lake City by 1900. The Mormon Church, on the other hand, maintained an integrated structure—Blacks as well as Whites were members of geographically defined wards—but its denial of the priesthood to Black members precluded the development of leadership and institutions that could serve its Black constituency. As racial consciousness gained expression in Utah through the development of Black institutions, a policy of separatism may have ironically assisted Protestant denominations in their appeal to the local Black community.

Mother Augusta (Anderson) during her tenure as mother superior of the Congregation of the Sisters of the Holy Cross. Photo courtesy of the motherhouse of the order.

3

MOTHER M. AUGUSTA (ANDERSON)
Doing What Needs Doing

Sister M. Georgia (Costin)

Sister Georgia (Costin), historian for the Sisters of the Holy Cross, has a master's degree in English from Marquette University and a master's in Criminal Justice from Michigan State University. The University of Notre Dame Press has recently published her book Priceless Spirit, *a history of the Congregation from 1841 to 1893. In 1995 she traveled to Brazil to write a history of the order there. During the genesis of this book, one of the local historians we approached was Bernice Maher Mooney, author of* The Salt of the Earth: The History of the Catholic Church in Utah, 1776–1987. *She identified Mother Augusta of the Sisters of the Holy Cross, who lived in Utah for only three years, but she established several schools and a hospital, some of which are still serving the state. Feeling that her story could best be told from the motherhouse of her Congregation, Mooney referred us to Sister Georgia, who graciously agreed to join us. She says that as she researched the life of Mother Augusta, she came to realize how much her experience in Utah reflected the rest of her life, devoted to "doing what needs doing."*

When the Reverend Lawrence Scanlon arrived in Utah in August 1873, he found himself pastor of the most extensive parish in the United States, with probably the smallest Catholic population. The area for which he was spiritually responsible covered 85,000 square miles — the entire state of Utah and the eastern third of Nevada. There were about 87,000 people in the area. If they had been spaced out evenly there would have been one (and a very small fraction of a person) in each square mile. But Father Scanlon's parishioners numbered only 800 of these people; if the Catholics of Utah had been spread out evenly they would have been 108 miles apart. The 1911 edition of the *Catholic Encyclopedia* in its article on Utah says, "In Salt Lake and Ogden there were, by actual count, 90 Catholics; the remainder were dispersed along railroad divisions, in mining camps, and on the ranches." Later on, the same article praises Father Scanlon's accomplishments:

> The Catholic population of Utah is sparse; nevertheless the bishop [the same Father Scanlon] has achieved marvels. He brought the Sisters of the Holy Cross from Indiana to Salt Lake City, to Ogden, to Park City, to Eureka. In Park City and Eureka the Sisters teach select and parochial schools; in Ogden they conduct the Sacred Heart Academy; in Salt Lake City the Sisters conduct St. Mary's Academy and also Holy Cross Hospital. The Kearns St. Ann's Orphanage, built by Senator and Mrs. Kearns, has, since its completion in 1900, been under the care of eleven Sisters of the same order.

All of this began when Father Scanlon decided that the ninety persons in the Salt Lake-Ogden area were enough to make a beginning. He decided that this would be the headquarters of the parish and that there had to be a school there. Religious sisters were needed to teach in the school. The Sisters of the Holy Cross, originally a French group, now with an independent motherhouse at Saint Mary's, Notre Dame, near South Bend, Indiana, were establishing a fine reputation as teachers. Father Scanlon and his immediate superior, Archbishop Joseph S. Alemany of San Francisco, agreed that if these sisters could come and organize it, the school would be a good one. They wrote to the sisters.

The letter was received in early April and presented to the sisters' council, the governing body of the congregation, on April 10, 1875. There was discussion for and against the request, but unfortunately no verbatim account of it can be found. Finally the council voted in the affirmative: the school would be accepted. At first, two sisters would go — Sister Ferdinand (Bruggerman) and Sister Guardian Angels (Porter).

So this might have been an account of the heroic western adventures
of Sister Ferdinand or Sister Guardian Angels, except that in the end neither went. Sister Ferdinand asked to be excused from the assignment. The
council then looked within its own membership and asked its secretary,
Mother M. Augusta (Anderson), if she would go. She agreed. Then she
somehow got the point across that while Sister Guardian Angels would
no doubt be very useful on the assignment, Sister Raymond (Sullivan)
might be just a little better. On May 13, Sister Raymond was named to
replace Sister Guardian Angels. It was also noted at the meeting on that
day that the Salt Lake area "seems to promise a great field. Both school
and hospital seem to be desired."[1]

Sister Augusta had been moving west all her life. She was born in
1830 in Alexandria, Virginia, and baptized Ann Amanda, the youngest
of the four Anderson children. Her mother died when Amanda was four,
and the father put the children in a prairie schooner and set out in a
wagon train for Kansas. Somewhere between Alexandria and the town of
Lancaster, Ohio, Amanda's eight-year-old brother John was kidnapped
by roving gypsies. After a six-day search and a ransom contributed to
by every family in the wagon train, John was restored to his thoroughly
shocked and frightened family.

An aunt of the Anderson children, the sister of their dead mother,
had married a Mr. Lilly and now lived on a farm near Lancaster. The An-
dersons stayed some days with the Lillys while the wagon train made an
extended stop. Mrs. Lilly suggested that it was too dangerous for Amanda
to continue the journey, and her father reluctantly agreed. Amanda therefore remained behind with the Lillys and grew up in Lancaster, though
she was always in touch with her father, brother, and two sisters. The Lilly
farm was the Catholic center for that part of rural Ohio. Mass was offered
there once a month by an itinerant priest, Father Casper H. Borges, later
third bishop of Detroit. So Amanda was brought up in a firm and lively
faith.

The city of Lancaster was not just another midwestern farm town.
Among its distinguished inhabitants were several who affected the life of
Amanda Anderson and the order she would some day join. Chief among
these were the Ewing, Blaine, and Gillespie families. Thomas Ewing,
lawyer and judge, had served as secretary of the treasury in the brief ad-

ministration of President William Henry Harrison and for part of the administration of President John Tyler. Later, under President Zachary Taylor, he became the first secretary of the newly organized Department of the Interior. The Ewing family accepted William Tecumsah Sherman as their foster son at the age of nine when his own father died.[2] In 1850 Sherman married Ellen Ewing, daughter of Thomas.

Two sets of Ewing cousins, the Gillespies and the Blaines, also became part of Amanda's destiny. James Gillespie Blaine was a presidential candidate in 1884. Neil Gillespie was one of the first to graduate from the University of Notre Dame, and his older sister Eliza became Sister Mary Angela in 1853 and is generally regarded as the American foundress of the Sisters of the Holy Cross.

Eliza Gillespie had studied music in Lancaster under Mrs. Harriet Redmon, whose daughter, also named Harriet, had married a Mr. Lilly. There is no record of a relationship between the farm Lillys and the town Lillys, but it seems strongly likely. When Harriet Redmon Lilly's husband died, she decided to follow her friend Eliza Gillespie into the convent. On her trip from Lancaster to South Bend, Harriet was accompanied by Amanda Anderson and Mary Caren, both of whom also hoped to become Sisters of the Holy Cross. Amanda Anderson (Mother Augusta) and Harriet Lilly (Mother Elizabeth) each had a profound effect on the later history of the community. Mary Caren did not remain.

After the required year in the novitiate, Sister Augusta began her apostolic life by teaching grade school in Chicago. She then returned to Saint Mary's to serve in the "manual labor" school for girls who would have to earn their own living. She was given charge of a girls' academy in Morris, Illinois, but was suddenly removed from that work in December 1861 to join the sisters who were already nursing in the hospitals of the Civil War. She described her arrival at her first hospital assignment:

> Although we were tired and sick for want of sleep, there was no rest for us. We pinned up our habits, got brooms and buckets of water, and washed the blood-stained walls and scrubbed the floors. Dr. Burke sent some men to carry away the legs, arms, and other pieces of human bodies that were lying around. We had no beds that night, but we slept as soundly as if we had

feathers under us. The hospital was full of sick and wounded, but after some days we succeeded in getting it comparatively clean.[3]

Sister Augusta remained at military hospitals throughout the war and beyond. She was in charge of the Overton Hospital in Memphis from June 1862 until August 1865. She then went to Cairo, Illinois, and took charge of a "pest house" which contained wives and children who had contracted small pox while trying to reach soldiers on either side of the recently erased line of hostilities. She got back to Saint Mary's briefly but returned to take charge of a newly opened hospital in Cairo in 1867. From this stay she brought back with her two orphaned children who simply had nowhere else to go. The boy, Florian DeVoto, was educated at Notre Dame, which in those days took elementary and prep as well as college students; his sister, Rose, went to Saint Mary's. Rose later taught at St. Mary's Academy in Salt Lake City. Florian remained to teach at Notre Dame for some time, but moved to Ogden, Utah, where his son, the brilliant historian Bernard DeVoto, was born in 1897.

There is no historical basis for the story that as a result of her nursing activities in the Civil War, Sister Augusta became a favorite of General Grant. It is likely, though, given her Lancaster connections, that she may have met General Sherman, especially since his family moved to South Bend and his daughter attended Saint Mary's during the war.

In 1870 Sister Augusta left Cairo to take up a position as general secretary and stewardess (buyer and provider) for the congregation. It was from this work that she went to Salt Lake City with Sister Raymond in 1875.

The Golden Spike had been laid in Promontory just six years before, so the sisters were able to take the train all the way to Utah. They were met by Mr. and Mrs. Thomas Marshall, who took the sisters to their own house. There the sisters stayed until their convent was ready, which was not long. The house which the men of the area built for them was "a little adobe cottage, as unpretentious as the home of Nazareth."[4] From the beginning the sisters were enthusiastic about their first western location. "I think this is one day to be a great center,"[5] Sister Augusta wrote back to the Reverend Edward F. Sorin, C.S.C., her highest superior and founder of the University of Notre Dame.

The sisters had been instructed that if possible they were to buy the property on which the school would be located. This would enable them to set up a "select school," for which they would take full responsibility: admitting the pupils, setting the course of study, selecting the textbooks, collecting the tuition, and paying the bills. This plan did not meet with the approval of Archbishop Alemany, who preferred a parish school, administered by the pastor and supervised by the archbishop. In either case, because of the great distances to some Catholic homes, the school would have to take boarders as well as day students. For this reason they were starting out with girls only, hoping to take small boys as soon as possible. Children would be accepted at whatever academic level they had attained, so there would be a wide range of ages and intellectual development.

Sister Augusta wrote back to her motherhouse that, when the rest of the faculty arrived, they would need "one first-class teacher." Her preference would be one of the following sisters: Pauline (Moriarity), Rose (Crowley), Blanche (Bigelow), and Rita (Brennan). She also specified Sister Anna (Crowley), a sister of Sister Rose, to teach drawing. She seemed intent on getting people she knew. Scrambling her syntax a little, she wrote, "I very much dread to have a Sister sent to this queer, far-off place that I do not know."[6]

Her next concern was to fund the school. Salt Lake City was surrounded by mines—Bingham Canyon, twenty miles to the southwest, was one of the richest copper deposits in the world and also contained lead, zinc, gold, and silver. While many of the miners did not have their families with them, some of them did; and even those who did not were willing to support a Catholic school. Father Denis Kiely, Father Scanlon's first and at that time only assistant, guided and accompanied Mother Augusta and whatever sister went with her among the outlying mining areas, explaining to the men what the sisters hoped to do. Usually they returned wearily at the end of a day, but sometimes they were gone as long as a week. It was on these expeditions that the sisters realized why a hospital had been mentioned in the original letter along with a school.

Mining was a dangerous business, and there was no central place to take the seriously injured and care for them. When Mother Augusta spoke of starting a school, some of the miners told her that a hospital was what was really needed. She promised them that there would be a hospital, too.

She usually met with good results. The men were chronically short of cash, but promised donations on the next payday. And they kept their word. "Miners," she wrote back to Father Sorin, "are *not* like fashionables, who sometimes think the name enough without the money."[7]

The school building was going up with amazing rapidity. Fort Douglas, an army post nearby, had an architect in the person of Captain G. C. Davis of the Fourteenth U.S. Infantry. Mother Augusta described what she wanted, and Captain Davis drew up the plans. Excavations began on June 21, 1875. The first shovel of ground was turned by Mr. D. C. McGlynn, who had made the first money donation toward the school. He also donated the tin for the roof. W. S. Potter served as foreman, carpenter, and overseer of plans and specifications. S. W. Carlisle was the stonecutter, and Louis Moser and John Snell laid the first stones of the foundation June 27.[8] Window frames, sashes, stairs, and casings were the work of Joseph Salisbury, William Berklon, and Henry Raddon. Roofing material other than the tin was provided by M. B. Callahan. J. M. Allen took care of heating and plumbing and W. Lemmon did all the painting.

By July 12 they had enrolled fifteen boarders and fifty day students. Not all were Catholics. Mormons and Protestants were showing an interest in the new school. Father Scanlon officiated at the laying of the cornerstone in August, assisted by Father Kiely, and named the school Saint Mary of the Assumption.

Sisters Pauline, Anna, Josepha (McHale), Holy Innocents (McLaren), and Petronella (Piggott) arrived in mid-August. Sister Holy Innocents was to teach music and Sister Petronella was a cook, which ensured regular and substantial meals.

It seems incredible that the structure could have had a roof on it by the first week of September, but opening day was set for Monday, September 6. On Sunday, September 5,

> a Mormon Bishop proclaimed from the pulpit that no Mormons
> would be permitted to send their children to the Sisters' school

under penalty of being cut off from the church. Consequently, few returned for school, though many parents had registered their daughters. The Catholic population of the city consisted of nine or ten families, but so generous was the non-Catholic patronage that by the end of the first week of school the enrollment was one hundred day pupils and six boarders. At the end of the first year there were twenty-five boarders.[9]

The first student enrolled was Nannie Marshall, daughter of the family who had given the sisters hospitality on their arrival.

It will be seen that even if Mother Augusta functioned as full-time administrator and fundraiser, and Sister Holy Innocents taught music all day, the pupil-teacher ratio was a little better than forty to one, which was average or better than average for Catholic schools in those days. Nevertheless, the sisters must have been counting on a continuous increase, for before September was over, the motherhouse sent three more sisters: Sisters Eugenie (D'Orbesson), Gertrude (Kunze), and Martha (Ready).

Two months after the young ladies began their classes, an addition was ready on the little adobe house and Sister Gertrude opened a school for small boys. Mother Augusta's office was nearby, in case Sister Gertrude needed any backup, but Mother Augusta probably did not teach. She had too many other responsibilities.

She was able to rent a two-story brick house on Fifth East Street in which to make a start on a hospital. In October 1875 Sister Holy Cross (Welsh) and Sister Bartholomew (Darnell) came from Saint Mary's to begin setting up the hospital and receiving patients. Dr. Allan Fowler, Dr. D. Benedict, and his brother Dr. J. M. Benedict agreed to treat the patients without a fee. The hospital was soon overcrowded. Sometimes the only available beds were the two being used by the sisters; then the sisters gave up their beds and slept on the floor.

Miners subscribed to the hospital at the rate of one dollar a month, "paid regularly while in health."[10] It was an early form of health insurance.[11] The care for those who subscribed was entirely free, not only the doctors' services, but room, nursing care, food, and medicines. Those who chose not to subscribe were charged ten dollars a week plus physicians' fees. The sisters had flyers printed and distributed in the area with this information clearly stated. The three doctors were described in the flyer as "a corps of the best Physicians of the City."

Sister Martha left the group at the school to become cook at the hospital—not only for the two sister nurses, but for all the patients. She only stayed one year. In 1876 Sister Alcantara (Evans) and Sister Martina (McMahon) joined the original pair. Both are listed as nurses. For that year the four sisters apparently shared the cooking duties.

For the year 1877–78 Sister Petronella came from the school to take up the cooking chores. Sister Holy Cross, the superior, and Sister Bartholomew, her assistant, shared the nursing duties with Sister Martina. Other kinds of help were provided: Sister Gonzales (Meagher) took over all the laundry work, which must have been considerable, and Sister Zita (Murphy) did most of the housekeeping.

This was the situation in Salt Lake City when Mother Augusta left the city. The three years she had spent in founding the hospital and the school were a longer time than she had expected to spend. Like all of her work, the tasks were done well. Both institutions had long lives ahead of them.

Because pioneers do not have much time for writing things down, there is not much in the written record about these three years. An account from a much later student gives us an idea of St. Mary's eventual development. Ann Bassett apparently enrolled in St. Mary's Academy on October 22, 1898. She later wrote:

> Father decided to send me to a Catholic convent in Salt Lake City, Utah. . . . I was met at the station by the Sisters [and later] tabulated and turned out among 400 girls of every age and size, from tots to twenties. . . . Our clothing was beautifully pressed and placed ready to wear. . . . And what thrilling sensations I experienced listening for those innumerable bells to ring! . . . At the slightest symptoms of illness or fatigue we were gently whisked away to another part of this endless building, to the infirmary.[12]

We learn from the records of later years that there was a great Pontifical High Mass in St. Mary's Cathedral in Salt Lake City when Sister

Holy Cross died in 1898, with Bishop Scanlon as celebrant and Father Kiely as homilist. In the oratorical style of the day, Father Kiely reviewed the sister's life in Salt Lake City.

In a building on Fifth East for a temporary hospital, her labors began.
There she labored most devotedly, and under the most trying circumstances for seven years. With only one Sister to assist, they had at times as many as fifty patients to be watched, cared for, and nursed. Often to meet pressing demands, she gave up her own apartments, and slept on the floor; still oftener would she be a week without rest, or sleep, save only perhaps a few hours in the day, when she would entrust her patients to other hands. Her broad charity, tempered with the greatest patience, and entirely devoid of selfishness, won for her the affection, love, good will and generous support of all who knew her.[13]

While her school and hospital were growing in Utah, Mother Augusta returned to Saint Mary's, where she was assigned to serve four one-year terms as superior in four different establishments, adding to her experience in both school administration and nursing administration. She was then elected to a six-year term as mother superior of all the Sisters of the Holy Cross. Then, with a change in the sisters' constitutions, she served another six-year term with the title of superior general, leaving major office in 1895. During her twelve years in charge of the congregation she added to its missions five parish schools (three of them in Utah),[14] five academies (three of them in the West), and four more hospitals.

She lived twelve more years and died at 8 P.M. on Christmas Eve of 1907. There were no Pontifical High Masses or lavish homilies for her. Many of the bishops, priests, and religious leaders she had worked with were themselves dead by then. The motherhouse records contain copies of articles about her death from the South Bend *Tribune* and the South Bend *Times*, the Cairo (Illinois) *Bulletin*, the *Catholic Columbian Record* of Columbus, Ohio, and the Saint Mary's *Chimes*. There was also one from the *Intermountain Catholic* of Salt Lake City, an editorial written by her old friend Father Kiely, remembering her work and praising her virtues. Twelve priests of the Congregation of the Holy Cross order were on the altar for her funeral mass, including the Reverend Gilbert Francais, fourth superior general.

The school which Mother Augusta had opened in 1875 became Saint Mary's Academy and later the College of Saint Mary-of-the-Wasatch. The college closed in 1959 and the high school in 1969. In 1994 circumstances necessitated the sale of the Holy Cross Hospital to Health Trust of Nashville.

The Sisters of the Holy Cross are still serving the people of Utah, but in less institutionalized ways. Many are working in smaller towns and rural areas, following, as Mother Augusta did, the precept of their founder, the Reverend Basil A. Moreau, "Do what needs doing."

Eliza Kirtley Royle, age 46, in 1893. Photo courtesy of the Ladies Literary Club.

4

ELIZA KIRTLEY ROYLE
Beloved Club Mother

Patricia Lyn Scott

Patricia Lyn Scott received a B.A. degree in history from Southern Utah University, an M.S. degree in library science with a specialization in archival administration from Wayne State University, and an M.A. in history of the American West from the University of Utah. She has been with the Utah State Archives since October 1984 and serves as Utah's local government records archivist. She provides consultant services and training in every aspect of archival and records management to Utah's counties and school districts. She is the author of several history articles and the book A Hub of Eastern Idaho: A History of Rigby, Idaho. *She has also produced eleven bibliographies on Utah history, contributed articles to the* Utah History Encyclopedia, *and is currently co-editing a book on women in Utah. She serves on the editorial board of the* Journal of Mormon History. *She selected Eliza because in 1983 she presented a paper on the Ladies Literary Club. At that time she felt: "I wanted to know more about these women. Who were they? Where did they come from? Eliza Kirtley Royle is the logical first choice. She was the club's first president and was its beloved 'Club Mother.'" Scott found Eliza left little about herself, but among the few records she was quoted frequently as maintaining, "The club is my life."*

During the last quarter of the nineteenth century, hundreds of women's literary clubs were founded across the United States. These clubs provided a means for women to promote sisterhood, confidence, and skills

44

in speaking, researching, and writing, giving women a "sense of worth and enabl[ing] some members to move on to more political activity."[1]

Eliza Kirtley Royle was a leader in the women's club movement in Utah. Though she received numerous honors during her lifetime, including national recognition for her contributions to women and acknowledgment as "one of the most brilliant women in the west," she has been largely forgotten in Utah history.[2] She was a strong, well respected woman. Her life was spent being a devoted daughter, a loving wife and mother, a steadfast friend, an enthusiastic student, a leader, and a committed club woman. She was a force for bringing Utah women together out of their isolation into the world of learning and culture.

Eliza Kirtley was born on April 6, 1835 to Sinclair and Mary Ann Kirtley in Columbia, Missouri. She was the second of five children, four girls and a boy.

Columbia, located in central Missouri twenty-seven miles north of Jefferson City, is the Boone County seat. In 1840, it boasted a population of 1,000 and was said to be the social and educational center of an agricultural district of "unsurpassed fertility."[3] Eliza described Columbia as "a little town containing many refined and cultivated people and a town of some ambition," a place where "cultivated judges and lawyers from all over the state" were entertained.[4]

Sinclair Kirtley was a prominent, well-respected attorney, a Whig who served three terms representing Democratic Columbia in the Missouri State Legislature and one term as state senator. He was known as Captain Kirtley, a rank he had earned in the U.S. Army during the Black Hawk War in the 1830s.[5] He was born in Kentucky, graduated from the Transylvania University of Lexington, then studied law, and was admitted to the bar in 1825.[6] He moved to Columbia, Missouri, to practice law and there on February 3, 1831, married Mary Ann Breckridge Peebels. She was only sixteen, half his age, and her only education was from a country school. Eliza later recalled that her mother "deplored the fact that she had no opportunity of securing a finished education, but her very appreciation of her loss made her a student and a woman of self-culture and as she grew older became the pride and ornament of the hospitable home . . . [to which] distinguished people of the state were the frequent and always welcomed guests."[7]

Captain Kirtley had a keen interest in horticulture and obtained plants from eastern nurseries for his orchards and gardens. He organized a drama club at the state university, serving as its leader, manager, instructor, and participant in many productions. Eliza later described him as "a man 'before his time.' He was much in public life, not for the honors or instruments of office, but for the good he could do for his country and his state."[8]

Eliza does not describe her education, but her sister Mary recalls that early on Eliza manifested a love of good literature and reading books "because she keenly appreciated and enjoyed the beauties of the style, or the 'truth of nature' of the plot, or the high and noble thoughts portrayed by the author."[9]

Since Captain Kirtley served on the board of trustees for the Columbia Female Academy, it could be assumed his daughters attended this institution. The academy was a combined elementary school and high school operating on the educational philosophy of "the establishment of right principles, the cultivation of reasoning facilities in due proportion and the storing of the mind with useful truths." Junior students received training in English grammar, rhetoric, algebra, geometry, botany, philosophy, chemistry, astronomy, geography, history (ancient, modern, and American), and human physiology. Competition between students was minimized while each student was judged on the basis of her own abilities.[10]

The Kirtleys were a religious family. Every member of the household, including the servants, assembled for morning prayers and hymn-singing. They belonged to no church until the early 1840s when they were baptized in the Presbyterian Church. Within a few weeks, Captain Kirtley was elected an elder, a position he held throughout his life.[11]

The Kirtley home was not large, but was set in the grounds of two whole blocks. The large yard contained both fruit and shade trees creating a "delightful children's playground."[12] Mary recalled, "Our house seemed to have been the rendezvous for all the numerous children in our neighborhood, and often, late in the afternoon, or at twilight . . . my father would get his flute . . . [and] play for them to dance on our large back porch, every child there being as much at home with him as were his own children." She added, "Never were children reared under happier auspices or in a sweeter home."[13]

The Kirtleys left their "idyllic" life in Columbia in 1847 and moved to St. Louis, where Captain Kirtley entered a law partnership with his brother-in-law, Edwin Ryland. Little is known of their life in St. Louis except that Eliza's education continued at the "Young Ladies Select School."[14] Later the Kirtley children viewed this move as a mistake, noting how their father "missed his horses, his fruit culture and flowers and, not least, the dear, life long friends of his early married life in Columbia." His health eventually suffered.[15] When his physicians advised him to move to the more favorable California climate, he left Missouri in 1852, planning to establish a home for his family in Sacramento. He planned to have fruit trees and flowers, a place to cultivate a garden even more beautiful than his "old, beloved one in Columbia." On April 30, 1853, Captain Kirtley died only a few days after writing his last hopeful letter. He was buried in Sacramento.[16] After their father's death, the Kirtley family moved to live with Grandmother Peebels in Lexington, Missouri.

The Kirtley daughters enjoyed the "delightful society of the Young People in the pleasantest of Missouri towns"[17] where Eliza married Jonathon C. Royle on April 23, 1857 at the First Presbyterian Church of Lexington.[18] Jonathon was born in Kentucky, the son of an English woolen manufacturer. He had received little formal education but had read constantly in his youth. After choosing law as his profession, he read law with the well-respected Judge Woods. Admitted to the bar in 1853, he became Wood's partner.[19] Judge Wood had been a friend of Eliza's father and undoubtedly introduced her to his young associate. Being an attorney's daughter, Eliza was well prepared to be an attorney's wife.

The Royles recorded little of their early life together in Lexington. Jonathon became a circuit attorney in the Sixth Judicial Circuit while Eliza undoubtedly lived a traditional domestic life as the mother of three sons: Sinclair, born in 1858, Frank, born in 1860, and Edwin, born in 1862.

The Civil War immediately changed the course of their lives. Jonathon enlisted in the Confederate Army and was made judge advocate with the rank of colonel. While it is not known how long he served in the Confederate Army, he was called "judge" throughout the rest of his life.[20]

Missouri was a bloody battlefield with countless skirmishes, raids, and battles. The Royle family found themselves practically destitute after various "alarming vicissitudes" and "left the farm and moved to St. Louis." When circumstances became precarious, Judge Royle left and went westward to Colorado. Thirty-eight miles west of Denver he settled in Central City, a booming mining town where he soon became an expert in mining law. A year later, Eliza and their three little boys joined him.[21]

Gold had been discovered in Gregory Gulch in 1859, and Central City had emerged as the hub, surrounded by mines, mining, and the robust towns of Black Hawk, Nevadaville, and Russell Gulch. Compared to other settlements in the area, Central City was the "epitome of respectability." Though its streets contained the typical trappings of a boisterous, wide open mining camp—saloons and variety halls, prostitution, and gamblers—the raw violence that marked other camps was nearly nonexistent in Central City. By 1870, Central City boasted a population of four thousand.[22] The famous journalist Bayard Taylor called it "the most outrageously expensive place in Colorado. You pay more and get less for the money than in any other part of the world."[23]

While little is known of the Royles' life in Colorado, it was marked with both sadness and happiness. Not long after their arrival, four-year-old Frank died, the child who had most resembled Eliza's beloved father. In 1868, Eliza bore their only daughter, Martha. Because Central City's elevation of eight thousand feet proved unhealthy to Eliza, the family moved to California in 1870.[24]

But the Royle family moved to Salt Lake City only a year later, arriving on March 13, 1871. It was a city reluctantly opening to the outside world. The railroad had reached Utah in 1869, ending Mormon isolation, but there were fewer than one thousand non-Mormons in the entire Utah Territory. In 1882, Judge Royle recalled that "a few 'Gentiles' . . . had been permitted to live in Utah," suggesting his awareness of being an outsider.[25] There is no evidence that either he or Eliza participated in any of the anti-polygamy crusades common during the 1870s and 1880s. In fact, Judge Royle was later described as having "cordial

relations with the Mormon people . . . [and having] never entered into
the bitterness and strife which was all about him."²⁶

Almost immediately Judge Royle formed a partnership with Judge
Thomas Marshall. Marshall and Royle became an eminent firm, handling
a great deal of big mining litigation. He became the local attorney for
both the Central Pacific and for the Wells Fargo Company.²⁷Royle's reputation was a fine one. He was said to "be a liberal in all his business
transactions, and untiring worker in behalf of his client . . . an exemplary
citizen [with] a large following of personal friends."²⁸

On November 12, 1871, Rev. Josiah Welch organized the First
Presbyterian Church of Salt Lake City, with a membership of eleven including the Royles. A decade later, Judge Royle recalled that in 1871
"the Presbyterian Church discovered that it had mission work in Utah
requiring intellectual strength, fervent piety, and executive ability."²⁹
Though vacant houses and halls were scarce in Salt Lake City during
the 1870s, "Welch and his flock" organized to build a church. "Poor
in the current funds of the world, but rich in faith," the women of the
church "addressed a call for help to their sisters in the United States"
and Rev. Welch went east to solicit contributions. Through the small
congregation's united efforts, the Presbyterian Church purchased a lot,
constructed a building, and dedicated their church on October 11, 1874.
The following April, the church established a Presbyterian school in the
basement, where thirty pupils including the Royle children received instruction from Professor and Mrs. John M. Coyner and their daughter,
Emma.³⁰

Despite these opportunities, Eliza suffered from the remoteness and
the lack of intellectual stimulation she felt in this desert city. Her sister,
Mary, later described Eliza "as feeling keenly the dearth of intellectual
pleasures and interests in that city of Mormons." As a result, "with four
of her intelligent lady friends . . . [she would] meet together in her parlor
every Friday, for two hours," where they "read and discussed . . . world
literature, history, art, ceramics, and a wide range of other interesting
topics."³¹

In 1875, Eliza joined a small group of women who met at the home
of Mrs. Jennie Froiseth, wife of Bernard A. M. Froiseth, geographer and
cartographer of the region. There they formed the Blue Tea, Utah's first

women's club. Mrs. Froiseth, raised in English literary circles, frequently lamented the lonely life in Utah. While visiting a New York friend, Julia Ward Howe,[32] it was suggested she organize a women's club and call it Blue Tea, reminiscent of "bluestocking fame" and "dainty pink teas."[33]

The Blue Tea was essentially an exclusive literary and cultural club with a membership limited to twenty-five. The women met to discuss literary works and to read papers that the members had researched and written. Meetings were held weekly on Thursday afternoons for three hours. On September 14, 1876, Eliza was elected vice-president and presided during Mrs. Froiseth's extended illness in November and December of that year.[34]

Among the members of the Blue Tea were a few women who believed a non-exclusive women's club was needed in Salt Lake City, not only for the literary elite, but also for women who were just learners. Eliza later recalled, "Very soon the few who were determined that a club should stand for the education of the many rather than culture for a few, seceded from the original society."[35]

In February 1877, three Blue Tea members and a few friends met at the home of Mrs. Tina R. Jones and organized the Ladies Literary Club for the purpose of "literary pursuits and mental culture." Eliza was elected its first president and its first plank was said to be the "open door," placing no restriction of education or number of members. No minutes survive from the years prior to 1879 and little is known of these first meetings, but a constitution was drawn and officers were selected.[36]

On March 29, 1877, the members of Blue Tea discussed Eliza's six-week absence and authorized the secretary to write to the vice-president and inquire "if she intended on resuming her duties."[37] There is no evidence that she responded to this query nor were any other absent members discussed.

On April 19, members of the Blue Tea adopted a motion stating that "the ladies one and all who took part in the 'secession' and have not been present at our meetings for more than two months, be expelled from membership. The following names were [then] stricken: E[liza] K. Royle, H[enrietta] Billing, C[atherine] F. Robertson, G[eorgia] Snow, M. H. Hemingway, S[arah] Gamble, M. M. Barker."[38]

Unlike most literary clubs formed during the 1870s and 1880s, the

Ladies Literary Club members were not "older women who had joined after their families had grown," but for the most part were young mothers with young children.[39] Most of these women were the wives of prominent businessmen, government officials, and religious leaders, and had resided in Utah for only a short time. A few were single professional women, but all were said to be non-Mormons.[40] Neither Mormons nor any other group were excluded from membership by the club's constitution or bylaws, but by what was said to be a common understanding. Gentile women, a tiny minority in the entire territory of Utah, felt a need to form a sisterly enclave.[41] Eliza later recalled:

> A few warm-hearted, large-minded women of Salt Lake felt that nowhere did women in a community more need the help of sympathetic and cooperative intellectual work than in Utah. In those early days they were cut off from the new and progressive methods of culture, which centered in the large cities of the East, and feared that without a struggle they would be left behind their Eastern sisters. Thus the Club was organized for intellectual culture and upon the principles of deep sympathy and broad charity.[42]

Eliza later described this new organization as "an Infant truly crying, in the night; an infant crying for the light."[43]

Until 1895, the club met every Friday for two hours. History was the chief subject of study. The club made a careful and systematic study of the history of Rome, Germany, France, Florence, Spain, England, Russia, and South America. Members researched and wrote papers on club-selected topics and presented them during the club meetings. One or perhaps two meetings a month were devoted to art and to other topics. The club year ran from September to May allowing for a three-month vacation. The business of acquiring knowledge was an all-absorbing one and not until 1897 was an entertainment committee appointed. Mrs. George Y. Wallace, a founding member, later recalled: "I think the first subject we ever took up was Rome. We studied Rome until I could nearly find my way blindfolded through its streets. I had to write a paper, about it, and I can remember that, while I didn't mind writing it, I tried to get someone else to read it. She wouldn't, so I had to do it myself. I was scared to death, but I managed through it."[44]

Two of the most important functions of the club were broadening their members' outlook and developing their poise. The club seemed to bring out talents and abilities that might otherwise have "lain dormant."[45] This reflected a national trend. Karen J. Blair noted in *Clubwoman As Feminist* that "the task of freeing women from inhibitions about speaking publicly was not an easy one. For generations women had been taught that silence in public was a virtue."[46]

Eliza's devotion to the club was second only to her devotion to her family—her husband, daughter, and two sons. Then, in 1879, at the age of forty-four, Eliza bore her last child, a son. He was named Jonathon for his father.[47] After twenty years of childbearing one phase of Eliza's life ended.

On December 20, 1882, the Ladies Literary Club was incorporated under the laws of the territory of Utah. The Articles of Incorporation included the original constitution, plus expanded bylaws. The new purpose stated that the club was created to "establish, maintain, and carry on a society for the promotion and general diffusion of knowledge among its members and the public in matters of science, art and literature, and other branches of higher education of women."[48]

Twenty-eight active members signed the Articles of Incorporation. Only six charter members remained since the formation of the club in 1877; besides Eliza they were Annabel M. Black, Laura C. Douglas, Mary C. Gilmer, Tina R. Jones, and Mattie S. Woodward. Membership always fluctuated dramatically in the early years. Many women lived in Utah for only a short time, then moved on as their husbands' professions required them to relocate. It was a rare meeting that did not include the resignation of a departing member.

The club meetings were first held in members' homes, but by the end of 1877 membership had doubled to twenty-four, requiring more space. For twenty years, the club led a nomadic life, meeting in more than twenty different locations, first in donated space, then in rented rooms. After incorporation, the women discussed buying a lot and constructing a clubhouse, but lack of funds delayed such action.

Eliza loved the Ladies Literary Club and it became an essential part of her life. Not only was she elected as its first president, but she also served a second term from 1889–90, two terms as corresponding secretary (1881 and 1885), and five terms as historian. She also headed the art committee (1880), served as a member of the ways and means committee (1882), and served on the original building committee in 1882. Eliza remained active throughout her life and the club's minutes are replete with her involvement. She regularly attended meetings, presented papers, participated in discussions, and always demonstrated her full commitment and knowledge.

Eliza's interests were also not exclusive. In addition to her involvement with the Presbyterian Church and the Ladies Literary Club, she was also an honorary member of the Salt Lake Women's Club.

While the Ladies Literary Club was founded for self-improvement, members soon became interested in outside projects. Their first was supporting the fledgling Masonic Library, a subscription library which the Masonic lodge had opened on September 1, 1877 for the "use and benefit of the craft and general public." The new library contained 1,786 volumes.[49] On December 11, 1879, Eliza was appointed to chair a five-member committee to obtain library subscriptions for club members. A week later the committee distributed subscription certificates to all club members.[50] The club continued its support of the Masonic Public Library and then of its successor, the Pioneer Public Library Association.

In 1893, the Club sponsored a three-day "Kirmess," an annual fair, to raise funds to purchase two thousand volumes for the library. Eliza hosted the Italian booth, providing food and entertainment. The Kirmess netted $3,100, and two thousand new volumes were carefully selected with the recommendation of the superintendent of schools.[51] In January 1896, the club helped draft legislation which would authorize cities to levy taxes for the support of public libraries and lobbied for its passage. In March 1896, the measure passed and became law on January 1, 1898. A provision of the law required one thousand signatures in the jurisdiction to make it operational. The club spearheaded the effort in securing the signatures.[52] Across the nation, women's clubs were achieving similar successes:

In the face of ridicule and censure, women learned that silence was no longer the virtue it once had been. . . . women found it smarter to probe first about the problems in the arts, and then about the problems of women in society. . . . Club life succeeded in reaching and assisting a large body of American women to grow, by altering their expectations of both their societal functions and their ability to carry out change.[53]

In 1892, the Ladies Literary Club became the first Utah women's club to become affiliated with the General Federation of Women's Clubs. Mrs. Clarence E. Allen, a former Ladies Literary Club president, was made Utah's first state director. The Ladies Literary Club was one of seven women's clubs in the state that responded to the call to organize the Utah Federation, on April 7, 1893. Their action made Utah only the second state federation in the nation.[54]

In 1895, club president Eurithe K. La Barthe, who would be elected to the state legislature the next year, appointed a permanent clubhouse committee chaired by Isabel C. (Mrs. Arthur) Brown. In September 1897, the committee purchased a lot on Third East between First South and South Temple for $1,500 and hired a builder to construct a building for $3,200.[55]

On January 7, 1898, the club's first clubhouse was opened with ninety-three members and twenty-one guests in attendance. Dedicatory services were brief and simple. Isabel C. Brown, chair of the building committee, formally presented the clubhouse and Club President Mrs. W. A. Neldon accepted the building on behalf of its members. A short program included the reminiscences of three charter members, followed by music and poetry recitations. Eliza, one of the speakers, proclaimed: "This is indeed a day of joy! A day of joy for all, but especially for the few who are left of the little band of hopeful women who attended the birth of the feeble infant, whose majority we so gloriously celebrated today, for it is the year of 1898 that this child of our love reaches for [its] twenty-first birthday. . . . Loyalty and devotion to the Club's interests have been . . . one of its most marked characteristics." She spoke with pride of the fact that a number of flourishing clubs had been founded by former members of the Ladies Literary Club in the West and North and even in cultured Boston.[56]

From June 21 to 27, 1898, the fourth biennial conference of the General Federation of Women's Clubs was held in Denver with 835 delegates representing 690 women's clubs, whose combined membership topped sixty thousand. During the afternoon session on June 23, Eliza Kirtley Royle was made an honorary vice president of the General Federation for life. She was only the fourth woman to be given this honor, a recognition of her contribution to the "establishment of women's clubs in the West."[57] This honor would only be the first of many bestowed on Eliza.

In March 1901, Eliza resigned as historian of the Ladies Literary Club, saying, "I feel assured that my health will not permit me to do the work required by the position this year."[58] The nature and seriousness of this illness is not known or how long Eliza's activities were curbed, but the club's minutes reported her attendance in the fall.

The club celebrated its silver anniversary on February 2, 1902. Every seat in the little clubhouse was filled and the hall was festively decorated with flowers and national colors. Eliza had planned the program and chaired the day's events. She told attendees that she had previously "glorified the club's past" but was proud to recognize "the glory of the present." She noted the benefits of club life and the business sense that club activity developed in women. Proudly, she announced that the club's building debt had been paid. Letters were then read from absent past presidents, short speeches were made by those present, songs were sung, poems read, and gifts presented to the club. Each club member donated twice as many pennies to the club as the number of her years, totalling 3664.[59] Members were obviously loath to admit their ages—even to themselves. The average age of members of that day was calculated to be just twenty-three years.

Just a few weeks later, the club, in a touching and beautiful ceremony, presented Eliza with a loving cup in grateful appreciation of her long service as the "club mother." Eliza was sixty-seven years old and had been a staunch member of the Ladies Literary Club for twenty-five years. Her acceptance included these prophetic words: "I shall not be with you, but God willing many of you will be here to celebrate our beloved club's golden birthday. Then you will say with me, 'the Ladies Literary Club has been a blessing to me and mine.' "[60]

The "mine" to whom Eliza referred were her husband and four surviving children. Just as Judge Royle's solid and respectable legal profession assured the family's economic and social status in the city, so Eliza's club activities with their emphasis on self-improvement and community betterment created a parallel standing in the female world. While Eliza and the children might have remained isolated from the larger Mormon community, these voluntary affiliations provided a network of associations in which the children grew up, with their accepted places in the society created by their parents.

Her four children were all well educated and successful. Sinclair Kirtley became a prominent New York physician. Edwin (Ned) Milton became a nationally renowned dramatist and author living in Connecticut. Martha Royle King Palmer was an accomplished professional musician—a vocalist and composer. She was married twice: to Lorin King, a Utah druggist, and after her divorce to Eugene B. Palmer, a newspaperman and realtor. She was the only child to settle in Salt Lake City. Jonathon C. managed the Denver office of the Associated Press.[61]

On April 23, 1907, the Royles celebrated their golden wedding anniversary by holding a reception in the music studio of their daughter, Martha, at the Commercial Building. Newspaper accounts described the room as "radiant with beautiful flowers." The chief decorating color was yellow, in honor of the golden wedding anniversary. Beneath a canopy, the judge and Eliza received more than two hundred friends. On display were trousseau gowns Eliza had worn fifty years before and one of their wedding invitations. The Judge read a six-stanza poem of tribute he had written, "To Eliza K. Royle—My Dear Wife."[62] Friends described them as "true companions, inseparable for even a day." Their marriage was simply described as "beautiful." Their son Edwin dedicated his novel *The Silent Call* to his parents: "To my father and mother who have preserved the spirit of old-fashioned romance throughout their fifty years of wedded life."[63]

On June 6, 1910, Judge Royle died of chronic nephritis at the age of eighty-one.[64] He was said to have been in "feeble health for a long time, but had been confined to his bed for only a few days."[65] Judge Royle left an estate worth only $14,618.03, not a large sum, and designated Eliza as his sole beneficiary. He wrote in his will: "It is my wish that my wife, who has been so much with me, and who has for so many years borne with me the burthens and the joys and sorrows of life, shall, as far as I can compass it, at my death be free from poverty, dependence or pecuniary anxiety. I am satisfied that my estate will not be large enough to divide between my wife and my children, and still leave her, in such division, sufficient means from the income and proceeds thereof, to live upon."[66]

After fifty-three years of marriage Eliza was alone. Her husband's death left a void which could not be filled—as friends later wrote: "a sorrow, from which she never recovered"—although she was too serene in her Christian faith and rich in intellectual resources to become emotionally crippled. She first traveled east and visited Sinclair in New York and Ned in Connecticut and her two sisters in Denver. She then returned to make her home with her daughter in Salt Lake City.[67]

Just six months after her husband's death, Eliza died on December 10, 1910 after a brief illness at seventy-five.[68] While her death certificate listed the cause as "cerebral hemorrhage," her friends noted, "it was the heart's yearning to be with her companion of fifty-three sweet years." Newspapers called her "one of Utah's most prominent pioneers and one of the most brilliant women of the West."[69] Her legacy to Utah was the Ladies Literary Club.

By 1910, club membership had increased to 250 and discussion began on plans to enlarge the clubhouse. Enlargement proved infeasible and on March 10, 1910 a committee was appointed to dispose of the clubhouse and to make preliminary plans to build a new one. In April, the committee sold the clubhouse for $8,250 to the Pexiotto Lodge No. 421, Independent Order of B'nai Brith and later that year purchased a lot at 850 East South Temple for $8,500. For two years the club attempted to raise money to begin building. The minutes are very sketchy for this period and do not indicate where meetings were held.[70] In January 1911, the club drafted the following resolution of respect in memory of their beloved "club mother":

> Whereas it has pleased God to remove into His blessed preserve our beloved friend and co-worker Eliza Kirtley Royle.
> Resolved—That the membership of the Ladies Literary

Club give expression to our sense of the loss we have sustained. She was one of the Founders and was the First President of the Club and has always been its most loyal friend and adherent; and throughout her thirty-four years of her connection with it, has ever been the club's most gracious counselor. She was strong in her convictions of right, keen and clear in her judgment, quick in her perceptions, ready always with her sympathy, equal to every occasion, swift and generous in her commendation, and above all things, charitable. We admired her as a strong and earnest club worker; we admired her as a woman, and we loved and cherished her as a warm hearted steadfast friend.

The resolution was "spread upon the minutes of the club and a copy was sent to her daughter, Mrs. E. B. Palmer."[71]

As the Ladies Literary Club heralded the opening of its clubhouse two years later, members again recalled their first president and beloved "club mother." On April 25, 1913, following the formal acceptance of the building by Mary W. Critchlow, club president, Martha Royle Palmer presented a memorial chair, a "touching tribute of love," in memory of her mother, saying, "Next to her family, my mother loved this club, and it is only fitting that as a token of that love . . . I should present this tribute to you in memory of her . . . a practical gift which should prove useful to the club every day of its meetings."[72] The chair was made of fumed oak, upholstered in brown leather. The wood was carved in a design of oak leaves and acorns and the Kirtley crest and coat of arms was carved on the high back near the top, with the letters "E. K. R." and the club monogram, "L. L. C.," below.[73]

Mrs. Critchlow responded: "May [Eliza's] sweet mantle of charity and optimism, adherence to right and steadfast of purpose, loyalty in friends, fidelity to trust and faith in God fall upon all . . . May her spirit, symbolically breathed upon us today, be with us always in the coming year; and may the sanity, justice and love which were so evident in her life direct the wheels of progress and development in this club."[74] Eliza's chair remains a cherished possession of the Ladies Literary Club and is used by the president at each general club session.

After one hundred and eighteen years, the Ladies Literary Club continues as Utah's largest and most active women's club, true to its past, but looking to the future. One cannot enter its clubhouse and not feel the presence of all the women that have entered its doors and of that small band that began its efforts. As Charlotte Perkins Gilman, feminist author and lecturer, observed, "Club women learn more than to improve the mind; they learn to love each other."[75]

Eliza would heartily agree.

Sarah Elizabeth Carmichael. Photo courtesy of the Utah State Historical Society.

5

SARAH ELIZABETH CARMICHAEL
Poetic Genius of Pioneer Utah

Miriam B. Murphy

Miriam Murphy is a native of Salt Lake City and a graduate of the University of Utah, where she edited the school newspaper, The Utah Daily Chronicle. *She worked for several years in advertising in New York and San Francisco, returning to Utah in 1970 to become the associate editor of the* Utah Historical Quarterly. *She has, in addition, published poetry, histories, and numerous reviews. She recognized the importance of Sarah Elizabeth Carmichael to Utah poetry several years ago and wrote this essay, which originally appeared in the* Utah Historical Quarterly 43 *(winter 1975) and is reprinted here by permission. She became intrigued with Sarah: "A lot of people were writing poetry in that period, most of it pretty dreadful sing-song stuff with twisted language, but she had poetic genius. She had a modicum of success nationally and a tragic life, including a breakdown that ended her poetry."*

The poetry of Utah's pioneer days lies for the most part forgotten in the periodicals of the day and a few slim volumes of verse preserved in local libraries. While a surprising number of early Utahns wrote poetry, only a handful of their poems survive—most notably in hymns such as the familiar "Come, Come Ye Saints" by William Clayton. Of the poets themselves, Eliza R. Snow is the only one whose name is mentioned with any frequency today. The neglect of pioneer verse is readily explained by reading the poems. Many of them reflect the sentimentality and didacticism that sometimes marred nineteenth-century poetry; additionally, these Mormon poets tended to explore religious themes with a dogmatic zeal that no longer appeals to most readers. Sarah Elizabeth Carmichael—Lizzie, as she was called—overcame these faults to produce poems of genuine literary merit. Regrettably, her work has been obscured in the general eclipse of pioneer poetry.

Two facts about Lizzie Carmichael emerge: she displayed a poetic brilliance that was admired by her peers both in Utah and elsewhere, and she lived with a tragic heritage that darkened her life during what should have been its crowning years. While brief sketches of her life have appeared from time to time in local publications, research has uncovered additional material on both the poet and her husband, Jonathan M. Williamson, that will flesh out her story and correct some misconceptions.[1]

Lizzie was born in 1838 at Setauket, Long Island, New York, a daughter of William and Mary Ann Carmichael. Her destiny was shaped in large measure by the family's flawed heredity. Her parents were double cousins, and of a reported seven children born to them only Lizzie with her superior mind and a sister of below-normal intelligence survived infancy. Just when and where the Carmichaels were converted to Mormonism is not certain. However, in October 1842 the family joined the Latter-day Saints at Nauvoo, where father Carmichael worked as a carpenter on the Nauvoo Temple. By the spring of 1847 the family was living at Winter Quarters, Nebraska; and in 1850 they made their final move to Salt Lake Valley, settling in the city's Eighth Ward. Lizzie was then twelve years old.[2]

The earliest plan of Salt Lake City shows William Carmichael as owner of a lot on the northwest corner of State Street and Fifth South. This location opposite the Eighth Ward Square gave Lizzie an ever-changing view of incoming settlers who camped there prior to establishing permanent residence elsewhere. In 1851 an adobe school where Lizzie may have attended classes was built on the north side of Fourth South near State Street. She may also have used the facilities of the fledgling territorial library housed in Council Hall. Despite the limited educational and cultural resources of Zion, the "pretty, big-eyed retiring girl" began her solitary, self-taught career as a writer.[3]

That the tender bud flowered, given its environment, indicates a personal persistence and a commitment that ran very deep. Edward W. Tullidge called Lizzie's birth "in the severest sense untimely; she was reared in these valleys of Rocky Mountain isolation, where the poet, the musician and the painter were told to go to the canyons with ox teams for wood to earn their daily bread."[4] On the Mormon frontier the struggle for survival made the arts expendable. If, as some have suggested, her home life was characterized by misunderstanding or even resentment, the fact would not be difficult to understand.[5] Artistic genius and domestic order are fitful companions at best. Nevertheless, some communion—fostered perhaps by parental pride—did exist. A charming picture of Lizzie's father describes him "with his dinner pail in one hand and the manuscript of a poem written by his gifted daughter in the other, [with which] he might have been seen almost any day going to work and stopping at the newspaper office to leave the manuscript."[6]

Beginning in 1858 more than fifty poems by Miss Carmichael were published in the *Deseret News* over a period of eight years. Her first offering was apparently so well done as to cast doubt upon her authorship. The poet sought the help of a "high church official" who assured the editor of the girl's genuineness and Lizzie became a frequent contributor.[7] The first poem to carry her name was "Truth" which appeared in the March 10, 1858 issue. Then a young woman of twenty, Lizzie found her work readily acknowledged by the pioneer intelligentsia, and in 1859 the powerful Eliza R. Snow made her approval public:

> Make room for the rising minstrel-
>   List, list to her minstrelsy;
> Its numbers are rich and truthful.
>   And pure is its melody.[8]

As Lizzie's genius continued to unfold, it brought her a measure of fame but at the same time exposed areas of tension between the artist and her family and the church.

The early published poems of Miss Carmichael are remarkable for their lack of distinctively Mormon subject matter. Often homiletic in character, the verses treat friendship, love, personal integrity, writing,

Indian pride, and similar topics from a humanistic, nonsectarian point of view. Even the poem "Pharaoh," where man's contending with God is explored, she avoided heavy-handed parallels between the exodus of the Israelites and that of the Mormons.[9] And in a rare poem on a Mormon subject—Brigham Young—Lizzie retained control over her topic, refusing to be overawed by his power. The result is a poem that praises but does not cloy:

> We do not call thee chieftain
> We do not name thee king,
> We wreath no brilliants for thy brow,
> No ermine round thee fling[10]

The verse continues, expanding the theme of the Mormon leader as a beloved man who belongs to the people: he is "ours." By contrast, there is a remoteness to Brigham Young in these lines by Eliza R. Snow:

> Servant of God, most honor'd—most belov'd:
> By Him appointed and of Him approv'd.
> Prophet and Seer—You stand as Moses stood,
> Between the people and the living God.[11]

A recently uncovered document asserts that Lizzie "often sought the society and literary counsel of Sister Eliza." Sometime after the 1856 publication of Eliza Snow's first volume of poetry, the two visited Brigham Young, seeking help for "a similar recognition of the youthful aspirant for literary honors." The church president advised the girl: "Use your gifts to build up truth and righteousness in the earth and your gift will be preserved as long as you shall live. If you prostitute your powers to gain fame or gold, your light will go out in darkness." This should not be construed as indicating antagonism on Brigham Young's part toward Lizzie and her work.[12] The practical man of affairs probably knew far better than the two women that the world honors poets with laurel wreaths and love but seldom money. Then, too, he may have recognized that despite a close bond of sympathy, the young poet would never emulate the older woman's perfervid zeal. One cannot imagine Lizzie penning lines such as these:

O God, bless Brigham Young;
Bless him, and all that bless him;
Waste them away, O God, we pray,
Who, rising to oppose him,
Contend with Thee.[13]

The times generally favored zeal over art.

From her earliest years, Lizzie must have longed for the benefits of a broader education. Her facile mind absorbed what it could from the limited resources available in Salt Lake City, but it craved more. John R. Young remembered meeting Lizzie, probably sometime in 1858, when he attended a school taught by Sister Pratt and here became acquainted with Miss Carmichael, "one of Utah's most gifted daughters."[14] Far from desiring merely "fame or gold," Lizzie may have wanted, even at this early date, to earn money from her poetry to pay for further education in the East.

While little is known of Lizzie's personal life in the early 1860s, the "rising minstrel" mixed with prominent members of local society, winning their admiration and acceptance. An elaborate program of speeches and music celebrating Independence Day 1862 included her poem "Life and Liberty," read by John T. Caine. A few weeks later, similar activities commemorating Pioneer Day brought from her pen not a poem but a brief address to the pioneers read by William Clayton.[15] She had entered the most productive, challenging, and ultimately tragic decade of her life. National recognition, marriage, and travel lay ahead of her, but by the end of the 1860s her life — the life of her mind — was essentially over.

Edward W. Tullidge may have been the most perceptive of Lizzie's contemporaries. He saw her as a genius whose powers of improvisation carried her to the heights, but the patient shaping and reworking of a master such as Keats "cannot, we fear, be justly accredited among her higher poetic gifts and graces."[16] While she appears to have "lisped in numbers" as naturally as Pope, many lamented along with Tullidge that "the poet was born out of due season."[17] Had her intellectual environment been more challenging and critical, her powers might have matured more fully despite the brevity of her creative years. Nevertheless, the poet did grow. She began to see her subjects in dramatic terms, using conflict, contrast, and irony in an increasingly sophisticated way. "The Daughter of Herodias," "Esau's Petition," "The Stolen Sunbeam," and the "Feast of Lucrezia Borgia" reveal a growing command of her art. A few lines from the latter poem will illustrate how the muse was maturing:

> Wine! wine! it flowed in a crimson stream
> Through the crystal cups, till its ruby gleam
> Shadowed a blush on the soft white hand
> That raised the glass from the marble stand.

As the bacchanal progresses and the wine takes effect, the guests become fearful:

> They spurn the wine with a frenzied ire,
> Their hands are ice, and their lips are fire.
> There's a mantle of blackness above them spread
> They hear a chant for the dying and dead;
> They see priests moving; wan tapers gleam;
> But each life-pulse stands like a torpid stream;
> And they gaze with a stupor of brain and heart
> As the gorgeous curtains are torn apart,
> And a form of velvet of sable dye,
> With the forehead bound by a jeweled tie,
> Stood looking upon them with eyes severe,
> And they shuddering whisper: "Lucrezia's here."

But the poisoner's triumph over the nobles is brief; Lucrezia's son is one of the victims.[18]

Miss Carmichael's advancing skill eventually brought her recognition outside of Zion. William Cullen Bryant published "The Stolen Sunbeam" in his two-volume collection *A Family Library of Poetry and Song.* Retitled by Bryant "The Origin of Gold," the poem has been justly acclaimed for its fine conceit depicting heaven's fallen one tearing a plume from the setting sun and burying it in the earth where it becomes gold. Another anthologizer, May Wentworth, selected two Carmichael poems, "A Christmas Rhyme" and "Sorrow," for her volume *Poetry of the Pacific* in 1867. In addition to the anthologies, some have claimed that Lizzie's poems were often reprinted without credit by the eastern press. In any event, ample evidence exists that the Utah poet was recognized and respected in the literary circles of mid-nineteenth century America.[19]

Like many other writers of the period, Lizzie was profoundly moved by the Civil War. The conflict that set brother against brother captured her imagination and brought from her pen vivid, dramatic poems such as "Ashes to Ashes." The war indirectly affected her personal life as well. Miles from Zion the call to arms led Jonathan M. Williamson, a surgeon, to enlist with the California Volunteers in San Francisco on September 27, 1861. A year later the doctor entered Salt Lake City with troops under the command of Col. Patrick E. Connor. Lizzie may have caught a first glimpse of her future husband at that time, as the soldiers marched up State Street past her home.[20]

Williamson surfaced in the local news early in 1863, following the Battle of Bear River, when he traveled fifty miles north with another physician to meet the wounded. One can only speculate on the doctor's activities during the following year and a half. In the summer of 1864 the Camp Douglas post newspaper reported his return from California where he had been "for some time past." A few months later the surgeon was mustered out of the service, his three-year enlistment having expired. Wanting to take a more active part in the Civil War, Williamson signed on as a surgeon with the artillery brigade, 16th Army Corps, under Gen. A. J. Smith and saw action in the "great campaign of 1864–65." In August 1866 he returned to Zion "in his own conveyance," reportedly making one of the quickest trips on record.[21]

One uncertainty remains: when and where did the bright poet and the army surgeon meet? Evidence suggests the couple became acquainted during the doctor's stay at Camp Douglas, in the year and a half between the Battle of Bear River and Williamson's trip to California in 1864. This assumption better explains references—many of which are highly overdrawn—to Lizzie's conflict with church and parental authority.

Beyond question feelings ran high when Connor and his men

marched into Salt Lake City. The Mormons felt harassed and viewed the troops with suspicion. Many of the soldiers saw the Saints as traitorous lawbreakers and enjoyed poking fun at their beliefs and their leaders. Despite the atmosphere of mutual distrust, social contacts must have been made. Williamson evidently read the poems Lizzie was then writing with some frequency for the *Deseret News*. Perhaps the dazzling "Feast of Lucrezia Borgia" charmed him as it did so many others.[22] If he actively sought her acquaintance at this time, he probably found his status as a physician rather than an ordinary soldier an asset. While he was both a Gentile and an army man, Williamson posed no personal threat to the populace. Indeed, his interest in the poet may have been welcomed by some of the city's social leaders as a sign that bridges between the two hostile camps could be built.

In 1863–64 Lizzie was in her mid-twenties and unmarried in a society that had little place for that kind of nonconformity. Her wide acquaintance with the city's influential families makes it difficult to believe that no one had proposed marriage to her. As a plural wife Lizzie would have added distinction to a family, and any artistic temperament she displayed could have been easily accommodated by a husband who need not share her company except when he wished. A refusal to marry into a local family and her subsequent alliance with a Gentile probably would have exasperated her family. Reports by Beadle and others that it nettled Brigham Young sufficiently to ban her works or moved Mormons generally to dissociate themselves from her are questionable. Evidence abounds that Lizzie remained a loved and admired figure locally despite her negative feelings about polygamy—feelings shared by at least one other notable woman poet of the period.[23]

While Lizzie may have encountered some closed doors and cold shoulders, her poetry never fell out of favor. Indeed, Utahns were eager to claim her as their own. For example, Mormon historian Brigham H. Roberts heaped praise on Miss Carmichael's "President Lincoln's Funeral," asserting that it "is not anywhere surpassed in the literature—prose or poetry—that the sad event produced; no, not even Walt Whitman's 'O Captain! My Captain.'" The poem did attract national recognition following its publication in the San Francisco *Golden Era*. The famous actress Julia Dean Hayne, who frequently appeared at the

Salt Lake Theater, came on stage during one performance "in appropriate mourning dress, and read the poem with a pure pathos and perfect elocution, considering the immense capacity and imperfect acoustics of the room. It requires genius to read as well as write good poetry." The elegy merits acclaim. Its expression of grief achieves a solemn dignity in lines such as these:

> Bands of mourning draped the homestead,
>   And the sacred house of prayer;
> Mourning folds lay black and heavy
>   On true bosoms everywhere:
> Yet there were no tear-drops streaming
>   From the deep and solemn eye
> Of the hour that mutely waited
>   Till the funeral train went by.
> Oh! there is a woe that crushes
>   All expression with its weight!
> There is pain that numbs and hushes
>   Feeling's sense, it is so great.[24]

If Lizzie were out of favor with Mormon leaders over polygamy or, as some have suggested, her espousal of the Union cause, they were strangely unsuccessful at keeping her poems from the public. During only one extended period of time, from late 1864 to early 1866, did the poet fail to publish with some frequency in the *Deseret News*. Most likely the anti-Mormon press seized upon Lizzie's distaste for polygamy and her early failure, with Eliza Snow's assistance, to interest Brigham Young in publishing her poetry and blew that incident out of all reasonable proportion. J. H. Beadle, for example, had Lizzie leaving Utah under the safety of a military escort to marry Dr. Williamson. And as recently as 1969 Stanley P. Hirshon uncritically asserted that Brigham Young banned her works until they were so well recognized that he "finally offered to help her, but the proud girl refused." From many sources it appears that Lizzie's home life was marred by a lack of understanding. Evidence also supports the notion that she rebelled against her parents and the establishment by marrying outside the Mormon faith and aligning herself with the perceived enemy at Camp Douglas. Far from being a sign of yet another malevolent Mormon plot, Lizzie's conflict with authority seems de rigueur for a poet of any intellectual pretension.[25]

The publication of Lizzie's only book of poetry sometime in mid-1866 ushered in a series of events that greatly altered her life. The slender volume, entitled simply *Poems*, was "published with the consent—somewhat reluctantly given—of the authoress, by a devoted circle of her friends and admirers, who design thus to preserve an early memento of her talents and genius as a writer; and by its circulation among kindred spirits, who as yet are strangers to her muse, secure for her poems a more extended acquaintance and recognition."

Included among the twenty-six poems selected for publication were the frequently praised "April Flowers," "President Lincoln's Funeral," "The Stolen Sunbeam," and "Moonrise on the Wasatch," which is among her best descriptive poems, as its opening section illustrates:

The stars seemed far, yet darkness was not deep;
Like baby-eyes, the rays yet strove with sleep;
The giant hills stood in the distance proud—
On each white brow a dusky fold of cloud;
Some coldly gray, some of an amber hue,
Some with dark purple fading into blue;
And one that blushed with a faint crimson jet—
A sunset memory, tinged with cloud-regret.
Close to my feet the soft leaf shadows stirred;
I listened vainly, for they moved unheard—
Trembled unconsciously; the languid air
Crept to the rose's lip, and perished there.
It was an hour of such repose as steals
Into the heart when it most deeply feels;
When feeling covers every shred of speech
With one emotion language cannot reach.
And Nature held her breath and waited there,
An awed enthusiast at the shrine of prayer;
Like a pale devotee, whose reverent lips
Stifle the breath that burns her finger-tips.[26]

Much of the book's story can be traced in the columns of the *Daily Union Vedette*. On August 6, 1866, the Camp Douglas newspaper carried a review of *Poems* by Carrie Carlton, originally published in the San Francisco *New Age*. Praising both book and poet, the reviewer noted that "true to a refined and heavenly instinct she stands up bravely to resist all example, all entreaty, all parental authority." According to the reviewer, Miss Carmichael hoped to be able to enter Vassar College. The following day the *Vedette* reported that Aaron Stein, who evidently handled the book's sale, had sent Lizzie $581.15, proceeds from subscriptions to her volume of poetry. Stein said that he and another "gentleman" who had been responsible for promoting the book felt rewarded for their efforts and pleased by the "flattering reception given it by a critical press."²⁷

The *Vedette* continued to take an interest in Miss Carmichael's poetry, publishing several of her poems during September and October 1866. On November 20 the newspaper was pleased to report that *Poems* had been well received in Boston by a "high authority in matters of letters" who believed the poet was destined to achieve greater prominence in the field of literature.²⁸ The future must have looked bright to the poet who had every reason to believe at age twenty-eight that she had many years left to develop her art to its full potential. The doctor must have felt pleased with Lizzie's modest success and hopeful that as her husband he might help her sustain it. The dream was not to be.

Not long after his return from the East, Williamson became embroiled in a controversial claim-jumping case. Albert Brown, a former cavalry captain, and the doctor had claimed an unoccupied piece of land west of the Jordan River. Late one night they were surrounded by forty men and forced down the bank of the river. When Brown was recognized by one of the men as having treated him kindly while on provost guard in the city, the would-be settlers were helped from the water on their promise to immediately leave the country. This potentially tragic event must have discouraged any plans Williamson had for settling in the area at that time.²⁹

In late October 1866 a probable obstacle to the doctor's marriage with Lizzie was removed. Mary Ann Carmichael, mother of "our distinguished poetess," died of a heart attack at age fifty-eight.³⁰ On November 4 Williamson and Lizzie were married at Fort Bridger by the well-known

Judge W. A. Carter. The *Vedette* gave its blessing to the occasion: "The happy couple are both well and favorably known in this community, the gay Benedict as the late Surgeon of the Second Cavalry C. V., and the worthy bride as the sweet poetess of Utah. May their path through life be strewn with flowers, and every step a fountain of friendship gush forth to water them."[31]

Nearly a year later, the *Vedette* reported that the Williamsons were living in Ohio, the doctor's native state. The newspaper reprinted a letter, "evidently from the pen of the accomplished Mrs. J. M. Williamson," originally published in the Cincinnati *Commercial* denouncing polygamy and claiming that Lizzie had bearded the Lion of the Lord in his den: "I am no Hagar wandering desolate from the tent of a Mormon Abraham, but one of the few women who have grown up in the shadow of Brigham Young's despotism, and dared to defy him in the presence chamber of his power."[32]

Reportedly, Williamson wanted his wife to write a history of the Mormons, a project that never got beyond the planning stage, as most sources agree that Lizzie went into a severe mental decline about a year after her marriage. The Williamsons showed up next in Pioche, Nevada, a booming mining town, the naming of which has been credited by several authorities to Lizzie.[33] Then, some time after 1870, the couple returned to Salt Lake City, where they lived out the remainder of their lives. Dr. Williamson continued his medical practice and cared for his wife and sister-in-law, Mary Carmichael.[34]

Whatever the nature of her mental debility, Lizzie apparently enjoyed periods of lucidity. In 1874 Mary Jane Mount Tanner, a childhood friend, visited the invalid and described her manner:

> She is better now but not well enough to take her place in Society. Poor Lizzie! It made my heart ache to see her. She was so changed. The light of intelligence had gone from her eyes, and her voice had a strange sound like some one speaking in the distance, but she talked intelligently and wanted me to come again. She has a beautiful home nicely furnished. Her husband's mother and sister lives [*sic*] there to take care of her. It made me

feel very nervous to see her, and my health is so poor I do not think I can go again.[35]

In 1880 the doctor's mother, Abigail Williamson, died and two years later death came to him. J. R. Walker and Boyd Park were executors of his "considerable property." When home care for Lizzie became too difficult, she was sent to the state mental hospital at Provo, where she had "special privileges and attendants." Ellen L. Jakeman saw her there in the 1890s, "a slender figure in a close fitting black dress, with a white crepe shawl over her shoulders, at Sabbath services—with them, but not of them." Finally, after more than thirty years of mental instability, Lizzie died at her Salt Lake City home on November 10, 1901.[36]

With no family to mourn her, the city's newspaper provided generous eulogies and recalled for their readers the achievements of her youth. The *Deseret News* praised "the once brilliant poetess whose literary gifts placed her name among those of the best writers of the nation." The *Salt Lake Herald* called her "a literary genius and born poetess, who at one time was ranked the peer of American writers, and whose work has been characterized as the spontaneous outbursts of a poetry-filled soul." The *Tribune* opined that "had she retained the brilliant mind of her youth she would have found a place in the foremost ranks of American literature."[37]

The headstone on her forgotten grave in Salt Lake City Cemetery has disappeared, and the poetry that brought a heightened sensitivity to the crude frontier eludes all but the persistent seeker. Lizzie penned her own best epitaph in these haunting lines that foreshadow her mental collapse and the obscuring hand of time:

Pale, blighted flowers, the summer time
    Will smile on brighter leaves;
They will not whither in their prime,
    Like a young heart that grieves;
But the impulsive buds that dare
    The chill of April showers,
Breathe woman-love's low martyr prayer—
    I kiss your leaves, pale flowers.[38]

Despite changing literary fashion, Lizzie's best poems break the bonds of time and place to speak with a voice readers today can appreciate. Certainly the genius of nineteenth-century Utah literature merits a permanent place in the state's pantheon.

Chipeta and Ouray in a studio portrait. Photo courtesy of the Utah
State Historical Society.

CHIPETA
She Didn't Want to Come to Utah

Susan Lyman-Whitney

Susan Lyman-Whitney is a native of Utah and a graduate of the University of Utah. She has worked for Network *magazine and is currently a feature writer with the* Deseret News. *She frequently writes about family and social issues, including women's issues. The Associated Press and Sigma Delta Chi have recognized her excellence with awards for her articles on topics ranging from rape to the zen of housekeeping to the Wilberg mine disaster. When she heard of this project, she was interested in contributing, but had no woman in mind. She explored possibilities through conversations, articles, and books, and settled on Chipeta when she realized that most of the things, particularly news reports, written about her reflected the bias of White authors and politicians who presented this Ute woman in whatever way served their own purposes. As is the case with most native Americans, little unbiased, factual material exists about Chipeta, but, Lyman-Whitney observed, "She was an interesting person, for all we don't know about her." An earlier version of this essay appeared in the* Deseret News.

When a delegation of Utes visited the capital city in the early months of 1880, the Washington, D.C., reporters described the event as one big party. But for Chipeta, a woman in that delegation, the trip must have been far from festive. Her husband was dying of kidney failure. This would be Chief Ouray's last trip to Washington and he was negotiating a treaty which was to end a way of life for the Utes. He knew it and she knew it. The best they could hope for was to lessen the losses. On behalf of their people, they would be giving up sixteen million acres of Colorado grasslands and mountain meadows, ending a life of hunting and trading and self-determination. Ouray was setting the stage for a treaty which would banish his people to the desert of the eastern Utah Territory.

The White people, too, must have realized it was the end of an era. They were, after all, about to become the recipients of all that gorgeous, fertile, mineral-laden land. The Eastern press chose this time to romanticize the Utes and their visit. In newspaper articles of the day, and later in the poetry of a slew of would-be Longfellows, Chipeta became a legend.

Unfortunately for those who wish to know her as she really was, the accounts of Chipeta's life tended to grow more colorful with each telling. When she arrived in Washington, D.C., on January 11, 1880, reporters gushed over her. "A ripple of cheers greeted the dumpling Chipeta in her beautiful doeskin dress." The Washington Press already had decided to make a heroine of Chipeta, implying that she was the power behind Ouray's throne and telling a pretty tale that Ouray had refused to come East until President Hayes invited 'Queen' Chipeta too."[1] They described her in the same terms they used to describe European royalty, listing the gifts she was given during her several visits—expensive clothes, furniture, and silver—and the dances and receptions she attended. It was during her 1880 visit with Ouray that she was labeled by White people as "Queen of the Utes."[2] She was their darling, and then she was not.

Thus, Chipeta is described differently by different reporters. She was beautiful; she was gross. She was a queen; she was a savage. She was intelligent; she was simple. She loved White people; she was disloyal to them. Several biographers describe her as being slim and beautiful when she was young, and fat and ugly when she was old. In fact, she looks remarkably the same in photos taken of her throughout her life: She was a short, broad-shouldered woman—not thin, not fat—who usually wore a pleasant expression, an expression which could have masked any number of emotions.

The reporters and historians of her day had a much more difficult time romanticizing her after her husband died and she left the relative richness of Colorado to live in a dusty, desolate reservation in eastern

Utah. They began to search for her sins, possibly to assuage their own guilt. While she was alive, her biographers began to blame her for her own altered circumstances. In their efforts to glorify her, then to fault her, then to turn her into a legend after she died, writers have spent more words on Chipeta than on any other Ute woman. But for all those who wrote about her, about what she thought and what she felt, hardly anyone actually asked her any questions. "The people who wrote about her got their information from documents," says Clifford Duncan, Ute historian. "They didn't get input from Indian people."[3] Chipeta's fate is similar to that of many native Americans. George Howe Colt observed, "Pocahontas left behind no words of her own and as years passed her life became a template that Americans felt free to embellish according to their own agendas."[4]

What we know for certain about Chipeta's life is just a sketch, a brief outline. And today, seventy years after her death, she has still not taken her place in history as a full human being. Chipeta was born in 1843. Modern Utes believe she was born a Kiowa Apache, taken to be raised as a Tabeguache Ute (also called Uncompahgre Ute) after the Utes killed her parents in a raid. At the time she was growing up as a Ute, her people were prosperous and thriving. Their horses were fast and hunting and trading and food gathering were easy. They were mobile people, living and traveling in family groups, only getting together as a tribe several times a year. Whites called these people the Utes, and they called themselves the People. There were, at the time of the first White settlers, perhaps twelve distinct bands roaming in an area of more than 225,000 square miles. Their homeland stretched beyond the borders of present-day Utah and Colorado. At the time of Chipeta's birth, the Uncompahgres lived in central Colorado. Then gold was discovered near Denver in 1858. In 1863, the U.S. government negotiated a treaty to move the Uncompahgres west, out of the way of progress. They were promised cattle and money, none of which they got.

Chipeta married Ouray in 1859, when she was sixteen and he was twenty-six. At the time of their marriage, Ouray was already a favorite of the Whites. He had been acting as an interpreter since he was a boy. The son of a Jicarilla Apache father and an Uncompahgre Ute mother, Ouray was raised near Taos, New Mexico. He spoke four languages: Ute,

Apache, Spanish, and English; and apparently he moved easily between cultures.

Ouray had been married before, to a woman named Black Mare. It was not uncommon at the time for Ute males to have more than one wife. There is some confusion among White biographers as to what happened to Black Mare, whether or not she was alive when Ouray married Chipeta. Part of the legend is that Ouray was riding near a river one day when he saw a beautiful Ute maiden drawing water. He was supposedly so smitten with her that he braved the wrath of Black Mare and took Chipeta for his wife.

Clifford Duncan tells a more prosaic story. He says Ute people know Black Mare and Ouray were married and had a son together, a boy named Queashegut. The Utes believe Black Mare died when the boy was very young. In those days, the Utes had a practical and common way of taking care of the widows, widowers, and orphans in their midst. According to tradition, if a young woman died, one of her female relatives would be chosen to watch over the children. A sister or cousin might actually marry the widower and help him raise the children. Thus, after Black Mare died, the Utes say, it was arranged that Black Mare's sister, Chipeta, became Ouray's wife and Queashegut's mother.[5]

Most biographers agree that Ouray's son did not live very long with Chipeta and Ouray after his mother's death. Queashegut was kidnapped by the Sioux when he was somewhere between the ages of two and twelve years old. Eventually Ouray was able to enlist the aid of his friends in Washington to search for Queashegut. But when the government agents located a young man they thought was Queashegut, living with the Arapahoe, the lad refused to admit the possibility he could be Ouray's son. He would not even meet with Ouray.[6]

And what of Chipeta? What was in her heart when she became Queashegut's adoptive mother? What was in her heart when he was kidnapped, lost for years, then found and lost again? Nothing is recorded of how she felt, of course. We are left to guess, knowing only this: Chipeta never bore any children of her own.

In the early days of their marriage, Chipeta and Ouray may have been able to live the traditional, cyclical ways of their people, following the deer into the mountain in the summer, gathering nuts in the fall, living in the lower elevations in the winter. But as more White settlers came, the government increasingly relied on Ouray. They counted on him to be not only an interpreter, but a mediator. Biographers write about him as if he were the accepted leader of the Uncompahgre. In fact, the Whites were the ones who chose him. And if the Uncompahgre did not recognize him as a leader, he was even less recognized by the White River and other Ute tribes. Yet the Whites often expected Ouray to speak for other Ute tribes as well as for his own.

Modern historian Floyd O'Neil observes, however, "Chipeta and Ouray were not always on the inside." At the time Ouray was chosen by the White people to be spokesperson, he was not considered by Utes to be influential. He reminds, "He was half Apache."[7] Chipeta's great-great-grandnephew, Roland McCook, adds: "There was a negative side to Ouray, from the Indian's viewpoint. He was a White man's Indian. So his wife was looked upon as that, too."[8]

Nonetheless, in 1868, when seven Colorado Ute tribes negotiated a new treaty giving them about one-third of the state, Ouray was one of the main negotiators. The government paid Ouray $500 a year, perhaps as much as $1,000 a year for a few years, while he acted as an intermediary. It was a princely salary. In addition, the government built a home for Chipeta and Ouray. The government no doubt thought to ensure his loyalty.[9]

During the late 1860s and early 1870s, Chipeta and Ouray farmed, as the government agents encouraged the Utes to do. The government wanted the Utes to be settled, though at the time no treaty required them to stay put on one piece of land. In fact, Ouray and Chipeta still did leave home to hunt and to travel, at least some of their days, with their own people. What they thought about becoming "civilized" and what their fellow Uncompahgre thought of their farm and their friendship with the White people has been recorded only by Whites. It is all glowingly positive. Chipeta and Ouray must have learned, on their diplomatic visits to Washington, how numerous and how powerful the White Americans were. They always tried to convince their people that cooperation was the only way to survive.

In 1872 gold was discovered in the San Juan mountains and Ute land was flooded with miners and speculators. Chipeta, Ouray, and eight others went to Washington to work out yet another treaty in which the Utes gave up a large portion of their land. They were still supposed to be allowed to hunt on the land they gave to the Whites, but now the pressure of White settlers was increasing. Indian agents in the Colorado Territory were stepping up their efforts to keep the Utes from their traditional hunting grounds, and squatters were constantly trying to stake claim to Ute land.

At the same time, writers were fueling the Chipeta legend. The story of the Meeker captives gives an indication of how that legend grew.[10] In the Washington papers in 1880, mention was made of Chipeta's daring as she saved the lives of three White women. Arvilla and Josephine Meeker and Flora Price were held captive by a group of White River Utes after the Indians killed ten men at the Indian Agency. Later, biographers told of Chipeta riding one-hundred miles, bareback, in a nonstop race to save the White women. In fact, there probably was no such ride. If there was any truth to the story about Chipeta's daring ride, it may have been that she rode to find Ouray, or more probably, sent someone else, after she heard about the deaths at the Meeker agency. Chipeta did not physically rescue the women, though she and Ouray were influential among their people and definitely lobbied for the release. It was government agents who gathered up the captives and brought them to stay at Chipeta and Ouray's house on their trip home.

The incident started because Nathan Meeker, the Indian agent for the White River Utes, was adamant about making farmers out of them. When an Indian named Johnson refused to plow and plant his horse pasture, Meeker sent a man out to plow it for him but Johnson's son drove the man away by firing a rifle over the head of the fellow who came to plow his father's pasture. Johnson was married to Ouray's sister, so it was actually Ouray's nephew who started what came to be known as the Meeker incident.

Nathan Meeker was not about to have his authority challenged in this matter. He sent for help and when army troops arrived, the Utes feared attack and ambushed the troops. Then, knowing the worst had begun, a group of White River Utes went to the Indian Agency and killed Meeker and all the White men who were there and took the women and children away with them.

It was, in a way, just what the government and the White settlers had been waiting for. Now government agents had an excuse to seize the land. They wanted not just White River lands, but all Ute lands. The fact that Ouray and Chipeta and the other Uncompahgre had nothing to do with Nathan Meeker's death made no difference. The fact that the Meeker women considered Ouray and Chipeta their friends made them heroes but did not save them from the reservation.

After the Meeker incident the White women who had been held captive were freed by the negotiations of various army officers and Indian agents. They were taken to Chipeta and Ouray's home for a night or two on their way out of Indian territory. Then they went to their homes in the East. Later, when they were called to Washington to give testimony about what happened, each of the women talked about finding shelter with Chipeta and Ouray after their ordeal. In her official testimony, Flora Ellen Price gave the nation a glimpse into Chipeta's home: "We were treated well at Ouray's house. It has Brussels carpet, window curtains, stoves, good beds, glass windows, spittoons, rocking chairs, camp stools, mirrors and an elegantly carved bureau. We were received as old and long lost friends. Mrs. Ouray wept for our hardships and her motherly face, dusky but beautiful, with sweetness and compassion, was wet with tears. We left her crying."[11]

Modern historian Floyd O'Neil is distressed by the way White people described Chipeta's home. He is distressed by their assumption that she would want to imitate them in all things and their surprise that there were rugs on the floor. In fact, he says, Navajos had long been making rugs and putting them on the floors of their homes. It is but one of many examples of how Chipeta was treated as a curiosity, even as a savage who had no culture of her own and who could only be considered to be living a good life to the extent that she could be taught to follow the ways of the European Americans.[12]

But that is what she was, especially on her last visit to Washington—a curiosity. During their several months' stay in Washington in 1880, Chipeta and Ouray gave testimony about the Meeker incident and Ouray negotiated the terms of the reservation. One reporter wrote of Chipeta's last visit, "She was the rage for the season, and the epistolary correspondence from attaches of the English legation to the court journals of London bespoke for her a hearty reception from the peerage of England should she visit that country."[13]

But it seems Ouray and Chipeta were thinking more of Colorado than of England. In the midst of the negotiations, when he could see their land would be lost, Ouray ceased to wear the European clothes he had been given. He dressed only in his beaded buckskins. He refused White physicians and went home to die. He asked his people not to reveal to the Whites where he was buried. When Ouray died in August of 1880, *The Denver Tribune* observed:

> In the death of Ouray, one of the historical characters of Colorado passes away. He has figured for many years as the greatest Indian of his time, and during his life has figured quite as prominently before the country as has any white man in the Rocky Mountains. It is therefore meet and proper that on the occasion of his death, his life should be remembered. The record of his deed is one of simple parts, yet he has proven himself elevated so far above other men of his race and time that his acts stand out in bold relief. Ouray is in many respects — indeed, we may say in all respects — a remarkable Indian; a man of pure instincts, of keen perception, and apparently possesses very proper ideas of justice and right, the friend of the white man and the protector of the Indian, even standing up and boldly asserting the rights of his tribe, and as continually doing all in his power to create favor for the white man with the Indians.[14]

After her husband died, in the traditional way of her people, Chipeta cut her long hair. For the rest of her life, and she lived 44 years after Ouray died, the photos show her with shorter, shoulder-length hair. Short hair is a sign of mourning, explains Clifford Duncan. "Long hair signifies a good life." Traditional Utes also give away their possessions when a loved one dies. They feel like orphans, Duncan says. They make themselves as materially bereft as they feel.[15]

Roland McCook says he knows little about this woman who was his great-great aunt, but he does know something about the trek to the reservation. He doubts Chipeta was allowed to bring a wagon so she probably did not bring many household goods with her. McCook says, "They were herded out there by the cavalry. If they had horses, they rode. A lot of people just walked."[16] In September of 1881, 1,458 Uncompahgres were removed from Colorado. It was left to the soldiers who escorted the people to Utah to report on the chaos of the trip and on how the people cried. Those who chronicled the journey did not mention Chipeta by name. One can only guess at the depth of her loss. Modern Utes believe it broke their grandparents' hearts to have to leave the place they called the Shining Mountains. Chipeta may or may not have lived with White River Utes when she first came to the reservation. However, for most of the rest of her life, Chipeta is known to have lived with her own family. Chipeta's brother, named McCook, lived near the Book Cliff mountains. They raised sheep on one of the prettier but more remote parts of the reservation.

Sometime not too long after leaving Colorado, Chipeta was reported to have married again. Duncan says the Ute people are not sure whether or not this is accurate, but White historians say she had a second husband, Toomuchagut. Toomuchagut was a White River Ute who had been fairly wealthy in Colorado. If Chipeta were living with Toomuchagut and other White River Utes when she first came to the reservation, she was part of the group of Utes who were most unhappy about reservation life.[17]

For several years her White friends hardly saw her and they blamed her. *The Denver Republican*, in August 1887, told the story of "Chipeta's Downfall," talking about how desolate her life had become and attributing her poverty to the fact that she married again.[18]

Some biographers say she maintained her friendships with White people. Others say she was withdrawn and bitter. Floyd O'Neil says both versions probably contain some truth. "She ran sheep out on Bitter Creek. She was terribly isolated. But when she came to town, she probably did look up old friends." During the 1960s O'Neil interviewed many members of the tribe, including Chipeta's nephew Ouray McCook. They did not talk about Chipeta, however. At the time she was not thought to be especially significant. O'Neil is from Uintah County, locale of the Ute reservation, and says his father, who was born in 1903, could speak Ute and knew both Chipeta and the McCook family. He does not remember his father talking much about her, yet, just from knowing her circumstances, O'Neil is sure she spoke English. The fact that she used an interpreter on state occasions, which confused some White biographers into writing that she could not speak English, can be easily explained, he says. Most people feel more comfortable in a formal interview speaking their own language.[19]

Duncan is also sure Chipeta spoke English. He is sure, also, that Chipeta took a double loss in status when Ouray died and she moved to the reservation. "She was used to being up front with her husband. After he died, the whole thing disappeared. She was not in a position where she would be noticed."[20]

Roland McCook knows Chipeta was well known in Colorado, among Whites and Utes. He assumes she maintained some notoriety after she moved to Utah. In the McCook family, he says, what they remember of Chipeta is this: "Simply that she was a brave woman, of course. She accepted the situation that her husband, and his influence, would bring on her. She was loyal to her husband, stood by him all the time, even when his purposes were futile. He did prolong the inhabitance of Colorado. . . . I think she filled her role adequately."[21]

One fact her biographers agree on: In her old age, Chipeta was blind and living in a tepee. There are a few more facts known about her. One is that she did visit an old friend, Mrs. Charles Adams, in Colorado Springs, in 1912. The two women had a photo taken together. Chipeta apparently visited Colorado several times after she went to the reservation in Utah. She appeared as "Queen of the Utes," a curiosity in rodeos, and she attended festivals.[22]

Chipeta was, several times, photographed surrounded by her family members. In several photographs she appears with a small girl by her side. Some White biographers have said she was lonely in her old age, but the photos seem to prove otherwise. Clifford Duncan says he doubts she was lonely. "She had a lot of friends and family." In the way of Ute families, still today, people consider their great-nieces and -nephews to be grandchildren. Thus, even though Chipeta had no children, she had grandchildren. Furthermore, a grandchild often went to live with a grandmother or grandfather, to be an apprentice and learn whatever skills that relative possessed. The little girl in the photos with Chipeta was probably the child of one of McCook's children and probably lived with Chipeta, says Duncan. She was not treated as a servant but as a daughter, adopted by an elder to learn the spiritual ways as well as the crafts of the tribe.[23]

In 1916 the superintendent of Indian Affairs interviewed Chipeta, through an interpreter. Finally, someone was asking her to reflect on all she had experienced, to reflect on a life that saw the most tumultuous change in the history of her people. In this, her first and last, interview, Chipeta is quoted as saying something rather enigmatic: "Never have I had an unkind feeling or an unkind thought toward the government in Washington, and if I were to express what I have in my mind, someone would misunderstand and think that Chipeta's heart has changed and that she is no longer friendly toward that government." Chipeta mentioned that she was promised a good place to live in Utah but that the promise had been forgotten. When the agent asked her if she needed anything now, she said, "I desire nothing. What is good enough for my people is good enough for me. I expect to die soon."[24]

Chipeta died at the age of 81, on August 16, 1924, the same year the Utes were granted U.S. citizenship. Later, her body was moved to Colorado and a monument was dedicated to her and Ouray. Roland Mc-Cook sees the exhumation of her bones as proof of two things: first, that she was still important to Coloradans; second, that even after she died, the White people continued to disregard her wishes. Ouray had specifically asked his people not to let the Whites give him a funeral. McCook believes Chipeta would not have wanted one either. She certainly would not have wanted her remains moved. "That's not done, in the Indian sense of things." He does not know who revealed the site of Chipeta's grave. He assumes it was someone in his family who did not understand the Whites were planning to disturb her body.[25]

The reburial on May 24, 1925, however, was a source of celebration. It included "an Indian ceremony that lasted four days, followed by a Christian Service that was half-Catholic and half-Protestant. . . . The ceremonies were attended by the largest group of whites and Indians to assemble on the Southern Ute agency up to that time."[26]

Five thousand people came to the ceremony. Poetry flowed. The people of Colorado may have been overjoyed to see the Utes leave their state, but they could not wait to commemorate them. And as for Chipeta herself, who knows what she might have made of the celebration. She might have been honored — if not by the reburial, at least by the remembrance. She might have been saddened by the irony that she could not live in Colorado, but she could be buried there. We have few of her actual words. But McCook points out that we have few words from any Utes of that day. "Even that little bit that was afforded her was not afforded anybody else." Especially not any other women. He says, "Chipeta had privileges other women did not."[27] How she really felt about her life, about the government, about how it felt to try to live in two worlds, we will never know. Perhaps the Ute Tribal Council spoke for her, when, in 1968, they issued a statement of purpose that said, in part, "Our ancestors would have preferred to have kept their land."[28]

Elizabeth Claridge McCune as a young woman. Photo courtesy of the Utah State Historical Society.

The McCune mansion by Susan Mumford.

ELIZABETH ANN CLARIDGE MCCUNE
At Home on the Hill

Carol Ann S. Van Wagoner

Carol Van Wagoner is currently the Community Relations Director for the Salt Lake Tribune, where she oversees special events, promotions, and the Newspaper in Education Department. She was reared in Los Angeles, graduated from Brigham Young University in liberal arts, and taught school in North Carolina. Her greatest joy and challenge is raising her three children "in a house slightly smaller than the McCune Mansion." She spends free time traveling around the world; a recent adventure included driving to the tip of Baja California with her two young daughters to watch a total eclipse of the sun. She is "intrigued by Utah's older mansions and the women who lived in them." One of the most magnificent of those mansions still overlooks Salt Lake City from a hill just below the State Capitol. The house is a genuine reflection of its builder, Elizabeth Ann Claridge McCune because she faced no financial limitations, had her choice of location, and worked constantly with the architect to produce exactly the home she wanted. In this unusual approach to a biography, Van Wagoner interweaves Elizabeth's life with a tour of her home, entering by the front door, progressing through the main floor, and then moving upstairs.

The exterior finish is dark red brick with brown stone trimmings and a dark brown tile roof of Holland tiles. The house is located on a corner of the hillside, which overlooks the whole city and gives a view from the windows which impresses one with panoramic grandeur.[1]

Anyone who spends much time exploring the downtown area of Salt Lake City, Utah, will surely discover an intriguing mansion at 200 North Main Street. Built on a "heaven-kissing hill," the McCune mansion stands as a regal symbol of an era of entrepreneurs and elegance — the era of Elizabeth Ann Claridge and Alfred McCune.[2]

Elizabeth was born February 19, 1852 in Hemel Hempstead, Hertz, England, to religious parents who attended, but never joined, the Baptist Church. Her father, Samuel Claridge, was a grocer who had Latter-day Saint customers. After reading their literature, Samuel said, "It made such an impression on me that I said to my wife [Elizabeth Hopkins], 'It seems to me just like the truth,' and from that time I could not leave it but wanted to read all the books I could get, and in six weeks, I was baptized by that poor old messenger George Coleman."[3]

Samuel joined the Ten Pound Company, a program to help Saints in England emigrate to America. The individual paid ten pounds and the church subsidized his or her emigration. The Claridge family used this system to emigrate to Utah in 1853. Elizabeth was two years old when her family arrived in Salt Creek (today called Nephi), Utah. Her youth was spent playing with friends Elizabeth "Bessie" Jeffries Sparks and Mary Ellen Love Neff. Elizabeth, known as Lizette to her friends, had a talent for drama. Mary Ellen recalled, "Lizette was always quick at repartee, always humorous and full of droll sayings. She could mimic any one so perfectly that her companions could tell who the boy, girl or adult was she was telling about by her dramatic portrayal of them. . . . She was very kind-hearted and did not do this to hurt anyone, simply to make fun for the crowd."[4]

She worked as adroitly as she played. During the summers, Lizette and her friends chatted at spinning wheels as they spun skeins of yarn. The girls seldom were idle. They spent hours sewing, knitting, crocheting, doing chores, playing, walking, riding, sleighing, and dancing in the winter time. According to Mary Ellen Neff, "The boys at Nephi were all good companions and cavaliers."[5]

When Elizabeth was thirteen years old, she and her friends

developed the desire to become musicians. Having heard someone play a concertina, they planned to glean in the wheat fields to get money to buy one. Despite their hard work, they did not secure enough money. What they earned was put into savings.

The next year, the girls decided to give up their musical ambitions and invest the wheat money for nice clothes. Elizabeth Sparks recalled the summer: "As we had heard much about the pretty things to wear that could be purchased in Salt Lake City, our next ambition was to go up to spend our cash. It took us three days to reach Salt Lake and we stayed with a cousin of Lizette's, but spent our time walking up and down Main Street gazing at the most beautiful things we felt sure that were ever displayed in shops in the world."[6] They might have wondered if they would ever have such beautiful things in their homes.

The home is entered through a heavy pair of bronze gates. On the left of the entrance vestibule is the reception room; passing through the vestibule, the main stair hall is entered from which open the sitting room, dining room, library and drawing rooms. Back of the main hall is the rear hall stairway leading from basement to attic and back of this is the family breakfast room, kitchen, butlers' pantry, servants' sitting room and back porch.... The main hall is finished in English Oak. The wainscotting here is probably the finest piece of work of the kind in the United States.

At 15 years old, Elizabeth and her friends learned to be telegraph operators. They studied, practiced, and perfected the art of telegraphy so well, that, by fall, they were hired, but each by a different office. The separation was dreaded until they realized that they might still keep in touch by chatting over the lines after business hours. "You may better believe we made good use of this opportunity," wrote Mary Ellen Love Neff.[7]

In 1867 a group of Utah leaders, including President Brigham Young, visited Nephi. They were greeted with music, flowers, and banners. The company ate dinner at the Claridge home. Elizabeth's autobiography records their feelings. "How we girls flew around to make everything nice for the stylish city folks! As soon as they were seated at dinner, we slipped upstairs and tried on all the ladies' hats. I would venture to say that could the ladies have seen us next Sunday, they would have been struck with the similarity of styles in Nephi and Salt Lake City millinery."[8]

At that afternoon's religious meeting, names were read of men who were called as missionaries to go and settle the "Muddy," a primitive site in Nevada. Elizabeth records:

> I did not hear another name except "Samuel Claridge."
> Then how I sobbed and cried, regardless of the fact that the tears were spoiling the new white dress.
> The father of the girl who sat next to me was also called. Said my companion, "Why, what are you crying about? It doesn't make me cry. I know my father won't go."
> "Well, there is the difference," said I. "I know that my father will go and that nothing could prevent him and I should not own him as a father if he would not go when he is called."
> Then I broke down sobbing again.[9]

Elizabeth's mother and sister remained in Nephi as their father and his second wife headed for the "Muddy." Elizabeth and her brother joined their father for the journey. On the day they were to arrive at St. Joseph, their destination, the wagon train ascended a mile-long hill where a huge rock loomed at the top. As the horses could not climb the steep rock, they were unhitched and led to the top via another winding route. A heavy log chain was attached to the wagon so the horses might raise it.

Unfortunately, the wagon tongue gave way, and the wagon dashed past Elizabeth, caught her dress on the wheel, and almost crushed her to death. The wagon rolled further and plunged over a precipice, scattering provisions and her clothing across the prairie. Elizabeth's father had not spoken a word up to this point. He turned to her and said, "My daughter, I prophesy that the day will come when you will have much better clothes than those to wear."[10] He might well have added that she would have beautiful places in which to wear them, too.

The vestibule itself is finished in old English oak with beamed ceilings. . . . Halfway up the stairway is a balcony overhanging the stairs which recalls the picture of Romeo and Gelt. . . . the ceiling over the main stairs is composed of deep oak panelling filled with

beautiful art glass which is artificially lighted for night use. Under this balcony is another alcove with seats and rug. . . . The dining room is English Renaissance in design, the woodwork being of old mahogany and the ceiling hand painted. . . . It is by far the richest room in treasures in the house, (if we except the statuary in the drawing room), and together with its furnishings would make a complete subject for a magazine article.

While Elizabeth was with her father and brother in the Muddy, hardworking 19-year-old Alfred W. McCune, claimed one acre and 9 rods of land in Nephi in 1868.[11] His father, Sergeant Matthew McCune, had moved the family to Nephi shortly after Alfred's birth. Matthew had been with the Bengal Artillery of the East India Company when he attended a study group, accepted the doctrines of Mormonism, and decided to emigrate. He was not fond of farming, however, so he and his brother Henry organized a freighting group to haul goods for the new railroad lines.

In 1871, when the settlement at the Muddy was abandoned, Elizabeth Ann went to St. George to be the telegraph operator. Susa Young Gates, the 48th child of Brigham Young, had been sent by her father to St. George with her mother and sister to make a winter home. The girls met and became close friends.[12]

Elizabeth Ann and Alfred William had been maintaining steady contact all through her mission to the Muddy and at the St. George telegraph office. Alfred was almost twenty-three and Elizabeth had turned twenty when she left St. George to return to Nephi and to Alfred. They were married on July 1, 1872 at the Endowment House in Salt Lake City.

They made their first home in Nephi, where their first child, Alfred William McCune Jr., was born April 3, 1873. A second child, Harry Bertrand, was born August 26, 1874, but died within two months.

The driving of the Golden Spike played an important part in launching Alfred into his successful business ventures. In 1878, he and his business partners contracted to supply graders, track layers, provisions, hay, and grain for teams as the track laying approached Nephi. His ventures were sometimes daring, but almost always successful, making Elizabeth's building possible.

The drawing room . . . suggests the French palaces of Louis XIV. The long windows, draped with priceless hangings; the exquisite furniture of hand embroidered tapestry, made in France; the little tables, the cabinets filled with rare and costly curios; the rose satin brocaded walls with the exquisite panels of Watteau paintings set over the doorways. . . . Back of the drawing room is the Library. The small reception room which opens from the drawing room is octagonal in plan and finished in San Domingo mahogany. The walls are hung with green moire silk. The ceiling is composed of eight panels each having four figures in relief representing the seasons. . . . Above the large window seat is one of the most beautiful and costly art glass windows in the west. . . . This room is modified empire in design and is the gem of the whole house.

The size of the McCune family was expanding. A third son, Earl Vivian, was born on November 12, 1875 and a fourth son, Raymond, on March 29, 1878. On March 6, 1880, their first daughter, Sarah Fay, was born.

Alfred's business ventures were also expanding. He created a successful railroad grading company, invested in a livestock company, and began mercantile business. Not only merchandise was offered, however. Alfred embarked upon a contract to furnish timber for the Lexington Mills in Montana. Loggers were hired, choppers employed, and forests selected. Alfred and his brother Henry were separated from their families in Nephi during these times, but they went home for Christmas in 1883 on the narrow gauge railroad train from Butte to Ogden. The trip lasted two days before they arrived at Salt Lake City. Then they traveled to Nephi, arriving Christmas Eve, returning to Butte January 3, 1884 and arriving on the sixth of January to very cold weather and four feet of snow. [13]

Five months later, Lottie Jacketta was born in Nephi on June 16, 1884. On July 22, 1887, their young son, Frank Claridge, died at almost five years of age. All the while, Alfred's ventures in railroads and mining continued. He contracted to furnish wood for the Anaconda Mining Company and invested in mines in British Columbia. By 1888, 39-year-old Alfred was not only well known in Utah, but throughout the United

States and Canada. He was building a fortune that would allow dreams to come true.

The breakfast room which opens into the dining room connects each to the other with broad sliding doors. It is a small room, octagonal in shape, located between the dining room and the butler's pantry with a small conservatory on the east. The fireplace in this room is of Irish marble in one corner. . . . It is such a room as Wm. Morris might well have designed.

In 1888, when Elizabeth was thirty-six years old, the McCunes moved to Salt Lake City into a home near the Union Pacific depot. Their eighth child, Matthew Marcus, was born March 10, 1889 and their ninth, Elizabeth Claridge, was born September 17, 1891. Elizabeth's interests continued to be centered around her family and the LDS Church. She accepted a church position as a counselor in the Young Women's Organization and was interested in missionary work. Alfred, exploring new possibilities, converted Salt Lake's trolley car system from mule power to electric power.

In 1897 the McCunes took their large family for a year's trip to Europe. Stopping first in England, the family leased an elegant residence at the seashore in Eastbourne, some 63 miles from London.

Returning from the trip to Europe in 1898, the McCunes moved into the Gardo House, a famous Salt Lake house built for one of Brigham Young's wives. The home was leased from the LDS Church for $150 a month. Sometime during this period, the McCunes decided to build a home for their family. Alfred gave Elizabeth carte blanche on its construction and furnishing. She hired a young architect named S. C. Dallas to tour the world for architectural ideas and materials.

The chambers are dreams of beauty. The principal one belonging to Mrs. McCune is furnished in a white enamel and is pink brocade and white lace in its finishings and furnishings.

Mr. McCune's room is oval in plan and was designed as much for a den as for a chamber of rest. It has a large fireplace of Utah onyx while the finish of the room is of specially selected red mahogany. The three concave doors of this room are cut from one log. . . . There are six other private and guest rooms on this floor and it would be difficult to decide which is of the greater merit.

Alfred made an unsuccessful attempt to become one of Utah's United States senators in 1899. In those days, state legislatures chose senators by majority vote with as many candidates running at the same time as legislators desired. A novice at politics, Alfred became embroiled in controversy during the process and was not nominated.[14] The election process had exhausted Alfred. He took his campaign manager, Fisher Harris, and other intimate friends to Europe for two months as a reward for their efforts on his behalf. They returned the later part of May to New York City, where Alfred met Elizabeth. Their paths crossed briefly.

Assignments in the LDS Church gave Elizabeth the opportunity to travel. She became a patron of the National Council of Women of the United States, an organization founded in 1888 and still in existence today, which works for the education and advancement of women in all areas of society. In 1899 she joined the International Council of Women, which had been founded the year before to promote the welfare of humankind and to work for women's right. She attended the International Congress of Women held in London in 1899 as a patron and a delegate from the LDS Church. The visit included an audience with Queen Victoria at Windsor Castle.

Friend Susa Young Gates praised Elizabeth, saying, "Equal to every occasion, she was as much at home on a board seat across a wagon box covering the dusty plains of Idaho or Mexico, sweetening every difficulty with a smile and cheering all discouraged hearts with her unfailing golden outlook on life—as she was in a palace sleeping car."[15]

In 1901 the McCunes moved into their new home at 200 North Main. Alfred later remarked that they really did not know exactly how much the home cost since they stopped counting after they had spent the price of $500,000.[16] In 1916 the architect, S. C. Dallas, described the building of the "bungalow":

> Both Mr. and Mrs. McCune are persons of definite personal ideas and strong personal preferences.
> In speaking of the plans, they always expressed themselves in the following manner; 'Simplicity must be the key note of the whole design; comfort, convenience, and economy the keynote of the plan; no attempt at vast display; no extravagant pretensions;

no stately or gorgeous effects are desired. We want the bunga-
low made up of delightful good taste, quite independent of
garnishes. We want a home that ourselves and family can live
in and enjoy. We want the fireplaces deep and cozy so that the
fireside will be the center of life in the winter season, and the ve-
randas are to be broad and spacious so that the family can enjoy
outdoor life in the summer season.[17]

On the second floor is the central hall sitting room with a
wondrously carved Flemish screen dividing it from the main stairway. . . . Going up to the ballroom one enters at once into the
vision of fairyland. There are four great alcoves, while the mirrored walls on every side reflect vistas innumerable. The artificial
marble called scageola, which forms most of the furnishings of this
ballroom required importation of a German from his fatherland,
and he was eight months in making this, at that time, practically
unknown composition.

The McCune family traveled to Peru in August of 1902, when Alfred took Elizabeth to view one of his interests — the Cerro de Pasco mine.
It was located at an elevation of 15,665 feet and reached by train and
wagon. Unfortunately, Elizabeth became ill with high elevation sickness
and a special engine was engaged to take her back down the mountain,
where she regained her health.

In 1905 Elizabeth was appointed by Governor William Spry as
a trustee of the Agricultural College of Logan, where she served for
ten years, the last two acting as vice president of the board. While
on that board she made a tour of the United States, accompanied
by Mrs. Susa Young Gates, to examine home economic departments
established in other schools. On her return and under her recommenda-
tion, a school cafeteria was established in the Agricultural College and
other improvements were inaugurated in the domestic science and art
departments.[18]

Elizabeth continued her LDS church commitments. In 1911, she
was appointed by President Joseph F. Smith as a member of the general
board of the Relief Society, an auxiliary of the church.

She visited all of the missions in Europe, Canada, Mexico, and in the Sandwich Islands, some of which presented difficult trips. As one friend expressed it, she was "such a good sport."[19]

With all of her travels, the mansion remained home for nineteen years. During those years, Elizabeth hosted small dinners and gala banquets. Private and public functions were held there.

Leading from the ballroom is the banquet room. This is a modified copy of a famous hall in an old English manor house. Finished in mahogany with beamed ceiling, the frieze extending from the top of the wainscotting is the most remarkable work. It portrays the hunting scenes, woodland and haunts of Robin Hood and Rob Roy.

Sometimes curious events occurred in the mansion. Elizabeth's granddaughter, Elizabeth Francesca McCune (Lynch) Fisher, remembered an armed robbery of the silver one evening while she stayed there. Grandmother Elizabeth—Nana, as she was called—told her to stay in bed because she heard gunshots.[20]

Another time, Alfred was sitting down to breakfast in the east family breakfast room when a shot rang out through the window, the bullet lodging in the dark mahogany wall board. Some person had taken a pot shot at him.[21]

In July 1917, a group of Mrs. McCune's closest friends were bidden to a week's retreat within the spacious home. None of the husbands were invited, except to dinner on the Fourth of July. When the guests entered, they were each presented with a simple gingham gown, which was to be the week's uniform. Not even the married children of the hostess were allowed to enter the doors; one came to take a few snapshots of the party, but was not allowed over the threshold. Each guest went about selecting her own bedroom and bath, and the busy editor guest had a special desk fitted up in the Gelt balcony. A poem with several stanzas was written by one of the guests, with the refrain referring to "the house that Elizabeth built."[22]

The family enjoyed the home but eventually Elizabeth was left alone for long periods after the marriages of her children, for her husband traveled extensively in his pressing New York business life.[23] On October 7, 1920, the McCunes wrote to LDS President Heber J. Grant, donating their home "on Main and First North Streets to be used preferably for the women's building, thus housing the three women's organizations [Primary, Young Women's, and Relief Society of the LDS Church], or for such purpose as may be deemed best."[24]

Almost immediately after donating their home to the LDS Church, the McCunes traveled to Los Angeles where they started searching for a home to buy. Perhaps surreptitiously, Susa Young Gates wrote a letter to Alfred suggesting he redirect his life:

> Action is the breath of your nostrils. . . . What about my dearly beloved Elizabeth; everybody loves her. . . . Her wisdom, her eloquence, and above all, her sweet modesty of deportment, her genuine spirit of social democracy makes her a name for good throughout this whole [LDS] church. . . . You know, Alfred, she possesses as great constructive ability for a woman as you do for a man . . . her magnificent enterprise of building and equipping that veritable palace on the hill. . . . She is a pioneer. . . . To build, to create, to assemble forces to beautify and glorify her surroundings, is as natural to her as creating great financial enterprises are to you.[25]

On November 16, 1920, Elizabeth wrote from the Hotel Van Nuys in California to her friend Susa Young Gates in Salt Lake City, saying, "Well here we are in the land of flowers and sunshine with considerable rain mixed in. . . . it's the flowers that appeal to me."[26]

The next month, they moved into a home at 626 South Kingsley Drive in Hollywood where they lived for three years. In 1923, with Elizabeth in failing health, they sold their Hollywood home and returned to Salt Lake City, where Elizabeth supervised construction of a new home on the northeast Avenues.

In the spring of 1924, Alfred and Elizabeth went on their last trip together, vacationing in Bermuda. Elizabeth became ill and they returned to Utah, where Alfred placed her in the Hotel Utah. The children and their families were cabled from all over the world. Elizabeth Claridge and family came from England, Jacketta and family from California, Matthew Marcus and family from Paris, Ray and wife also from Paris, and Fay and her family from California. They were all present when Elizabeth passed away on August 1, 1924. A grand funeral was held for her in the Assembly Hall on Temple Square. Then she was buried in Nephi. During early August 1924 Alfred addressed a letter to the mayor of Nephi in which he expressed his love and appreciation for the honor and sympathy shown at his wife's funeral. "Although the lives of my dear wife and myself have for some time past been in other localities, our hearts have always remained in Nephi."[27] Alfred William McCune passed away in Cannes, France, on March 28, 1927. His body was brought to Nephi where he was buried next to Elizabeth.

Elizabeth's mansion has endured many transformations: first the regal residence for herself and Alfred, the location for a young women's religious organization, a conservatory of music, a Brigham Young University extension center, and a reception center. Recently sold again, it still sits proudly on its "heaven-kissing hill."

Her Royal Highness Susanna Bransford Emery Holmes Delitch Engalitcheff seen here as a blond rather than with her usual brunette hair. Photo courtesy of the Utah State Historical Society.

The Gardo House by Jack Goodman. This picture previously appeared in Goodman's weekly column in the *Salt Lake Tribune.*

Susanna Egera Bransford Emery Holmes Delitch Engalitcheff

Utah's Silver Queen

Judy Dykman

Judy Dykman currently teaches World Geography and Utah History at Salt Lake City's Churchill Junior High, where she was selected as outstanding teacher of the year 1995. She earned her bachelor's degree in history from Weber State University and her master's degree in history education from Brigham Young University. Her interest in Susanna Engalitcheff began when she first heard stories of Utah's Silver Queen twenty years ago on a tour of Park City. "Her sense of humor, style, and intriguing personal history attracted me and I vowed I would one day write her biography. In her own unique way she greatly contributed to Utah's mining and social history." Susanna, who engulfed herself in the parties, travels, and social activities of the turn of the century, may be Utah's best representative of the Gilded Age. Dykman is currently expanding this essay into a book on Susanna Engalitcheff and the age in which she lived.

Her "Royal Highness" Susanna Egera Bransford Emery Holmes Delitch Engalitcheff was one of America's most colorful mining millionaires, and similar to others of the nouveau riche—the Vanderbilts, the Walshes, Margaret T. (Molly) Brown, and Baby Doe Tabor—her lifestyle frequently mirrored the excesses of the Gilded Age. As a child she crossed the plains in a covered wagon; as a teen she survived a stagecoach holdup;

and as an adult, she traveled around the world four times and lived in a palace. Married four times, she outlived all of her husbands even though two of the men were many years younger. By 1900 many American newspapers speculated that her shares in Park City's fabulous Silver King Mine made her Utah's wealthiest woman, but by the time she died in 1942 she was nearly bankrupt. During her prime, she met kings, queens, presidents and statesmen, conferred with Pope Leo, and conversed with Hitler and Mussolini.[1]

Affectionately known as "Susie" to her family and friends and as "Utah's Silver Queen" to the press, she was loved by some and vilified by others. For decades her social activities, travels, and personal tragedies made good copy. Because of this extensive press coverage some have mistakenly assumed that her life resembled an updated version of the Cinderella fairy tale. A recent magazine article even compared her to Princess Di or Liz Taylor; others have accused her of being cold hearted or callous to the needs of her daughter and her husbands. In reality she was typical of the cosmopolites of the Gilded Age, who had different values and perceptions than the average American.

The third of six children in the Milford and Sara Ellen Bransford family, Susie was born May 6, 1859 in Richmond, Missouri. Prior to the Civil War, her parents had property, owned several slaves, and operated a general store just outside Richmond, Missouri. When the Civil War broke out, her father enlisted in the Confederate Army and was commissioned a captain. Following his release from a Union prisoner of war camp he returned home, with broken health, to find that much of his property had been destroyed and that he was nearly penniless. Hoping for a fresh start and a chance to rebuild his fortune, Milford and his family joined a wagon train bound for California's gold fields. Approximately six months later they settled in Crescent Mill, a small mining community in Plumas County.[2]

Five-year-old Susie and her older brother, John, attended the town's small public school for several years. Later, when they were old enough to leave home, they were sent to San Francisco boarding schools to finish their education with several other children from the Taylorsville area. At sixteen, during one of her many trips to or from San Francisco, Susie was one of the victims in a stage coach robbery. The masked outlaws, probably friends, recognized her and assured her that they would not harm her, but Susie never forgot the ordeal and frequently joked about it years later.

As she matured, Susie blossomed into a very attractive young woman with beautiful expressive eyes, flawless skin, a trim figure, and long brown hair. Her-fun loving personality, self-confidence, and congenial manner enabled her to mingle easily with people. She attended many parties and social functions and became the "belle of Plumas." Considering her marital track record later in life and several flirtatious entries from numerous admirers in her autograph book, it is also likely that she had several romantic attachments in California before moving to Utah, but no record of these relationships exists.[3]

The summer of 1884 Susie traveled to Park City to visit some friends. She was twenty-five when she met Park City's handsome and popular postmaster, Albion Emery. Thirteen years her senior, Albion was an intelligent, ambitious man with a New England background. He loved classical literature and relished debating local political issues. His numerous Masonic contacts and political activities suggested he was destined to be wealthy and prominent. After a brief courtship they married in Ogden, Utah, on November 11, 1884 and settled in Park City.

The Emerys eagerly looked for investment opportunities after they married. Both were young and ambitious and hoped to find wealth and prestige. In 1885, Albion left the post office to work as one of the Daly Mine's bookkeepers. He also won a seat in the Utah Territorial Legislature and devoted many hours to Masonic activities. During the next five to seven years they scrimped to raise $8,000 to invest in Park City's Mayflower Mine. Eventually Susie raised most of the money by procuring loans from family friends like R. C. Chambers. Her father had grubstaked him earlier when both lived in Plumas County.[4]

During these early lean but happy years, Susie was childless until her younger sister, Viola Lamb, died in 1886. To help her brother-in-law, she volunteered to raise his infant son and christened him Harold Vernon Lamb. Motherhood appears to have been a good experience; two years later, at her insistence, Albion adopted a three-year-old girl they named Louise Grace. A policeman had found her on a doorstep, took her to a nearby Boston orphanage, and named her Louise Radford. Years later Susie explained that she had wanted a little girl for several years and was thrilled to have a daughter to dress in beautiful clothes.

In time, the Emerys' fortune dramatically changed. By 1893, the Mayflower Mine, eventually renamed the Silver King Mine, began to pay rich dividends to its investors. Their new wealth allowed the Emerys to travel and enjoy life. They bought stylish clothing and found a large new adobe brick home at 350 East 100 South in Salt Lake City. Albion's political career also skyrocketed. He was elected the Speaker of Utah Territory's House of Representatives in 1894 and the grand master of Salt Lake City's Masonic Lodge. Early in 1894, Susie's life seemed like a fairy tale come true. She was in love and happily married, had money and social status, a large new home, and a small family. Her blissful happiness soon ended, however. Her father died and only three weeks later, Albion, forty-eight, died suddenly on June 14, 1894 from heart and liver problems. Overwhelmed with grief, she lapsed into a deep depression. With the help of Albion's friends, she arranged for a large, impressive viewing and funeral in Salt Lake City's Masonic Temple and the Congregational Church. To accommodate his many Park City friends who wanted to attend the funeral, she chartered a special mourners' train to carry people from Park City to Salt Lake City. Following the funeral, Albion was buried in the Mt. Olivet Cemetery overlooking Salt Lake City.[5]

Albion's death in 1894 made Susie her daughter Grace's sole support and she was stunned to discover that he died intestate. Never anticipating an early death, he failed to leave a will clearly transferring his holdings to her. Just as the probate process was nearing an end, R. C. Chambers shocked Susie and Park City's populace by suing her for half of Albion's estate, $174,717. He claimed Albion borrowed half of the $8,000 he used to invest in the Mayflower Mine with the understanding that the two would quietly share the stocks and profits. Before his death Albion had paid Chambers $20,000, but Chambers felt he was entitled to more money.

Fortunately for Susie, Chamber's alleged agreement with Albion was an oral one and had never been legally recorded. Susie produced several cancelled checks to prove Albion had repaid the loan with interest. After the judge weighed all of the evidence he ruled in her favor. It now appeared that Susie unquestionably owned her husband's stock;

however, several weeks later, Chamber's attorneys appealed to Utah's Supreme Court to overturn the lower court's verdict. After several weeks of deliberation, the justices ruled in Susie's favor and gave her clear title to her husband's assets. Under Utah probate law, she and Grace now shared Albion's assets equally. Years later several eastern newspapers reported that Susie's estate in 1900, five years after the trial, was valued at $50,000,000 to $100,000,000, because they mistakenly believed that she had inherited 150,000 shares of Ontario stock. The Silver King Mine may have been valued at $50,000,000 by 1904, but Susie was only one of its original six owners. Her real assets by 1895 were probably closer to $2,000,000.[6]

Following her court victory, Susie personally managed her mining properties and other investments and began traveling to overcome her lingering depression. Albion's death also devastated eight-year-old Grace; the two had been very close. After his death the child developed several illnesses and became very insecure. Now that he was gone she needed more of Susie's time to compensate for his loss. Struggling with her own grief, Susie could not cope with her daughter's emotional needs. Grace brooded and grew resentful even though she and her foster brother, Harold, had everything money could buy. When Susie traveled, Grace was left with a governess; Harold by contrast was sent to a boarding school or stayed with his father who lived three blocks north and east of Susie in Salt Lake City.

During the next ten-year period, Susie tried enrolling Grace in two prestigious boarding schools hoping her grades and spirits would improve. Like many of the "nouveau riche" and Salt Lake City's established wealthy families, she preferred private schools as they suggested status. The first effort was disastrous; twelve-year-old Grace became hysterical when Susie insisted she live in a San Francisco dormitory with her governess and the other girls. Overwhelmed, Susie was grateful when her nephew, Wallace Bransford, offered to take Grace to Quincy to stay with his family. The following year Susie enrolled her in a respected boarding school in Washington, D.C., and found a nearby apartment. To fill her spare time, she attended many festive parties, traveled, and entertained lavishly. Susie tried to interest Grace in these activities, but she showed little interest. Instead she secretly wrote Wallace and complained about her mother. Frustrated at Grace's awkwardness in social situations, eventually Susie sent her teenage daughter to Europe hoping she would meet people and possibly make a royal marriage. At one point, Grace might have married the son of a European baroness, but Susie called her daughter home when the baroness proposed the marriage of their children. Susie felt the marriage was premature; Grace was only sixteen or seventeen years old and was too young to marry. Some have also speculated that she preferred the Swedish royal family for in-laws.[7]

Ironically, while Grace was avoiding people, Susie was enjoying an active social life. A year after the funeral Susie began accepting gentleman callers once more. Sometime in 1895, her business partner, Senator Thomas Kearns, introduced her to a wealthy Chicago businessman, Colonel Edwin F. Holmes. Holmes had lumber leases in Idaho, shipping investments in the Great Lakes area, stock in the Anchor Mine, and he was reported to have $8,000,000 in assets. Fourteen years Susie's senior, Holmes was also widowed in 1894 but had four grown children. Like Albion he was born in New England but was basically a self-educated man. After seeking Susie's hand in marriage for several years, the colonel decided to force the issue. They were dining with some Utah friends at the fashionable Delmonico Restaurant in New York City when he plucked a red rose from the table's center piece, tossed it to Susie and announced their marriage to the group. Moved to tears and startled by his persistence, she accepted his proposal. They married a few weeks later, on October 12, 1899, in the Waldorf-Astoria Hotel. After a simple ceremony and wedding party the newlyweds took a lengthy honeymoon trip around the world.[8]

During their years together, Colonel Holmes showered Susie with countless gifts, beautiful clothes, jewelry, and many collectibles. Susie began to concentrate on building an impressive wardrobe and jewelry collection on their honeymoon. When they returned to Salt Lake City, Colonel Holmes purchased Salt Lake City's Gardo House (Amelia's Palace) from the Mormon Church for $46,000 and presented it to Susie as a gift. Church architects had designed the house for Brigham Young to use as a center to entertain the church's many guests. One historian has described the house as a large four-story second empire mansion with more than forty rooms, over a hundred large windows, and a tower.

Following an extensive renovation, which cost $75,000, the Holmeses held a lavish open house and began to entertain widely. Their parties, recitals, luncheons, and Friday and Sunday "at homes" became the talk of Salt Lake City. Invitations to these affairs were prized possessions. The guest lists frequently included Utah's leading non-Mormon citizens and several state and local officials. [9]

She was generous to a fault with her family and participated in national and local community affairs. She built a home for her mother and took her on many trips, educated her sister, Nellie, and paid for her lavish wedding. She hired her brother John to manage her money and set him up in several real estate ventures. Eventually he became quite wealthy and was elected Salt Lake City's mayor in 1907. She also educated and supported her foster-son and nephew, Harold Lamb, and gave him a large, impressive prairie style home in one of Salt Lake City's finest neighborhoods after he married. Later she paid for the weddings of two of her nieces and gave them expensive gifts. Although a Democrat at heart, she generously contributed to the presidential campaigns of Woodrow Wilson, a Democrat, and Theodore Roosevelt, who was a Republican. For a time she also contributed to the Salt Lake City branch of the Salvation Army, the Orphan's Home and Day Nursery Association, and several other charitable groups, including the early Utah Symphony. A 1902 publication of prominent Utahns also commended her for her generosity to Salt Lake City's newspaper boys and the poor. After 1900 the membership rolls of the exclusive Ladies Literary Club and the Author's Club show she affiliated with both for some time. Each organization first worked to teach its members literature and history but also contributed money to community projects. [10]

When Grace turned eighteen in 1904, she startled Susie by announcing she intended to marry her cousin Wallace and wanted to manage her own money. Susie argued against the marriage because she felt Grace was too young to marry and repeatedly reminded her of the impressive "coming out party" they had planned. Next, she begged her brother John to intercede, but he declined and gave Wallace several thousand dollars as a wedding gift instead. Susie did not dislike her nephew, but he was not the son-in-law she had hoped for. He was young, unemployed, and could not offer Grace financial security. After some tense discussions, Susie finally agreed to host a small family wedding at the Gardo House on September 4, 1904. Following the marriage ceremony she divided her holdings with her daughter. When Grace and Wallace returned from their honeymoon, they moved into the Bransford Apartments across the street from the Gardo House. Sadly, when Grace returned home from her honeymoon she was noticeably cooler toward her mother. During their trip east, Wallace had told her that she had been adopted and was not Susie's natural daughter. Apparently Susie had concealed the adoption from Grace because she feared it would upset her. Throughout the next thirteen years, Wallace capably managed Grace's money, mining properties, and apartment houses.[11]

As Grace matured in her marriage, her relationship with Susie became more estranged. The women were polite to one another in public but apparently never had an opportunity to talk out their resentments privately. Grace died in October 1917 before the two could reconcile. Susie was distraught when she read the telegram, but cabled that she and Colonel Holmes were in Virginia, where he was taking a treatment for failing health and could not return. Some have criticized her for not rushing to the funeral but she may have been uncomfortable around Wallace because of his critical attitude toward her. After hearing several of his sarcastic comments about her lifestyle through mutual acquaintances she was very angry. Her husband's health also may have been more fragile than we know; he was seventy-four years old at the time. In retaliation Wallace buried Grace across the street from Albion in Mt. Olivet Cemetery so that she would not be buried near her mother in the future.[12]

But if Susie thought her troubles with Grace and Wallace were over when Grace died, she was sadly mistaken. With the reading of Grace's will, Susie discovered that Wallace had inherited all of Grace's assets. In response, Susie vented her pent-up feelings of resentment toward Wallace. Eleven months later, she took him to court to overturn the will, feeling her hard work to help Albion raise the money to invest in the Silver King Mine and her efforts to "bring up" Grace merited half of her daughter's assets. The trial that followed had a devastating impact on the rest of her life. The daily media coverage was frequently critical of her and colored many people's perceptions of her for the rest of her life.

Her relationship with her brother John's family was also everlastingly damaged. During the trial, both sides called numerous witnesses to support their views on the division of Grace's assets. Susie's attorneys alleged that Grace had subnormal intelligence and was too ill to make wise decisions. They claimed Wallace pressured Grace into leaving him all of her worldly goods and drove a wedge between Susie and her daughter. Wallace's attorneys claimed that Susie had misused Grace's money when she managed it and was a poor mother. They also maintained that Wallace and Grace had a happy marriage and were devoted to one another. After five months of conflicting testimony, the judge ruled in Wallace's favor and awarded him Grace's assets. Susie may have been seeking revenge by suing her nephew, but it is more likely that she simply needed the money. Colonel Holmes planned to leave all of his assets to his four children from his first marriage. After living on two incomes for many years, it would be difficult to live on one and maintain her standard of living.[13]

Following her bitter defeat, Susie and the colonel left Utah. They had allowed the Red Cross to use their stately Gardo House from the time the United States entered World War I while they spent most of their time at El Roble, their Pasadena winter home. After the trial, they sold the mansion back to the Mormon Church and donated part of the proceeds to the Red Cross. Never intending to live in Utah again, Susie also gave Harold, her foster son, Oakwood, her summer home on East Mill Creek. During the next several years she focused her energies on remodeling and refurbishing El Roble in grand style. With the help of a Los Angeles architect, she made the shake shingle home into a Tudor mansion.[14]

During the ensuing years the Holmeses traveled and entertained California's leading citizens. On Sundays, Susie hosted intimate gatherings of artists, writers, musicians, and politicians who discussed world affairs and what they called the "Seven Lively Arts." Her lively personality, amusing stories, and general attractiveness also garnered many dinner invitations. Because of her prominence in Pasadena, her picture was used on the cover of *California Life* twice. However, by 1923, the colonel's health had become a problem. Tensions also may have developed between the two about her spending habits as their mining dividends dwindled and both fortunes declined. Ill and tired of traveling around the United States and Europe, the colonel moved to Chicago to live with his two unmarried daughters when the hectic pace of entertaining and globe-trotting became too much for him. Susie received word of his death while traveling abroad with friends. She cabled his children that she could not return to the United States in time for the funeral and to proceed with his request for burial in the family plot next to their mother. Later she explained that she did not want to intrude on the family's grief at his passing, but there is evidence that she had a more pressing problem. Without revising his will or explaining the change to his children, the colonel had deeded some stocks to Susie to ensure her financial security after Wallace won the lawsuit. Perhaps she hoped her lawyers could negotiate a quiet settlement with his children later and prevent a confrontation at the funeral or when Holmes's will was read.[15]

Following the colonel's death, Susie carefully cultivated the illusion that she had vast wealth to preserve her social standing with her American peers and European friends and took pains to conceal the fact that she had less money. During the late 1920s, several articles appeared in eastern newspapers that listed her as one of America's wealthiest women. To stave off loneliness and for companionship in her declining years, several friends encouraged her to enter the matrimonial arena a third time. A striking figure with a trim silhouette and white hair, she soon met two Russian princes and several other unscrupulous men who were looking for a wealthy wife. One of the princes, Nicholas Vladomirovich Engalitcheff, or Nicki, claimed to be a descendant of Genghis Khan and a distant cousin of Tsar Nicholas II. Prior to 1900 he moved to the United States to work for Chicago's Russian consulate because the family estate in St. Petersburg could not support him. Within a few months he and Susie announced their plans to marry in *The New York Times*. Weeks later, when they tried to purchase the license, the state of New York refused to give them the document because the prince's second wife had mysteriously disappeared in Canada six years earlier and had not been missing long enough to be declared legally dead. Publicly embarrassed, they cancelled the wedding.[16]

Following this humiliating experience, Susie met another of New York society's most eligible bachelors, Dr. Radovan Delitch. Both the

French and Serbian governments had decorated him for meritorious service during World War I. After retiring from the military, he became a noted surgeon and cancer specialist with New York City's Fifth Avenue Hospital. When he married Susie in 1930, New York society was shocked; Susie, at 71, was thirty years older. Despite the disparity in their ages she was sure he would be the ideal husband and told family and friends she was very much in love. They had similar interests and shared the same friends. After a lengthy honeymoon trip around the world and a brief stop in Utah to introduce Rada to her family and friends, the Delitches moved to El Roble.

At Susie's insistence, Rada gave up his career in medicine so they could travel with their friends. It took only a few months for Rada to become very unhappy in the marriage. He stopped shaving, retreated to his study to read or wiite for many hours each day, and stopped speaking English. During the Great Depression Susie's mining investments and her income from her stocks continued to dwindle. Her servants reported that Susie and Rada frequently quarreled about money. Rada asked Susie to lay off several members of her staff at El Roble, but she generously refused, fearing some might not find work. Susie also found his possessiveness suffocating and stopped taking him to parties with her because he made a scene if she talked with other men. In retaliation he hired a detective to report on her activities. Finally, after fifteen months of marriage, Susie told him she had had enough. She wanted a divorce and sent him on a trip to Europe; when he returned the divorce would be final. Distraught at the turn of events, Rada committed suicide on Christmas Eve 1932 on his way back to the United States before the divorce was final. The ship's crew found him hanging by the neck in his stateroom; nearby was a tragic suicide note professing devotion to Susie.[17]

Susie received word of the suicide days later while she was lunching with her favorite niece, Nellie's daughter and her namesake, Susanna Hartman. Shaken and upset by the telegram, she decided not to cancel the lunch because her niece had been looking forward to it for many weeks; besides, as was common at the time, she had been schooled since childhood to conceal her emotions. Later she directed Culver Sherrill, her business manager, to take care of the funeral arrangements, and she retreated into seclusion. Sometime later, still upset about the tragedy, she told reporters he died of an illness and that they would have reconciled if he had lived longer.[18]

Less than six weeks later, Susie sold El Roble, her California estate, and many of her possessions and moved back to New York City. When friends and reporters asked how she could part with her beautiful California home, she replied that it now held too many sad memories. While this may have been part of the reason for the sale, by 1933, Susie also probably needed the money; the depression and income taxes had taken a major toll on her income from her investments. Sometime during the 1930s she also directed her business manager to sell her jewels and replace them with paste replicas to raise additional funds.[19]

After she returned to New York, Susie and Prince Engalitcheff set another date to marry—October 19, 1933. This time they were granted a marriage license and they had two weddings—a civil service and an elaborate Russian Orthodox ceremony. One news reporter claims the guests at the church service were amused when the prince's large gold crown slipped down over his nose, but Susie, delighted with the marriage, did not seem to notice. As Her Royal Highness Princess Susanna Engalitcheff, she had the excitement of sharing a Russian prince's title, which granted lasting social status.

By the time they married, it is likely that seventy-three-year-old Susie was more interested in a traveling companion and an escort than an amorous relationship. Unfortunately, both she and Nicki had strong personalities and he liked to be waited on. When they appeared together in public, Susie seemed to enjoy doting on him, but her fourth and last marriage lacked the love and affection that could have cemented them together. It ended soon after the honeymoon. They were separated when Nicki died on March 28, 1935 in a New York hotel. After decades of womanizing, heavy drinking, and smoking, he died of a stroke at the age of sixty-three.

Despite the fact that his obituary was printed in several major eastern newspapers and in Salt Lake City, Susie later told her western family and friends a humorous story about burying him at sea while they were traveling. Rather than return to the United States to bury him, she claimed she decided to stop in a nearby port and store his body in a warehouse, intending to retrieve it later on the return trip. When word of her plans leaked to the press, some Russian nationals insisted she bury their prince with the respect his rank demanded. To appease them, she rented a battle ship and arranged for a funeral. Next she hired a woman to dress in her clothes, wear a dark veil, and impersonate her so she would be spared attending the funeral. In light of their separation prior to his death, her "burial at sea" story seems significant; it clearly illustrates how much she had come to loathe him.

The prince's earlier marital history provides insight into their troubled relationship. His first wife was a wealthy American heiress from Chicago who divorced him after sixteen years when she discovered he was using her money to pay his mistress's expenses and debts. The second wife was a phony heiress who disappeared when he discovered she was penniless. Susie's business manager, Culver Sherrill, claims in his autobiography that Nicki left her for another woman in Denver. When the affair ended badly she refused to take him back but continued to support him quietly until his death. A second divorce would have been too humiliating.[20]

Culver Sherrill, secretary/business manager and devoted, loyal friend, was the last man in Susie's life. By the time she died in 1942, she was eighty-three and nearly destitute. She had less than $65,000 left of her fortune and a number of unpaid bills. After these were paid she was nearly bankrupt. At the reading of her will, the family discovered that she left them nothing but had left Culver and her former gardener the remainder of her estate. They talked of challenging the will because some felt she had become mentally unstable in her twilight years, but never did. A few relatives speculated that Culver may have used undue influence to gain access to her estate or may even have murdered her. As her secretary, Culver controlled all of her expenses and was not accountable to anyone. Others wondered if she had committed suicide since her death was medically unattended. Even though these theories add intrigue to her story, medical reports state she died of arteriosclerosis and problems related to old age. There is no evidence of foul play or that Culver was anything but kind and patient with her during the last years of her life.[21]

It is hard to explain why Susie left her relatives out of her will; earlier in her life she had been very generous with them. Her niece Susanna

Hartman recalls that Susie hoped to prevent them from quarrelling over her remaining assets. Susie probably also felt she had been very generous with them during her lifetime and did not feel a responsibility to them after her death. Part of the problem may have been that several of her relatives were openly critical of her as she aged. Undoubtedly some of her decisions, like marrying the prince and Rada, seemed foolish to the younger members of the family. Also by 1939, when she drew up her last will, all of her husbands and Grace and Harold were dead. Most of her brother John's family deeply resented her; she had earned their eternal enmity by challenging Wallace's right to Grace's estate in 1918. Sensitive to their critical barbs and comments, she probably did not feel welcome at family gatherings. Without close family ties, she turned to others outside of the family and took extended trips with her friends during her last years.

Culver, however, did not endear himself to her family after her death. When some questioned him, he told them there was no money and that all of her jewelry and many of her possessions had been sold for living expenses. He explained that the depression had devalued her stocks and mining investments making most of them worthless by 1942. But later, when he moved to California, he told the press a different story. He claimed that Susie had left him $4,000,000. In reality, the Mormon Church paid him $660,000 tax-free for her last piece of real estate, the Richmond (Sherrill) Apartments in Salt Lake City. The church later used the property to build its twenty-six story church headquarters. The dividends from Susie's devalued stocks provided Culver with some income, but when these dividends and money for the property were combined he had far less than he led the press to believe. He used his inheritance to lease and remodel a small villa in Taormina, Sicily. There he and a male companion named Angelo lived for ten years. During that time, Culver dictated his memoirs to Angelo and entitled the book *Crimes without Punishment*. Later the two men traveled extensively for several more years before returning to California, where they eventually separated. Following his return to the United States, Culver lived with relatives until his death in July 1981. One of his nephews claims that Culver, like Susie, was penniless when he died. His book failed to be a best seller even though a prominent New Yorker, Temple Fielding, endorsed it and promoted it.

Apparently, he used stories of great wealth, as Susie had done, to impress people.[22]

And so, all things considered, was Susie a cold, unfeeling socialite or was she a caring person? Was she an eccentric woman determined to live life to the fullest measure despite the convention of her day? She frequently quoted her first husband, Albion, whose precarious health led him to think, "Why live if you can't enjoy life?" Or was she like many of the nouveau riche, striving to belong? Her behavior suggests she was all of these things. The rich and famous of every era generally have little privacy and all of their mistakes, joys, and sorrows feed the newspapers almost daily and are often misinterpreted. To attempt to label her as one or another would distort her life.

Wealthy Americans during this period were greatly impressed with the court life of Europe's royalty and established their own, exclusive social clubs and cliques to imitate them. Some parents even tried to assure their children a place in society by marrying them to royalty. Susanna Hartman remembers Susie dreamed of marrying Grace into a royal family until she married Wallace in 1904. Each social organization rigidly enforced rules of etiquette and adopted criteria for membership. Groups such as Astor's 400 were routinely featured in the newspapers and its members achieved the celebrity status of twentieth-century movie stars. Half of the satisfaction of belonging to these formal and informal organizations was "getting in"; the other half was closing ranks and keeping others out. One of the greatest tragedies a wealthy person could experience was to be excluded or passed over by these prestigious groups. In the hope of averting this terrible experience, many worked tirelessly to become part of a group and once they were accepted worked just as hard to maintain their membership. Failure to attend the prescribed social events could cause them to fall out of favor with the group.

Like many of those who made their fortunes during "the Gilded Age," Susie rose to social prominence from modest circumstances. Her family had been prominent in the southern states for over a hundred years before it suffered financial reverses during the Civil War period. It would be natural for her to seek the same status and wealth her family had formerly enjoyed. On numerous occasions she reminded American and foreign wealthy contacts that she was "a daughter of the deep South" and imitated the South's hospitality. For decades following the Civil War there was marked bitterness toward southerners in some circles and few southern aristocrats were admitted into the highest social circles in Washington, D.C., or the other major northeastern cities. A search of Washington, D.C.'s and New York City's social registers from 1900–1935 indicates that Susie may have attended their parties and threw some lavish entertainments of her own, but was not accepted as a member of the group. Possibly some of her pretentious behavior was an effort to break through the glass ceiling that kept her and other southerners out. Wealthy Europeans by contrast welcomed all Americans into their cafe society if they were charming and entertaining.

The "old guard" in the Northeast were also wary of the newly rich and made it difficult for them to infiltrate their exclusive social circles. Just prior to 1900, all newcomers such as the Vanderbilts and the Rockefellers struggled to gain the acceptance of the Astors, Morrises, Cabots, and Lodges by staging elaborate parties and by boasting of their great wealth. Conspicuous consumption in homes, dress, and entertaining was part of the game of social climbing but vulgarity was shunned. The newly rich soon discovered it was important to know the "right people." For example, the Tom Walshes of Ouray, Colorado, were not accepted in Denver, Washington, or New York City until they had traveled to Europe. Once they had mingled with European royalty and the statesmen in Paris and Washington, they were given a chance to affiliate with the "right people" in Denver, Colorado. Washington's newspapers later touted Tom Walsh as the "king of entertainers" because of his elaborate entertainments. Having won acceptance, they saw to it that their children socialized with and married into the right groups to consolidate or increase their wealth.[23]

Originally, as *The New York Herald* pointed out in 1902, lineage was a prerequisite for membership in the exclusive social circles. Later, lineage became a minor consideration, "social prominence . . . was expressed . . . in terms of millions [of dollars] rather than in lineage." Stephen Birmingham, a chronicler of this era, called the years between 1890 and 1930 the "Era of the Great Splurge" because the newly rich were aggressively and competitively spending money as never before to impress each other. Mary Cable summed up the activities of the "nouveau riche" in the following statement. "The startling fact that slowly dawns upon the student of the era is that these people having made their piles, had nothing really serious or important to do. Nothing prevented them from an almost frantic schedule of heavy dinners, vast balls and formal calls. Laden with baggage they weekended with one another and made the rounds of selected watering places here and abroad, always with the 'people we know' and avoiding 'people we don't know'." This could explain why Susie tried to confuse and conceal the issue of her real net worth until the day she died. Would she have been accepted by her wealthy peers if they had known that her fortune was much smaller than she boasted?[24]

The wealthy were also absentee parents because many of them sent their children to boarding schools. They often shunned the public schools because they did not offer all of the opportunities of the private schools and included "the people we don't want to know." Generally, wealthy parents were too busy to spend much time with their children even during holidays or summer vacations. Governesses were expected to nurture the children and teach them manners and discipline. It appears that some wealthy people barely knew their children; their servants served as surrogate parents. Susie and her wealthy Utah friends sent their children to expensive eastern and western schools or enrolled them in local private schools like Rowland Hall. Offering their children such an education was almost a status issue.[25]

When Susie is compared with her peers, many of the excesses of her life become explainable. In addition, later in life she may have deliberately started some of the myths about her marriages, clothes, jewelry, and Park City origins as a joke. Surely some of her off-handed statements, like the one to Jennie Kearns, Senator Thomas Kearn's wife, about hanging her four wedding rings like a cluster of grapes in the bathroom, were intended to be humorous and earned chuckles from her friends. She also had a public image she felt she must maintain and was generally the life of the party at many socials with her sense of humor and entertaining stories. It is likely that humor may have allowed her to preserve her dignity in good and bad times. Unfortunately, the exuberant and spirited behavior that amused and attracted some of her European and western friends annoyed many of America's elite. Her outspoken comments and grand entrances offended some of society's grand dames. Such behaviors were thought unseemly for proper society women, and some dowagers of Newport, Palm Beach, and even Pasadena let her know of their disapproval. Intellect and charm were not thought to be essential and women were encouraged not to appear intellectual. One of the things that assured the Colorado Walshes a place among Astor's 400 was Mrs. Walsh's modest and quiet demeanor. *The Salt Lake Tribune*'s Jack Gallivan described Susie as gracious and self-assured in public and even felt her brilliant red dress at his wedding humorous when others thought it showed poor taste. However, her close family, friends, and servants believed she was a different person in private. Alone with those she trusted, she was quieter, more human and approachable. These extremes in her behavior later puzzled some who knew her well and revealed a very complex personality.[26]

A second scenario to explain Susie's eccentricities might be that she became senile as she aged. Some of her family feel this unlikely, but they were not close to her during the late 1930s and early 1940s and had few opportunities to observe her. Although the men who endorsed the changes in her will in 1939 claimed she was alert, Culver, her last business manager, quietly complained to Angelo that she was becoming increasingly confused and forgetful each year. Her last two unhappy marriages to Rada and the prince provide evidence that her judgment faltered toward the end.[27]

The following comment appeared in the *Salt Lake Tribune* on August 5, 1942, a few days after her death. It reflects the views of many who knew her during her lifetime. "Famed for a remarkable personality as much as for her extreme wealth, the princess was often described as a blend of grand dame, business woman, cosmopolite and breezy westerner, forming a striking and attractive combination."

Legendary in life, Susie is apparently not allowed to rest in peace even now. An interesting bit of folklore suggests that after the funeral some of her friends filled her coffin with silver dollars out of love and respect for her memory. Though the present Evans and Early Mortuary staff insists the story is not true, after her life of adventures — real and fabricated — it somehow seems fitting that Utah's illustrious Silver Queen who rose from modest circumstances in Park City to riches and lost most of it in the end, might be resting in a coffin filled with silver dollars. Over the years, members of Susie's family have complained to Mt. Olivet's Cemetery staff that their family headstones have been moved and are not in the right places. There is a logical explanation for this circumstance. A major water line for the cemetery's sprinkler system runs through the middle of the Emery and Bransford graves, making it necessary to move headstones occasionally to replace or work on the water pipes. The current superintendent at Mt. Olivet Cemetery, Mr. Daniel Valdez, is not sure if Susie's body actually rests beneath her headstone. No doubt Susie would be delighted with this situation. She loved to leave people guessing and enjoyed a good joke.[28]

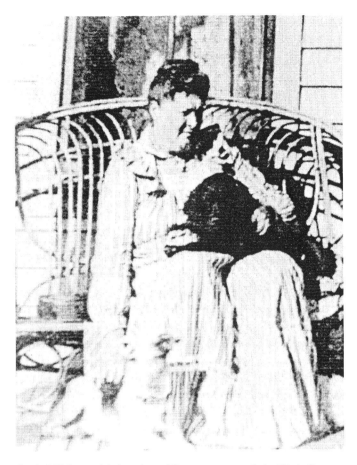

Rachel Urban with her dogs. Photo courtesy of the Utah State Historical Society.

MOTHER RACHEL URBAN
Park City's Leading Madam

Cheryl Livingston

Cheryl Livingston is an English major at Westminster College, expecting to graduate in 1996. She became involved in this project when she took a tour of historic Salt Lake City homes led by Floralee Millsaps, legendary tour guide for the State Historical Society and Heritage Foundation and one of the originators of this project. Livingston knew at once that she wanted to find factual information on Rachel Urban. She had learned of Mother Urban earlier when she toured Park City and heard some of the locals exchanging stories about the city's best known madam. She says, "I have always loved Park City and she is one of its most interesting citizens. I was fascinated by her and wanted to do more research." The problem for the researcher, however, was that little is documented about Mother Urban, as was often the case with "fallen women," but Livingston has collected here the folklore about her, much of which offers interesting insights into Park City's past.

Today in Park City, Utah, the whistles of the Union and Mackintosh mills are silent. Hardly anyone can remember the Sampson or the Little Bell, the Jones-Bonanza, or the Revelator mines. In canyons now filled with quaking aspens and ski runs, there once stood great stamp mills crushing out millions of dollars in silver ore. The story of Park City's first one hundred years is a story filled with strong women, astute men, and many colorful figures. Their stories still whisper from the old rough and broken cabins clinging to the hillsides. Perhaps one of the most endearing and colorful figures, winking at us through the dust of the ore wagons and the sounds of the steam engines, is the two-hundred-pound, wooden-legged madam known as "Mother Urban."

Her name was Rachel Urban and while many stories abound,[1] much of the concrete information ordinarily available about most people still remains a mystery for her. She was born in Ohio in 1864, the daughter of an Irish immigrant.[2] Much can be inferred from the knowledge that her father came from Ireland during the mid-1800s. Thousands of Irish people emigrated following the disastrous potato blight of the 1840s and many of them came to America. However, to be Irish and in America during that time period was not necessarily a pleasant situation. Anne Butler describes the situation:

> Although the Irish immigration began in the 1820's, the greatest numbers crossed the ocean after the famine of the 1840's. Between 1845 and 1855 death or migration claimed 2 million Irish inhabitants. Of those who sailed for America, little relief from the grinding poverty existed in the tenements of eastern cities. Not only poverty pursued the Irish, but the rancor and prejudice that haunted them in Ireland flourished in America. . . . with generations of social malaise to condition them, the women among the Irish group made excellent candidates for prostitution.[3]

Butler maintains that, in fact, "the most significant European pre-industrial influences upon frontier prostitution evolved from the Irish experience."[4] Surrounded by poverty and scorn, the Irish often migrated from city to city, many eventually going west. It is possible that similar circumstances brought Rachel to Park City.

Poverty fed prostitution. One of the chief reasons why women became prostitutes was that they had no other option for employment. "Observing that impoverished artisans sold the sexual favors of their wives and children, the Englishman Francis Place concluded that poverty and chastity were incompatible." Prostitution has always been a part of society, but it flourished in America until the end of World War I when "better wages and working conditions for women rendered prostitution less necessary for women."[5]

Most prostitutes were young women, usually between the ages of fifteen and thirty.[6] After that, they typically changed employment to related fields, possibly managing one or two girls. While no documentation has been found on her early life, it is likely that Rachel Urban had been a prostitute in her younger years. Her success as a manager is very apparent. Mother Urban conducted activities on what was known as "the row." "The row" consisted of her sixteen houses stretching up Heber Avenue at the mouth of Deer Valley with her parlor house located at 345 Heber Avenue. Because of its purple color, it was referred to as the "purple palace."

Rachel married a carpenter, George Urban, an immigrant from Denmark, in 1898. Census records show Rachel as having had six children, but only one, their son Richard, was still living in 1910. They moved from Ohio to Park City sometime after the turn of the century and by 1910 opened a bordello on Heber Avenue with eight to ten girls. They may have been in operation earlier. "Originally the brothels were on Main Street, but in 1907 an ordinance was passed to keep the 'soiled doves' a more respectable distance from town."[7] In the 1910 census, Rachel and George are listed as living with many young women "boarders." George and Rachel apparently stayed together on "the row" until his death in 1924.[8] George was probably her business partner as well; a carpenter had to have built those sixteen houses.

Heber Avenue was not far from the train station and legend has it that it came to be thought of as the "red light district" because many of its patrons were men from the railroad. They would leave their red railroad lanterns twinkling outside the doors or in the windows as a sign that the room was occupied.[9] Other signs of occupation were closed doors or blinds drawn completely down. If the door were ajar and the blind partially raised, a man "entered with $2.50 in his hand, or $10 if he wanted to stay the night."[10]

Rachel Urban was the most famous among all of Park City's "fallen angels," yet her birth year is surmised from census records and her family name is unknown. She died in Park City in 1933 and is presumably buried there. However, although an impressive tombstone bearing the name of Urban graces the Park City Cemetery, the caretaker can only report that George and Richard Urban and another man named Peter Howarth are buried there. The last occupant of the plot is unidentified. There may be a reason for this missing name.

Mother Urban was said to have kept to herself. This was probably prudent and even typical of those in her profession. "A prostitute's place in society seemed reasonably safe and accepted . . . if [she] did not flaunt [her] occupation." Those who forgot or ignored this important rule were often shocked at the consequences. "It might come as a distinct and unwelcome surprise to learn that the men who bowed to her on the street or paid her elaborate compliments when they visited her house would ask her to leave a gathering that included their wives."[11] Hubert Howe Bancroft, a nineteenth-century California historian reported the case of one who forgot. Belle Cora, one of San Francisco's most famous and successful madams attended a play at the American Theater with her husband, Charles. They were seated directly behind United States Marshal W. H. Richardson and his wife, and Mrs. Richardson insisted the Coras leave. The manager refused to evict them, so it was the Richardsons who left in anger. Belle delighted in her social triumph but two days later Marshal Richardson confronted Charles in a saloon where Charles Cora shot and killed him. Despite Belle's use of her considerable wealth and connections to stop the legal hanging, Charles was charged and jailed. On May 23, 1856, the "Second Vigilance Committee" took him from the jail, tried, and hanged him. Belle's story demonstrates that the repercussions of society on a prostitute who "forgot her place" could be severe and certain.[12]

Mother Urban apparently was unwilling to take such risks. If discretion is the better part of valor, she was valiant. Her life remained so low key that details about her are sketchy at best, but her prudence garnered respect from the public and the mine owners and allowed her to stay in business.

In Park City's early years, as was the case for most mining towns, entrepreneurship was almost a mania. For the astute there were empires to be built and fortunes to be made. Mining magnates like David Keith, Albion Emery, and Tom Kearns became millionaires. For women, however, the opportunities for employment were extremely limited. Perhaps only in prostitution did a woman's economic opportunities parallel those of a man's in frontier and mining occupations. And while prostitution was not designated as a "business" under labor statistics in the early 1900s, the madams who ran the elite parlor houses did so by saving up enough money to begin their own houses, and then by using executive abilities, talents that women during the time period had few opportunities to use in any other field. The fact that Mother Urban was managing sixteen houses indicates that she was extremely competent at business.

Her sixteen houses may have made her money, but it is the "purple palace" that indicated the quality of her operation. Jacqueline Barnhart categorizes early mining town prostitution into parlor-house residents, brothel prostitutes, dance-hall harlots, and streetwalkers. Of these, the women with the least security and the hardest work, "the worst paid and least professional," were the streetwalkers. Next in the hierarchy was the dance-hall harlot, who "had to provide her own room and very often did not receive a salary for her presence in the dive where she found customers." Brothel prostitutes might have their own rooms and possibly receive a salary for their presence. But the most elite by far were the parlor-house residents. Barnhart says that "the parlor house offered greater earnings from higher fees as well as an atmosphere of comfort and elegance. . . . the parlor house was traditionally the most desirable place to work . . . requiring the highest standards of professionalism. . . . in the very best houses everything was conducted with the utmost propriety" and a visit to a well managed house would resemble a visit to a nice home. "The parlor house resident had to be not only beautiful but accomplished, . . . witty and intelligent conversation was required of the prostitute, and when necessary the madam would school her in behavior and repartee. Occasionally one of the residents would play the piano, or there might be games. . . . the decor of the house would typically surpass other homes in the neighborhood in order to attract a wealthy and influential clientele."[13]

There is every indication that Mother Urban followed closely the ideas and rules of parlor houses. She is reported to have kept a tight ship with rigid rules. Her girls were never allowed to walk the streets. "She hired Mr. Reynolds, a crippled neighbor, to do their errands and shopping, for if she caught one of her protegees on the street, she would put her on the next bus out of town."[14]

To understand the important role of parlor houses in mining towns at the turn of the century, it is helpful to remember that until 1901 single miners in Park City were required by law to live only at the company boarding house. They worked long hours in the mines, seven days a week. There were not many opportunities for them to mingle with other people. Few families lived in town, and miners had only two days off all year—Christmas and the Fourth of July. Mother Urban always held a Christmas party for them and it was considered a respectable place where they could gather. It was also a place where they could go and have a letter written home, as many of them did not know how to write. And even if they did not go upstairs, they could always spend a pleasant evening there as the girls would know how to mingle.[15]

The mining companies' owners seemed to regard Rachel Urban as providing a valued and much needed service. They assumed that men would require sexual outlets and consequently would seek out prostitutes. Without Mother Urban, the miners might have made the long journey to Salt Lake City, resulting in absenteeism in the mines. When a mayor, formerly the high school principal, tried to shut the row down, an outraged Mother Urban complained to her prosperous and connected clientele. As the incident is now remembered, the superintendent of the Judge Mine used his influence on the City Council, and within a few days twenty-five "seamstresses" were ensconced in the little row of houses.[16] This was not a unique situation. Barnhart reports that in San Francisco, "although the parlor-house residents and their madams were among the best-known women in the city, they were almost never arrested."[17] The reason might have been the income they provided for the city. Mother Urban apparently paid her fines without complaint. In 1899, one typical month showed five dollars for assault, thirty dollars for gambling, and fifty dollars for prostitution.[18] Park City records show that fines were collected from the city's prostitutes regularly around the eleventh of each month. The rates apparently were $10 for "keeping a house of ill fame" (being a madam) and $5 for "resorting to a house of ill fame" (being a prostitute). A typical entry showed Francis Foster paying $10 for keeping a house and fines of $5 each levied against her "girls," Bessie

Scott, May Mitchell, Louise Wilson, Hilda Richardson, Hazel Morris, and Margaret Henderson. Mother Urban seems to have paid her girls' fines in a lump sum, the total sometimes reaching $120 per month.[19]

Other reports indicate that Mother Urban took good care of the girls who worked for her. In a pattern familiar in far more prosaic cultures, she was well known for her chicken soup. "Mother" was reportedly a term of endearment given to a madam out of respect or regard from her girls.[20] Her kindness extended beyond her girls. David Fleisher reports that Pat, "the old-timer," said, "If there was a death in the family, she'd come see you in the middle of the night and give you money if you needed it."[21]

The fact that she often called the doctor when one of her girls was ill or in need is reflected in an editorial that she wrote in 1913 for the *Park Record*. When Park City's Dr. E. P. LeCompte came under criticism for increasing his fees, it was Mother Urban who came to his defense. In her editorial, she praised him as a caring physician who never hesitated to come when one of her girls was in need: "Never in the history of the camp has a doctor been more attentive than Dr. E. P. LeCompte, and if he had just one-fourth of what is owed him he could undoubtedly move into Salt Lake with his family and live on Easy Street. I have called him hundreds of times to come over and see some unfortunate woman of the underworld and, unlike some of the other doctors, he did not ask me who was going to pay him . . . but he would come immediately and render all assistance possible."[22]

It might seem unusual to find an editorial from the local madam on the pages of the town newspaper, but the *Park Record* is not a usual newspaper. It is Utah's oldest continuously published weekly. It began its circulation in 1880, the same year that Park City was incorporated as a town. Its spirited editorials give us good insight into the nature of the young mining town. Like most mining towns, it was fairly tolerant toward prostitution in the early years. The *Record* contains sympathetic obituaries like the one for Eva Wilson, "a resident of Park City's immoral districts, . . . summoned to lay down her armor and pass through the dark valley."[23] This was very unusual because obituaries for women of any occupation or social class were not often included in the local newspapers.[24] In contrast, it did take a stand on what its editors perceived as community problems: "On July 31, 1986, the *Record* joined forces with the Masons, Protestants and Catholics. The joint venture was to rid the town of a nuisance. Wishing to be billed as 'the only gentile town in Utah,' the *Park Record* urged the ousting of the Mormons from the city."[25] In a paper with such fiery spirit, it was probably not surprising to find a letter from the local madam coming to the rescue of one of Park City's most prominent citizens. In fact, it might indicate that she was also one of its prominent citizens herself. Today she is most prominently remembered in the folklore of the area.

She reportedly walked with a cane and had a big Pol parrot which swore at customers from a perch on her front porch. When she drove into town, she was chauffeured by a uniformed driver in a limousine.

Area tour guides delight in telling about the time when two of the city's respected matrons were taking a stroll up Deer Valley road. As they passed Rachel Urban's house, the madam was sitting on the front porch. She recognized one of the women, Blanche Fletcher, who played the piano at the silent movies, and she motioned the ladies to come up for some tea. The ladies decided to accept the invitation, since no one else was there. After a pleasant time, the visitors said their good-byes. As they were leaving, Mother Urban asked Blanche's friend to introduce herself. When she said her name, Mother Urban smiled and said, "Oh yes, I know your husband well."[26]

Another story concerns Mike Carella, a Park City resident, who crashed his car into a tree and was thrown onto Mother Urban's porch. He loved to tell his friends, "I've been thrown out of these places before, but I've never been thrown into one!"[27]

When Park City residents recall their town's colorful past, they commonly tell of ghostly Tommy Knockers tapping in the mines to find their way out. They remember that seeing or talking to the man in the yellow slicker could mean death.[28] They remember that the women who worked in Park City's houses of prostitution were often called midnight angels, fallen angels, soiled doves, or the fair but frail, known by nicknames such as the Copper Queen, Trixie, or Frisco. The most endearing and famous among them was Mother Urban.

Mary Teasdel. Photo courtesy of the Utah State Historical Society.

MARY TEASDEL
Yet Another American in Paris

Martha S. Bradley

Martha Bradley was born and raised in Salt Lake City; she earned a bachelor's degree from the University of Utah, a master's from Brigham Young University, where she also taught, and a Ph.D. from the University of Utah, where she currently teaches architectural history. As a young woman she wanted to be a painter but was "side-tracked by motherhood," raising six children. She enjoys learning and teaching about painters and is particularly "interested in the lives of artists at the end of the pioneer period in Utah. It was extraordinary that several of the men traveled to Paris to study and even more remarkable that Mary Teasdel was able to follow and carve out a niche for herself." She explored this remarkable painter first in a paper for the 1989 annual meeting of the Utah Historical Society and it was subsequently printed in the Utah Historical Quarterly 58 *(summer 1990).*

During the winter of 1864 Elizabeth Jane Gardner traveled to Paris to study art. Upon her arrival she was taken aback by how different reality was from her dream: "It was the audacity and ignorance of youth . . . I never dreamed on quitting America that all Paris had not a studio nor a master who would receive me.

. . . I had forgotten, if I ever knew, that the few French and European women then familiar to the Salon . . . like the women painters who had preceded them were the wives, sisters or daughters of painters, and it was in the ateliers of their kinfolk they lived and worked."[1]

But Elizabeth was not willing to leave it at that. Determined to infiltrate the academies where one could learn the magic behind great art, but unable to enter a drawing atelier as her female self, she resorted to subterfuge—bobbing her hair and donning the clothes of a schoolboy, which required special permission from the chief of police. Finally a Parisian art education stretched out before her at a government school of drawing and modeling. A decade later, when the private Academie Julian opened its classes to women, she drew for the first time from live models under the tutelage of the prodigious Bougereau. More than the lively Miss Gardner's drawing technique caught her instructor's eye, and soon Elizabeth Jane Gardner Bougereau, like so many female artists before, mastered her technique under the instruction of her husband. She would later remark, "I would rather be known as the best imitator of Bougereau than not be known at all."[2]

The same winter that Elizabeth Jane Gardner first traveled to Paris a girl was born in Salt Lake City, Utah, who would grow up to share her dream. There is little in the story of Mary Teasdel's early life to distinguish her from hundreds of other Utah Mormon girls and to provide a clue as to why she chose such a new frontier. During her lifetime, many doors would open to women who wanted a career in art, but the obstacles were still great.

Perhaps the single most important factor of Mary's youth that allowed her to develop her talent in art was the relative wealth of her family and her father's willingness to lavish it on his daughter. S. P. Teasdel was a merchant, the equivalent of a present-day real estate developer, and an entrepreneur. As a girl, Mary lived in a beautiful, spacious home. Her family traveled extensively and enjoyed every cultural experience afforded in this western state's capital city. Hers was a liberal, generous home environment where she was taught the value of work, thrift, education, and the importance of planning for the future. She grew up believing she was indeed gifted and uniquely talented.

The Teasdels insisted Mary's education include what Alice Merrill Horne called the "accomplishments": music, both instrumental and vocal, fine stitching, and drawing and painting. Although her education was for the most part traditional and designed more to create an interesting woman than a scholar, Mary pushed it as far as she could and graduated from the University of Deseret in 1886 as an art and music major.

As one of the territory's first generation of college-educated women, Mary looked toward a career fully believing that the world was at her command. Within the context of her age, she chose one of the few "respectable" occupations open to single or impoverished genteel women who needed a means of support. After she finally made a commitment to the serious study of art, she proposed to "go abroad and study art from the foundation." Her father "reposed full confidence in his own powers to provide for his gifted daughter,"[3] which simply meant that money would not stand in her way.

Typical of his generation, S. P. Teasdel was proud of Mary's artistic talent but ultimately did not approve of professions for women. According to Horne, he believed that girls should be supported by their fathers and saw no reason why a woman should even desire to be independent in financial matters when she had parents or brothers to "gladly furnish her means."[4]

Mary Teasdel would eventually leave Utah to study art, but it would not be as simple as it had once seemed. S. P. Teasdel was one of thousands who lost their fortunes during the depression of the mid-1890s. Explanations of his misfortune vary but generally attribute it to a series of bad investments and internal fraud. He was frequently portrayed as the victim of unscrupulous men who took advantage of his generosity. Whatever the cause of his financial difficulties, Teasdel found it impossible to make good on his promise to support Mary's proposed art studies abroad.

Within a few months of her father's financial downfall Mary's two older brothers died. A month later her only sister died in childbirth. Surely it must have seemed that the world was tumbling around her. But in the midst of all the rubble she saw a glimmer of hope—one of her dead brothers, Harry, having no wife or children of his own, had left his savings to her. This sum, added to her own savings, was enough to fund three years in art school. At that moment, her commitment to a future career as an artist was tested more dearly. As she chose to leave her grieving parents and her last living brother, she must have believed that what she was about to do was important. A career in art was not for Mary a frivolous pursuit—simply a lady's accomplishment—but a way she could contribute something of worth to the world and, in particular, to Utah. Later in life, as she tried to express her feelings about the social role of the artist to an audience of young adults, she would begin with the words of Robert Browning: "For—don't you mark we're made so that we love first when we see them painted—things we have passed perhaps a hundred times nor cared to see; and so they are better, painted, better to us which is the same thing. Art was given for that—God uses us to help each other so, leading our minds out."[5]

Mary Teasdel had studied art in Utah with the best the state had to offer—J. T. Harwood. No other Utah artist possessed such natural gifts in painting. One art historian described Harwood's strength as "a fine sense of structure, a deeply rooted feeling for professionalism and craftsmanship, and a good control of muted color."[6] Harwood's students, including Teasdel, "prospered under his tutelage. He made us draw constantly and only the best work from a student was accepted. We would spend a whole week preparing a drawing of a ball."[7]

Harwood had advised Mary to spend at least one year studying at an American academy of art to become as proficient as possible in the rudiments of art before venturing abroad for more expensive training. Harwood himself had spent a number of years during the early 1890s in Paris at the Academie Julian, the first Utahn to do so, and the first to exhibit at the French Salon. Teasdel would be the third. After Harwood's studies in Paris he returned to Utah to open a studio and teach art, using the same methods as the French schools.[8]

In the 1890s a number of prestigious art academies in the eastern United States offered classes for women. The Pennsylvania Academy of Art, founded in 1805, permitted women to exhibit in the salon but did not admit female students until 1844. In those first female drawing classes women could draw from plaster casts of the Apollo Belvedere or Laocoon, but not before the instructor discreetly placed a close-fitting but conspicuous fig leaf over the "offending members." In 1868 the first life drawing classes with nude models opened to women, and by 1877 some schools allowed an occasional male nude model. In one instance the unprecedented action created a scandal in polite Philadelphia society. A letter written in 1882 to the director of the prestigious Pennsylvania Academy of Art epitomized public opinion:

> Does it pay for a young lady of a refined, godly household to be urged as the only way of obtaining knowledge of true art, to enter a class where every feeling of maidenly delicacy is violated, where she becomes . . . so familiar with the persons of degraded women and sight of nude males, that no possible art can restore her lost treasure of chaste and delicate thoughts. . . . The stifling heat of the room adds to the excitement, and what could be a cool impassioned study in a room at 35 degrees, at 85 degrees or even higher, is dreadful.[9]

This prejudicial view of the supposed adverse effects of life drawing classes on the morals of women was not an aberration that appeared in Pennsylvania and nowhere else. It was a belief perpetuated throughout the United States and Europe. May Alcott, the younger sister of Louisa May Alcott, angrily wrote while studying at the Academie Julian: "The lower school as it is called, or male class, no longer opens its doors to women, for the price, being but one half of the upper (womans') school, attracted too many, also, with better models, and a higher standard of work, it was found impossible that women should paint from the living nude models of both sexes, side by side with the Frenchmen."[10] Women were excluded from drawing from nude models except in extraordinary circumstances until the early twentieth century.

Mary Teasdel entered this world so full of restrictions on what a good woman could do in 1897—her thirty-fourth year—when she and her friend and fellow artist Cora Hooper boarded a train for New York City and the National Academy of Art. The National Academy had begun admitting women students after 1871 but did not open anatomy classes to them until 1914. For the most part women were limited to drawing from plaster casts in the "antiques" class.

Two years later, in 1899, Teasdel and another Utah artist, May

Farlow, traveled to Paris to study at the Academie Julian, following not only her teacher, J. T. Harwood, but the Mormon art "missionaries" John Hafen, John Fairbanks, Lorus Pratt, and Edwin Evans. The academic tradition can be traced back to Plato and Athens in the fourth century B.C. During the Middle Ages painters joined guilds to protect their rights as craftsmen rather than as creative artists. The origin of the modern academy of art is associated with Leonardo Da Vinci, who, at the end of the fifteenth century, hoped to elevate the status of the artist as a practitioner of the liberal rather than the practical arts. The academy in the modern sense really began in the seventeenth century when academies of arts and sciences surfaced throughout Europe. The French government established the Ecole des Beaux-Arts in 1648, and the Ecole dominated French art until the end of the nineteenth century. An artist's survival often depended on his acceptance at the biennial salons sponsored by the Ecole. Indeed it is difficult to find an eighteenth-century painter or sculptor still recognized today who was not an academician exhibited at the salons.

During the nineteenth century the salon occupied the absolute center of power in the art community. It functioned as the official arbiter of taste, passing judgment on the work of artists from around the world. Salons became vast affairs in which thousands of paintings covered every inch of wall space from ground level to the ceiling, paintings accepted by juries composed of presumably competent and occasionally distinguished representatives of the art community.[11]

Women were not permitted to study at the prestigious Ecole des Beaux-Arts until the end of the nineteenth century when a group of French women artists, organized as the Union of Women Painters and Sculptors, stormed the Ecole in 1896. The less prestigious Julian and Colarossi academies had opened their doors to female students a decade earlier.

From its inception the Academie Julian had expressed a more democratic attitude than the Ecole des Beaux-Arts. Its founder, Rudolph Julian, was a bookseller before 1868 when he opened a painting school in the Passage des Panamas. By 1877 it had become fashionable for young female artists to frequent the studios and ateliers of the Academie Julian. That same year a young Russian artist, Marie Bashkirtseff, first studied at Julian. She noted in her journal the courtship of Julian and his future wife, Amelie Baury-Sorel: "The spanish girl is at least 25 years old but gives herself 22. It could be thought that she is paid to wait upon everybody and to take care of the studio. She trembles when Robert-Fleury or Julian pay attention to any of the students."[12] In reality Madame Julian was not Spanish but simply eccentric, dressing in a wildly exotic manner with wide belts, enormous bows tied beneath her chin, and bold, vibrant colors. She took charge of the women's atelier at 51 Rue de Vivienne, founded in 1880, and later directed the school at Rue de Dragon which still bears the name Julian.

Teasdel and the other women students worked freely under the instruction of such salon-approved masters of the day as Robert-Fluery, Benjamin Constant, Jules Simon, and Bougereau. Although Madame Julian directed the female division, there were no women instructors.

Three study periods — morning, afternoon, and evening — divided the day. Classes were held from 8 A.M. to noon and from 1 P.M. to 5 P.M. Julian took care to allow students time to enjoy Parisian night life by creating the option of taking evening classes between 8 P.M. and 10 P.M., as elsewhere, or from 5 P.M. to 7 P.M. Serious students attended more than one class each day. Teasdel took four hours in the morning and three hours — from 7 P.M. to 10 P.M. — in the evening, not being one to frequent the Parisian cabarets.

Each week students positioned themselves around a live model, cast, or still life that they would draw for the next few days. Twice during the week, usually on Wednesday and Saturday mornings, the teacher would stage a critique, passing from student to student, commenting on each piece of work, giving a "short but telling criticism."[13] The student would patiently wait beside her work. John Hafen described the scene: "When the teacher comes to give his verdict, it is the custom for all to rise and listen with bated breath to the words that fall from this wonderful person. It is purely a one-sided affair for the student has nothing to say. All that he is or knows is drawn or painted on his canvas or paper. To be so presumptuous as to say 'The model moved' or 'The light was duller yesterday,' would bring the student in disgrace."[14] One student remarked, "It is truly wonderful how well these master minds understand the needs and failings of each student, and how readily they grasp the individual aim of each soul, thus encouraging individuality in each. Although the professors spend only two or three minutes on each student's work twice a week, they can readily discern the earnest, diligent workers and the aimless or idle ones. To the latter they are very severe in their criticism."[15]

One morning Benjamin Constant criticized the work of a young English girl in Mary's class. In a very general way he described to her the type of corrections she needed to make in her drawing. Perhaps overwhelmed by what he had said, she responded, "That is easy to say but hard to do." Constant, astounded that she would have dared to speak so impetuously, stormed out of the room and gave no more criticisms that day. He let it be known that no further criticism would be heard until the young Englishwoman left the class. Eventually the woman deferred to his superior status and begged his pardon to be allowed to stay.[16]

This type of drama helped to create the atmosphere instructors seemed to thrive on in the classroom. The American artist Cecilia Beaux described Robert-Fluery as if he were the key figure in a romantic novel. He was, according to Beaux, a "young middle-aged and very handsome man . . . his eyes, grey and deeply-set, smoldered with burnt-out fires. . . . The class, although accustomed to him, was in a flutter." Robert-Fluery drifted into class to criticize the women's work once a week, for which they were pathetically grateful. Once when Beaux was working on a full-length figure drawing, Robert-Fluery bent over her and began speaking in French, which she could not understand. (He was quoting Corneille.) "He rose not having given me any advice, but bent his cavernous eyes on me with a penetrating but very reserved smile and turned to the next."[17]

Classes were so crowded and instruction so brief and limited that the best students could expect at Julian was access to live models and plenty of time for practice. Painting in the studios was even more difficult than drawing and was often made impossible by the crowds of students that filled the ateliers.

At one time Teasdel studied under Jules Simon, considered by Alice Merrill Horne to be one of the greatest living artists. It was necessary to apply three months in advance for entrance into this very prestigious class which limited enrollment to the very best students. Among them were women who were associate members of the Champs de Mars, an important student organization.

Female students from the Academie Julian competed alongside their male counterparts for prizes from annual competitions staged by the Ecole des Beaux-Arts. There were also competitions within the Academie Julian itself and the best female students often were rewarded alongside the men. Prizes were handsome enough to tempt even the more wealthy students. Among those offered in an 1899 competition were a motorized three-wheeler with sidecar, first place; 100 frances, second place; 50 francs, third place; 25 frances, fourth place; and 15 bottles of champagne to be shared among six honorable mentions.[18]

In 1899 the American expatriate artist James MacNeil Whistler came to Paris after painting in England. He set up a studio in a quaint old house that he carefully decorated. After painting the walls in rich, warm colors, he chose draperies and furnishings described by Teasdel as both tasteful and refined. Whistler's studio was elegant, but even more important to Mary, disgusted by the filth of the Academie Julian, it was kept scrupulously clean. She would remember her days under Whistler as among her most pleasant in Europe.

Whistler, fully conscious of the awe he inspired among his students, dressed for effect. Immaculately assembled, smartly attired, and easily as elegant as his home, he lent a different formality to the routine of criticisms he gave to Mary's class while decked out in a dress suit with black kid gloves. She remembered being particularly careful that no spot of paint would splatter his suit or mar his perfection.

Whistler's studio could not have been more different from the ateliers of the French academies. Unlike other teachers he would often paint directly on a student's work to illustrate a point, insisting that his students paint with a pallet of colors exactly like his own so that his work would blend into theirs. Rather than having his students draw for months on end, he started them working with color immediately, learning from the first to model as in nature with hue rather than the more limiting (in his way of thinking) black and white. Whistler would remark that sculptors had an advantage because they were immediately given the medium they were expected to use. Teasdel remembered him rubbing a finger over part of a drawing and saying, "Why do you put that all (extraneous detail) in when you can come closer to nature by leaving it out?"[19]

Teasdel often felt dizzied by the confusing diversity of personalities and cultures she confronted for the first time in the ateliers of Paris. In her classes women from around the world mixed and struggled with the same design or color problems. Women from every station in life filled those sunlit rooms, "from the lady who comes with an equipage and footman, to the poor girl whose hard savings have brought her to the studio for a limited time. Yet it is the most democratic place in the whole world. The nobility are those who can draw and paint. Money, caste, education, and clothes, count for naught."[20]

The studios were often dirty, plain, and barren, with little if any furniture beyond a stool or easel. The stools were as plain and bare as the rooms themselves and ranged in height from six inches to three feet. In the center of the room a platform for the model was raised about two feet off the floor. The students formed a half-circle around this platform in three or four rows; the inside row of easels and stools was shorter than the outside ones so everyone could see the model. The female studios looked the same as those for men but rented for twice the fee. The proprietors insisted that the extra fee was used to keep the women's studios cleaner, but Teasdel found them to be just as dirty.

Mary easily fit into the routine of work at the Academie Julian. Classes began early Monday morning and continued until Saturday evening. What might have been a monotonous parade of male and female models was for Mary, at last, the chance to master drawing the human form. Hafen described his life drawing class:

Each Monday morning from three to ten professional male and female models are loitering about the ateliers waiting for a job. A few minutes before eight o'clock they mount the platform and show the contour of their figure and ability for posing. A vote is called, and the winning candidate engaged for the week. The manner of pose is also decided by a vote. Generally, but not always, there is a change in sex every other week. The model poses forty-five minutes and rests fifteen; repeating this from eight to twelve am, and from one to five pm every day in the week. When the school is full, . . . generally the case during the winter months, there is a model posing in each room and students are at liberty to work in any of them; but when a location is . . . chosen and the owner's name chalked on the floor under the easel, he holds a right to that spot . . . the entire week.[21]

Despite the fact that life drawing classes were open to women, and in some places even included nude male models, during the first decade of the twentieth century it was more typical to find a partially clothed model, usually one so young that he would pose no threat to the morality of the female artist. One atelier specified that male models wear "ordinary bathing drawers and a cloth of light material 9 feet long by 3 feet wide, which shall be wound round the loins over the drawers, passed between the legs and tucked in over the waistband; and finally a thin leather strap shall be fastened round the loins in order to insure that the cloth keep its place."[22] At a time when accurate rendering of the human body was central to art, one can appreciate how crippling these restrictions were. The widening of opportunities for women nevertheless led to an admirable flowering of fine craftsmanship, and at the turn of the century several American women artists were hailed by leading critics of the period as equals of men.

For the most part the instructors that Teasdel studied under at the Academie Julian were academicians whose traditional approach to work deviated little from the centuries before. In contrast to the more experimental light and color-filled work of the impressionists, they taught an aesthetic based on smooth surfaced, carefully modeled, detailed renderings of historical, biblical, and classical subject matter. The results were often standardized, stereotypical, idealized, sentimental renderings that resisted and at all times stifled the expression of individual personalities or ideas.

Later in life Teasdel would remember this time when impressionism was officially rejected by the salon but increasingly popular among painters themselves:

It has been said that the critics never were the first to discover a genius, but in every case they have been understood and appreciated by their fellow-workers, a long time before being accepted by those who always measure the present by past traditions. The French landscape school of Eighteen Thirty is an example of that fact. What is now acknowledged to have been a great epoch, was, during the greater part of the life time of the painters, one long disheartening, sad struggle for recognition.

Because their manner was a new one, and their ideas different from past periods; they were denied their true and just rewards until the public became more familiar with their works, the strangeness wore away and their eyes were opened to the appreciation of beauty unlike any other period.[23]

At the same time, Mary was most certainly aware of the new democratic, realistic spirit that entered European painting with Jean Francois Millet and others who began painting directly from nature, using scenes from peasant and farm life that elevated humble laborers into subjects of nobility and quiet dignity. These artists of the Barbizon school who lived and painted in the French countryside, studying the effect of outdoor light, inspired in Teasdel a broader, looser technique. The tradition of open-air painting was possibly the most important lesson Teasdel learned in France and one that would become central to her artistic career as she painted beneath the skies of Normandy, at the base of the Wasatch Mountains, and on the rocky crags overlooking the sea at Carmel, California.

During her three years in France, Teasdel spent the months of the school year in Paris, pursuing a rigorous schedule of class and studio work but spent her summers sketching and painting in Normandy. Paintings done during these sun-filled summers show that she was utterly charmed by the picturesque farm buildings, flower gardens, and sweeping expanse of sky-filled landscapes.

Mary and three other female students rented rooms in an old stone farmhouse surrounded by a lovely traditional French flower garden. Each afternoon the women would walk a mile and a half, stop for a picnic, and then walk another mile and a half, reveling in the changes evening brought. The three-mile hike back in the quiet twilight provided ample material for a series of memory sketches that Teasdel would execute upon her return. She set a goal for her summer work of at least one twilight and one evening color sketch each day.

During her stay in Paris, Teasdel won her share of laurels. In 1901 she became the first Utah woman and third Utahn to exhibit at the French Salon when the jury accepted a group of her ivory miniatures. The next salon admitted a portrait entitled *Dutch Woman Knitting*, and that same summer Mary entered two other ivory miniatures in the International French Exposition—the only Utah artist to do so to that date.

Almost as soon as Teasdel arrived home from Paris she became somewhat of a celebrity. Gov. Heber M. Wells appointed her to the board of the Utah Institute of Fine Arts, and within the year she was elected president of that body. The Institute (present Utah Arts Council) was the brainchild of Alice Merrill Horne, who wrote the bill and lobbied for its creation in 1899. This legislation created the first state-supported arts organization in the U.S. and called for an annual art exhibition, a state art collection, and public lectures on art.[24]

In 1908 Teasdel entered her impressionist painting *A View up City Creek Canyon* in the annual exhibition sponsored by the Institute of Fine Arts and won the top prize of $300. Edwin Evans described the painting as "one of the good things that have been done in Utah." J. T. Harwood also complimented the work of his former student, which won over his own submission, by saying, "The awards were just, and I think you show some great qualities in your work that none of the men have as yet exhibited." In the 1908 show Teasdel also won the award for best watercolor landscape as well as the best figure watercolor, which again received Evans's accolades.[25] Teasdel was easily as proficient a water colorist as an oil painter. Her watercolors have a spontaneous free spirit that recognizes the difference between the two mediums while allowing the peculiar beauties of each one to come forward. However spontaneous her work became, she was ever aware of plan, of composition, of design. "In great works of art every inch is the result of an intention by the master," she wrote. "Nothing happens by accident. Every line, every form, every color, every object is placed in a perfect balance and harmony with every other part. Nothing can be taken away or added without the picture suffering." It was the role of the artist, Mary Teasdel would say, to "seize the imagination and hold it captive." She continued, "imitation is not the principle aim in art, as many people think; selection, arrangement, and other qualities are even more important."[26]

Teasdel combined her career as a fine artist with that of a teacher. All Utah artists of this generation mixed their painting careers with teaching, photography, or some other venture to make a living to finance their art. Teasdel found it necessary to support herself after her return to Utah and did so happily as a teacher. Her students included Mabel Frazer and Florence Ware, both of whom would become not only well-known artists in their own right but teachers on the university level. Teasdel encouraged her students to become familiar with the work of the masters. "There must be some standard to which one can appeal, and this can best be found in those which are everywhere acknowledged to be greats."[27]

While one must judge Teasdel's work on the basis of contemporary standards, it is also important to place it in a historical context. Her work received the enthusiastic praise of her fellow artists. Alice Merrill Horne placed Teasdel alongside Harwood, Hafen, Fairbanks, and Evans as the best to come out of the local art scene. At the 1908 Utah exhibition a visiting artist, identified only as Mr. Potter, spoke highly of her work. Another critic described her lifetime work as "brilliant," and perhaps within the context of her culture it was. Horne saluted her success: "Often even men are not given credit for excellence in the field of art. Women painters are apt to be considered as only 'females.' It has been a great shock to this simple class of the dear public to see a woman given so many honors as Miss Teasdel has won both at home and in art centers abroad."[28]

Teasdel was a versatile artist, producing works in oil, watercolor, and pastel. Her works show her to be as accomplished with portraits and figure studies as with flowers and landscapes. But the bulk of her oeuvre was in landscape and reveals a great love of and intuitive emotional reaction to natural design. "It is not the province of the landscape painter, merely to represent trees, hills and houses—so much topography—but to express an emotion and this he must do by art," she wrote.[29]

Primarily a "fine artist," Teasdel also periodically played a role in the design process of large architectural projects, assisting in the planning, building, and decorating of several local homes. She believed that every object in the home should be carefully chosen because of its aesthetic possibilities since "true art always considers the uses of an object first, and constructs it so that it shall fill its part perfectly. Any decoration or ornamentation will be to beautify the fundamental form, but never to destroy it, or make it less useful." Furthermore, she stated, "There is always a certain simplicity in fine things, and perfection of the whole is greater and more difficult to obtain than elaboration of parts."[30]

She treasured the private, intimate dimensions of art, insisting that "true art is the personal expression of an idea in an artistic way. To be able to do this one must understand the language of art, its intentions and limitations." She continued, emphasizing what she saw as the three central tenets of all true art: "Art is infinite in its various expressions and should enter every part of our lives because art means harmony, beauty, and the eternal fitness of things."[31]

At one time or another Mary Teasdel won all the main prizes offered by the Utah Institute of Fine Arts. She spent the last two decades of her life painting and traveling between her homes in Utah and on the West Coast. As was true throughout her life, the paintings from this period formed a visual record of her travels, of the places she found so rich with beauty and intrigue. Her paintings of the California shoreline illustrate how far she had moved from her tight academic training in Paris to a more impressionistic, spontaneous, and spirited use of both color and textured brushstroke. She seemed to have finally come into her own.

Alice Merrill Horne spoke to the issue of style, describing it as the "golden fleece" with which the ambitious artist would wrap the canvas. And yet, she continued, an artist's individual, unique center will come through, for "not even a genius can construct a style for his use—rather he cannot get away from what he is—individuality is persistent."[32]

The central problem for all artists is that of finding one's own authenticity, of speaking in a language or imagery that is essentially his or her own. If one's self-image is dictated by one's station in life—by one's connections to others—it is impossible to find that individual voice. It is nothing short of remarkable that a woman like Mary Teasdel whose career and good fortune as a young woman often depended on her relationships with others was able to do this. The obituary honoring Teasdel upon her death attributed her success to study, travel, natural gifts, and indefatigable work.[33]

Her paintings honor her best. They speak to the issue of process, of a maturing of style and technique, of the many places she lived in and painted. The student studies painted in France, particularly in Normandy, are tight, determinedly academic, traditional in both outlook and style. Brightly colored and textured, they are obviously the work of an amateur or at least of a student learning her art.

Her later work, particularly her paintings of the northern California coastline, are much more self-confident and expressive of a free and unreigned spirit. Interestingly enough, they speak to the influence of the impressionists. While in France, her work was devoid of impressionistic detailing and more in line with the traditional training she received at the Academie Julian. Thirty years later she, like artists across the world, found herself drawn to the attention paid to light and color by the impressionists. Much of her Utah work, like the wonderful painting *Mother and Child* in the state art collection, is as much about color or light as it is about the more obvious subject of the two figures. It is reminiscent of the work of Mary Cassatt in its soft pastel palette and tender, quiet ambiance.

Utah has a few Teasdel works in its state art collection: *Mother and Child, Dutch Woman Knitting*, and a watercolor, *Monday Washday*, attributed to her. Outside of the few paintings from her California period that are housed at the Springville Art Museum the most extraordinary collection of Mary Teasdel's work is in a most unlikely place—the public library in Smithfield, Utah. In 1929 the Smithfield Town Council purchased 32 of her paintings for the paltry sum of $120. Only about eighteen to twenty of these paintings are on display at any one time. Although a few are large in scale, these paintings are for the most part small—usually between eighteen and twenty-four inches wide. Many are student studies done during her summers in Normandy. They remind us of her energy, her vision, and the great adventure her stay in France must have been.

Mary Teasdel was most certainly converted to her art. She sacrificed enormously to spend time in the galleries and classrooms of Paris. Though she was one of hundreds of American women who traveled to Europe at the turn of the century to study art, she was certainly not typical. But she did believe in the importance of her work and labored incessantly to make her dream become a reality.

Maud May Babcock. Photo courtesy of the Utah State Historical Society.

MAUD MAY BABCOCK
Speak Clearly and Carry a Big Umbrella

David G. Pace

David G. Pace holds a master's degree in communication and is a native of Utah, where he was a theater critic for ten years, first for The Private Eye *and later for* The Event Newspaper (Salt Lake City). *He is co-editor, with his wife Cheryl, of the American Theater Critics Association's* Critic's Quarterly. *The Paces are currently living in New York, where David works as a freelance critic and writer. He says he was led to write this essay on Maud May Babcock by the pastel-toned photos of "earnest, toga-ed women posed to dramatic and exaggerated effect in the first show put on at the University of Utah." He learned that the woman behind that little piece of history was Maud May Babcock, a tireless elocutionist who combined 'physical culture' with literature and dramatics with high moral purpose. That she influenced four generations of speech and drama teachers was the most likely reason for her notoriety, but David feels: "Those provocative 'poses plastique,' the photo reproductions which now hang in the lobby of the theater that bears her name are her greatest gift. The outing was one of the first times that the Utah community was able to see its own reflection in a performance text valued by the broader American culture—even if all the actors were in togas."*

When Brigham Young's daughter, the impetuous suffragette Susa Young Gates, enrolled in a physical culture class at Harvard summer school in 1891, she was captivated by Maud May Babcock, a vivacious 24-year-old elocution/physical culture instructor who must have reminded Gates of herself. Gates convinced Maud May to come to Utah. These "two soul mates of high purpose," recalls Mary Johnson Webster, an early student at the University of Utah, were not only early lobbyists for the woman's vote, but "wanted to improve their [women's] health . . . improve their looks."[1]

Improvement—physical, mental, and spiritual—was the calling card in not-so-remote-anymore Utah, still reeling from the renunciation of institutional plural marriage and sensitive to the critical eye of America. Buoyed by the "intense plea" of Gates, Maud May answered that call by coming to Utah as instructor of elocution at the University of Utah on an annual salary of $500.

She became the first female chair person among the faculty at the University of Utah, the founder of one college and two departments, producer and director of over 300 stage productions, a grand and tireless visionary and facilitator of the regional theater movement, and the first woman chaplain of a state senate. When she retired 46 years later, an honorary doctorate in hand, she had profoundly influenced four generations of speech and drama teachers, professional actors, and civic and religious leaders.

Maud May is a fascinating study of the early cultural and ideological precedents of a nascent, turn-of-the-century American community. Like her adopted Utah, she had to maneuver for respectability because she was a woman who, in typical fashion at the time, was only allowed into areas and interests legitimated by the academy or by social custom.

Who would have guessed that the fledgling, slightly lurid "fad" of physical culture which Maud May and others rigorously pursued would evolve from introducing women to bloomer pants into a spectrum of contemporary industries from weight loss programs and beauty pageants to sports medicine and professional bodybuilding? Even the Utah Jazz could, in a stretch, claim Maud May as their pioneer mother, for it was she who first organized basketball games in Utah shortly after acquiring the new court game's rules and plans during a visit home to the East.

Maud May Babcock was born in East Worchester, New York, on May 2, 1867, the oldest of two children of William Wayne and Sara Jean Babcock. She graduated from the National School of Oratory of Philadelphia and the Lyceum School of Acting, now the American Academy of Dramatic Arts in New York City, where she met and worked under the renowned Shakespearean scholar Alfred Ayres, who would become her greatest mentor. She also studied at Chicago University and for two years in London and Paris. She received a B.A. from Wells College in New York, and, in addition to her stint at Harvard summer school, taught at the Engleside School for Girls in the Berkshires in Massachusetts, Rutgers College, and the public schools of New York.

Before moving to Utah in 1892, Maud May, who was raised Episcopalian, had been piqued and even troubled by religious questions, particularly the issue of apostolic succession in the Catholic and protestant churches.[2] When she accepted the position of instructor at the University of Utah, her parents were more than a little worried. Their worst fears were realized when their headstrong daughter told them that she had joined the Mormon Church four months after her arrival in Utah. Mrs. Babcock referred to Mormonism as "that Hell Born sect." "I pray daily to God," her mother wrote to Maud May, "[that] if you open your lips to defend that cause in publick [*sic*] your tongue may be paralyzed." She signed the letter with a reproving, "Your Mama."[3]

Though she must have been wounded by her parents' stern disapproval, Maud May seems to have harnessed her heartache into a vigorous, at times militant, determination to make a name for herself and for the cause of physical culture and elocution in her new home. Not until Maud May came to the University of Utah did elocution, which included oral interpretation, public speaking, and pedagogy, become an entity unto itself. Her style of reading was initially influenced by the French theorist Francois Delsartè, famous for his dubious attempts to place elocution on a somewhat scientific basis through systems and notations of gesture which were used in what was then called platform readings.

Most likely, when the administration hired Maud May, it was not aware of what kind of force the woman would eventually become. Though she was not considered beautiful, she was striking and had a forcefulness, a rectitude, even a defensiveness that would calcify during the next 47 years into one of the most eccentric characters on campus. She was one whose rigid walk with her five foot, three inch height and protracted, elevated diction students would often mock, even though most would later gush about the profoundly positive influence she had had on their lives.[4]

The rest of the university community had at least a grudging respect for her. Bob Wilson, a student of Maud May's, reported that once while smoking on the corner of 200 South and Main Street he was unexpectedly beaned on the head with Maud May's umbrella. "Get that filthy weed out of your mouth!" she screamed at him. She often complained about students' lack of "gumption."[5]

In her efforts to legitimate a discipline that many were beginning to find artificial and outdated, she lobbied for moving the popular debate team from the English department to her own. In 1914, she got a little help from fate and her own shrewd politicking.

During commencement in that year, Milton H. Sevy, a graduating senior, "blasted" the university's president and its board of regents for being influenced too much by LDS Church leaders.[6] President Kingsbury disciplined the debate coach, C. W. Snow, who had worked with Sevy on the speech. That incident led to the protest and resignation of seventeen faculty members and ultimately to Kingsbury's own resignation. Before he resigned, however, Kingsbury moved the debate team to the department of elocution and changed its name to department of public speaking. His intention was to keep future speakers from being influenced by the English department, which he viewed as hostile to his administration, a bedfellow of the LDS Church. Kingsbury, who was good friends with the devoutly loyal Maud May, knew the she would help prevent a recurrence of the Sevy incident.[7]

Dramatics was even lower on the totem pole of respectable academic practice and discourse than elocution. Nevertheless, it was natural that Maud May would see the theater as an extension of her readings and a more comfortable home for her style than the forced praxis and often contradictory theories of the elocutionists. By 1893, her 300 pupils from the University of Utah, Brigham Young Academy, and private classes moved to the Salt Lake Theatre for an exhibition of "fancy steps, attitudinizing, muscular poses, drills, dances, steps, Swedish movements, Indian club and dumbbell performances," according to a *Salt Lake Tribune* report.[8]

Later, on June 6, 1895, at the Salt Lake Theatre, one hundred of Maud May's female students performed what was to become the first play produced by a university in the United States. *Eleusinia* was a modification of the earlier program but included "living pictures" of toga-ed figures in statuesque groups inspired by the Greek legends of Demeter and Persephone. The evening was a smashing success, leading an "enchanted" university president, James Talmadge, to remark to Maud May, "You are developing the taste of the public."[9]

Although Utah had a tradition of theatrical productions from its earliest settlement, developing the public's taste in a town only a few years removed from the frontier was no easy task, but Maud May seemed to latch on to the notion as she half finagled, half muscled her way into becoming the most influential catalyst to locally produced theater in the region. On December 14, 1897, three years before the university moved from its 200 West location (where West High now stands) to its current home on the hill, Maud May organized the University Dramatics Club, the most consistent and arguably the most prolific of its kind in the nation.[10]

The first show put on by the University Dramatics Club was a double bill of a one-act, *The Happy Pair,* and a "side-splitting" farce, *A Box of Monkeys.*[11] That theater was considered of somewhat questionable merit on a university campus is reflected by the fact that many of the club's shows were bombarded with vegetables from the rowdy sophomore class, which used to attend en masse. During a performance of Pinero's *The Amazons*, student actor Harold Goff, playing the role of Andre, took a thrown cabbage in the mid-section. "Afterward," reports Keith Engar in his master's thesis on the history of theater at the University of Utah, Maud May "sent word that the throwing should stop at once. Except for one little piece of celery, the vegetable deluge was stilled."[12]

Even so the "hoodlumism of the cabbage-throwers" led to a controversy played out in the student paper, *The Chronicle*, which included a "clarification" by Maud May on the true character of the exchanges at the theater, which resulted in the suspension of students.[13] Goff was eventually vindicated when the *Chronicle* editor was forced to resign over the incident and Goff was elected to replace him. The Dramatics Club staged a play nearly every year thereafter, including the regional premiere of G. B. Shaw's *Arms and the Man*, the western U.S. premiere of Shaw's *You Never Can Tell*, and, in 1912, Shakespeare's *As You Like It*, the most ambitious project to that time. The first "heavy" drama to be presented by the club was Ibsen's *Pillars of Society*. By 1913 the club was an amalgamation of students, alumni, and professors, essentially the first community theater in the state.

Desperate for rehearsal and performance space, the club eventually moved from the 1,500-seat Salt Lake Theatre to the Colonial and Garrick Theatres for its runs. Though there was talk of a new civic auditorium to be built, it never materialized, nor did Maud May's pipe dream of a 2,500-seat outdoor amphitheater with a 75-foot wide stage, a fledgling venture from which she herself emerged, as with other nixed projects, "considerably poorer."[14]

Maud May's disappointments, however, seem to have simply resurfaced as leverage for new ambitions. None of her "projects," though, were more important than her vaguely Greek notion of educating the whole individual. Good health, good sense, and good manners—the civic being—were all fused together in Maud May's mind, and her students reaped—some said, suffered—from her zeal to that end. She was not beyond paying tuition for a student who could not afford it, and she often would invite groups of students to her cabin in Brighton, southeast of Salt Lake City, where she would outdo them in climbing nearby peaks.

From his interviews with her former students, Ronald Frederickson commented that the vegetarian and largely Spartan Maud May seemed to have "literally willed her guests to conform to the same dietetic standards" as herself.[15] During visits to her cabin, students recall being served Maud May's (in)famous "mush" loaded with fruit and nuts and her warm lemon water taken every morning before breakfast. Though she was demanding and opinionated, the professor who never married was also a gracious hostess.[16]

In the classroom and at rehearsals she was ruthless; her verbal criticism to her students was withering, punctuated as it was by a pointed finger. And yet dozens of her students credited Maud May with their accomplishments. Utah governor Herbert Maw, who first met "Miss B," as her students called her, in 1912 was one of them. He credited her with encouraging him to find confidence in public. When Maud May learned of Maw's acute shyness, she immediately cast the freshman in the role of Theseus the King in *A Midsummer Night's Dream*. During his monotoned delivery she would shout, "STRESS!" "I didn't even know what she was talking about," confessed Maw years later, but by the end of what he described as "6 to 8 weeks of torture [rehearsal]," he was walking around campus like an Athenian king, or at least as Maud May imagined an Athenian king should walk.[17]

Not everyone appreciated Maud May's bullish style. One student who worked with her in the 1930s recalls that the queen of oral interpretation directed plays by reading every single line for the actor, who then had to repeat it exactly as she had intoned.[18] Harold Goff, who had suffered from the cabbage throwers as a student, had joined the elocution department in 1910 as an instructor. But he lasted only four years before citing Maud May's "excess of enthusiasm" among the reasons for his departure. And when she had heard of a faculty member's derision of the growing prominence of the department of speech, she went after him in the library "like Cicero going after Catiline," sending him to "figurative exile." Her victim later admitted that Maud May had won the argument, "since she was an elocutionist and I was only a professor of philosophy."[19]

In 1927 the department of public speaking became the department of speech (currently communication), of which Maud May was chair. There she reigned as with a holy purpose, encouraging the creation of the discipline's own discourse community, its national associations, its "scientific" validity, and its political fortitude—all to win a legitimate place in the academy. Although contested, the heritage of speech communication—from the oral tradition of the Greeks to the quantitative reductionism of speech champion C. H. Woolbert—was important if it was to have a future. Maud May was one of a very small group of leaders instrumental in ensuring that future, eventually becoming president of the National Association of the Teachers of Speech.[20]

More of a cheerleader and a disciplinarian than a theorist or intellectual, Maud May's strength was in finding the practicality of learning and refinement—the social and political uses of the Greek maxim "know thyself." When she first arrived at the University of Utah, she equivocated badly on the contradictions of Delsarte's mechanical gestures and the theory of Alfred Ayres, both of whom she vigorously championed.[21] "I don't think you could expect Miss Babcock to reconcile the two," stated H. L. Marshall, a student. "She wouldn't make any effort herself to reconcile them. She wouldn't necessarily be concerned that there was any incongruity there. Logic wasn't one of her strong points."[22]

And yet, like a true experimenter in her field, she would eventually let go of bad ideas, later admitting, "all the fool things I used to do!" when she recalled her early, Delsarte-inspired movements.[23] She was nevertheless firm in her opinions elsewhere, particularly in the fray when the differences between "impersonation" and "interpretation" were debated in the *Quarterly Journal of Speech*.[24]

Despite her work as the founder of the college of physical education (including dance) and the department of speech, Maud May's greatest notoriety is perhaps for her work in the theater which, like speech and physical education, needed an academic gloss before it could become a part of the constellation of higher learning. Pursuant to that, she linked the new regional, non-profit theater movement, known in her day as the "Little Theatre Movement," to the ideals of the early Mormon pioneer stock companies, beginning as early as Nauvoo.

Complaining bitterly about the "trash of [current] stock companies flooding the country," she spoke to the young women of the LDS Church about how the insurgent theater movement was more democratic, more in the realm of art, not just business.[25] After a short-lived experiment in 1915 called the Utah Theatre, she formed, independent of the Dramatics Club, the Varsity Players, which, between 1918 and 1922, was the first university subsidized, professional theater in the nation, a forerunner of the current Pioneer Theatre Company. James M. Barrie's *The Professor's Love Story* was the first production and starred Maurice Browne, father of the Little Theatre Movement himself. He appeared in more than one production at the old 300-seat Social Hall, where the high-output repertory group performed. So did Moroni Olsen, a local star who went on to national acclaim and whose own company got its start there.[26]

In 1930, eight years after the Varsity Players had disbanded, Maud May got her own university theater, fittingly named after the university president who had rewarded her with the debate team. The theater was named Kingsbury Hall, and the first mounting was Maurice Maeterlink's *The Bluebird*. With such an edifice as this, on the campus of the

University of Utah, Maud May must have felt a certain satisfaction. During the depression, season tickets at Kingsbury were sold at $2.10 for a five-show package. And the full-production facility turned out myriad shows, sometimes fronted with Broadway stars including the famous Otis Skinner and the first on-stage Peter Pan and Utah native Maude Adams.[27]

Still devoted to her beloved oral interpretation, Maud May continued for some time doing readings all about the region and wrote or compiled more than one book on the subject.[28] She also was busy acting as chaplain for the Utah State Senate, where many of her former students sat as legislators. She was probably the first woman in the country to be accorded the honor, and she wrote her short prayers carefully and undoubtedly delivered them with the same vigor that characterized virtually everything else she had done in her life.

In 1936, two years before "Miss B" retired, her former students gathered for an anniversary production of *Mrs. Bumpstead Leigh*, which was originally directed by Maud May in 1913. The identical cast was assembled, with only one exception; and it included Lila Eccles and Herbert Maw, by then the governor of Utah. The gathering was a tribute to Maud May of the devotion of her students, for as she had became an institution at the University of Utah and beyond, her unique zeal was matched by those of her disciples. They honored her not only with this production, but later by forming a Reading Society and christening the student stage at Pioneer Memorial Theatre in her name.[29]

Maud May was 71 years old when she retired in 1938. She claimed to have had the longest active service of any faculty member at the university, forty-six years. Her duplex on 11th East then became her new and only classroom, filled with an "amazing" doll collection, cloisonne, oriental rugs, carved chests and tables, crystal etched with gold, and a lace table cloth from China, which she had visited, among other places, more than once. It was there in her tiny apartment that she had hosted her father—who, like his wife, had been so hurt by their daughter's move west and her conversion to Mormonism—and also her brother Wayne, a distinguished Philadelphia surgeon, whom she tried to comfort at the untimely death of his son. Her devoted chow dog, Wu, and a crazy old parrot were her regular pupils after her retirement, but many of her past students visited to see how their eccentric friend was making out in the twilight of her life.

Four generations of college students and many others through her church service in the LDS Mutual Improvement Association had been brow-beaten and blessed by Maud May, a woman who was always sure she was right and pretty much convinced everyone else that she was. This moral highground was perhaps partly fueled by her own private fears of failure and also by the Mormon sense of industry and progressive community that she had been attracted to as a young woman. As it was, she was a perfect catalyst for the relatively quick establishment of time-honored institutions, attitudes, and "tastes" in Utah that would have otherwise been long in coming.

Whatever broad, societal agenda she may have had, however, her students were always the focus of her work. Though it took her twelve years to earn tenure, she was a model to many, including important directors, broadcasting VIPs and actors on both sides of the Atlantic. "My greatest accomplishment is the devotion of my students," she is reported to have said late in life.[30]

Everyone, perhaps, should have a Maud May Babcock for a teacher, the kind that can throw the fear of God in you by a mere glance, but whose interest in your well-being and development—however unpleasant at times—is unrelenting and full of expectation. Joseph F. Smith, a student and eventual successor to Maud May as chair of the speech department, wrote in a tribute to her shortly after her death in 1954, at age eighty-seven, that Maud May was "dedicated to the proposition that the only true and unfailing practicality is unswerving rectitude."[31]

Georgia Lathouris Mageras, Magerou. Photo courtesy of the Utah
State Historical Society.

12

GEORGIA LATHOURIS MAGERAS
Magerou, the Greek Midwife

Helen Z. Papanikolas

*A native Utahn, Helen Papanikolas graduated from the University of Utah,
where she had edited* Pen, *the literary magazine. Her publication of "Greeks
in Carbon County" in the* Utah Historical Quarterly *in 1954 broadened the
scope of Utah history and opened areas of study that many others have followed.
She founded the Peoples of Utah Institute and edited and contributed several
chapters to* Peoples of Utah *(1976). In addition to her extensive historical
studies, writing, and publishing, she has served on the boards and committees of
various civic organizations, including the Utah State Historical Society and the
Utah Humanities Council. Her work has been recognized with the Brotherhood
Award from the Utah Chapter of the National Conference of Christians and
Jews, a distinguished Alumnus Award from the University of Utah, an honorary Doctorate of Humane Letters from the University of Utah, an honorary
Doctorate of Letters from Southern Utah University, and an Honorary Associate
in Arts from the College of Eastern Utah. As Miriam Murphy points out in a
later chapter of this book, she is one of Utah's premier historians and a leading
authority in the United States on Greek immigrants. She revised this account of
the life of Magerou originally published in the* Utah Historical Quarterly *38
(spring 1970) and includes it here, recognizing "the importance of the midwife
to the whole community."*

In 1867, a baby girl born in a Peloponnesian village of Greece was fated, in the idiom of the Greeks, to leave her country, to come to a land called Utah, and to become a legend among its southern European immigrants. Often from the time she was a child, the girl, Georgia Lathouris, was sent up to the mountains beyond her village to take a bundle of bread and cheese for her father and brothers pasturing goats there. As she climbed a mountain slope one day in her fourteenth year, she heard a voice calling. In the entrance to one of the many caves on the mountain, a woman stood, calling and beckoning to her. Georgia was frightened and began to run; it was a Nereid, she was sure, one of the beautiful creatures of glens and woods whom it was dangerous to follow. The voice called insistently, "Don't leave me! Come, come!"

Cautiously the girl approached. The woman was not a Nereid but a woman from the village and in great distress. She had been gathering wheat when labor pains had started. The girl followed her into the dark cave and with the woman's guidance, delivered the baby. From then on she was affectionately called "*Mamí,*" the Midwife. In the following years she attended other women in her village of Ahladókambos (Pear Valley), a scattering of white stone houses and a few trees set in an arid landscape much like that of Utah, where she would live for a half-century. To midwifing she added folk cures. The village was poor, and she was paid in wheat and flour.

The *Mamí's* family could not provide her with a dowry, the means destitute countries used to distribute their little wealth. Centuries of foreign rule, the revolution of 1821 to free themselves from Turkish despotism, and the resulting chaos when the energies of the country were unrealistically channeled into futile attempts to regain their lands lost to the Turks and other European powers had drained their resources. The little *Mamí*, small, yet of great energy, seemed to be destined to remain unmarried and at the summons of the sick and of women who were fortunate to be wives and mothers.

But the young midwife's fate, which in Greek folklore is decided by the Three Fates during the child's first three days of life, was favorable. For the first time since Greece had been conquered by the Turks in 1453, a premier, Charilaos Trikoupes, came to power intent on reconstruction of the country.[1] Greece lacked people with technical skills, and foreigners came into the country to head construction crews. One of these foremen was a tall, young Austrian, Nikos Mageras. He was sent to the *Mami's* village to build a bridge over a nearby river.

Nikos had been a wanderer since the age of fourteen. His mother had died, and his father had married again. Rather than accept his stepmother, the boy left his town of Gospic, Austria, and traveled through Russia, Asia Minor, and the Balkans. On his journeys he had learned several languages and the principles of mechanical construction.

Young people of the village who were not pasturing the family goats and sheep in the mountains found work on Nikos Mageras's labor crew. The *Mami* was among them. The foundations of the bridge were built of stone, and the young people brought the plentiful rocks of the land to the construction site.

Soon after work was begun, the foreman went with the *Mami* to her parents' house. He asked to marry her and waived his rights to the traditional dowry. After their marriage, Nikos continued building wherever there was work in the Peloponnese. Four children were born during a time of great national instability.

By the end of the century, Greece's financial and political problems brought the country to national bankruptcy in 1893, humiliating defeat by the Turks in 1897, and impositions of foreign financial control in 1898.[2] All over the Peloponnese, bankrupt peasants were uprooting their currant bushes. Currants, the principal export of Greece, had fallen in price seventy percent in the year 1893.[3] The precarious position of the peasants in Greece was now perilous. The building of roads and bridges begun under the Trikoupes regime was halted.

The exodus of young men to escape the hunger and desolation of their mother country had always been constant, but now thousands were leaving to find work to help their families provide dowries and to pay off usurious mortgages. While Greece and other Balkan and Mediterranean countries were struggling desperately, America was just beginning to develop her immense and varied resources. Early emigrants from Southern Europe returned to their native lands as labor agents and emptied their villages and seaports of idle men and boys for work gangs in the New World.[4]

In 1902 Nikos signed a contract with one of these labor agents.

He left his family and, taking forty Greeks from all parts of the country, went to Fresno, California, to lay track for the Santa Fe Railroad. His goal was to save enough money to bring his wife and children to America.

Three years later he met an Austrian he had known in Gospic who told him that Nikos's brother and several cousins were working at the Utah Copper Mine in Bingham and at the Magna mill. Nikos, now called Nick, took time off to visit Utah to see his relatives and decided that the Midvale-Bingham-Magna area was a profitable place for a business. In that year of 1905 there were two thousand Greek men in Salt Lake County,[5] and each day more came. There had been only three Greeks in Utah in 1900.[6] The 1903 coal mine strike in Carbon County began the influx of large numbers of Greeks into Utah. These newest of European immigrants were unaware that an employer could be challenged as to wages, long hours, and working conditions. The *Wyoming Labor Journal* reported: "American and English speaking miners were driven from these camps. . . . The corporations considered Greeks better adapted to their needs than others and encouraged the employ of these by the hundreds."[7]

Greek labor agents advertising in Greek newspapers published in America and in Greece had an inexhaustible supply of countrymen for the West. Boardinghouses were needed in every company town. Nick opened a boardinghouse in Snaketown, west of Magna, the present tailings pond of the Garfield smelter. Greeks and other nationalities lived there in makeshift houses and tents. Nick offered food, lodging, and a convenient saloon.

The boardinghouse was a success with laborers, but not with a well-known Greek labor agent and his underlings. The labor agent had become powerful; at will he could decide who would be hired by the mine, mill, and smelter; how much tribute he would take from the men's wages; and where the laborers would trade. The boardinghouse was burned down.

Nick rented a second boardinghouse below today's Magna firehouse. This one was also destroyed by fire. The vendetta continued. The third boardinghouse, situated across the street from the present powerhouse, was set on fire at eleven o'clock on a payday night while Nick was in Salt Lake City attending to his duties as a representative for the Salt Lake Brewery. Thirty-five hundred dollars in gold and silver hidden in a trunk was melted into a mass. The money was Nick's savings for his family's future in America.[8]

At the time of the fire, the family was on their way to Utah. It was 1909, seven years after Nick had left them. Adhering to propriety, he had sent a friend to bring his family to America.

The family settled in Snaketown among three other Greek families. Two of these had German immigrant mothers who had learned to speak Greek. In the entire state there were fewer than ten Greek women, but Greek men and boys were streaming in to work on the railroad gangs, in the coal mines, the Midvale smelter, the Garfield smelter, the Magna mill, and the copper mines of Bingham.

Few of the men were married. Their families had sacrificed necessities to send them to America to fulfill the responsibility of providing dowries for their sisters. When this was accomplished and their parents helped, they could then send for picture brides.

Living in boardinghouses and shacks, the young men were extremely susceptible to disease. The influx of immigrants was overwhelming; their living conditions were not considered the concern of employers and townspeople. In tent colonies and shacks built by the workers from powder boxes and scrap lumber, water and sewage disposal were hazards.

In response to angry editorials in Greece, a Greek woman journalist visited Utah mining towns in 1914. It would take, she wrote, the pen of Edgar Allen Poe to describe the horrors of the Greek immigrant worker's life. R. C. Gemmel, general manager of the Utah Copper Company, replied to her complaints and demands that proper housing and hospitals be built for the Greeks and other immigrants: "They choose their own habitations. And if we built them new quarters, they would prefer to stay where they are."[9]

The journalist found that the workers were afraid of the company doctors. Although a dollar a month was deducted from their wages for medical care, they felt they were coldly treated, like animals, not human beings. Amputations were hastily performed. This was the men's great fear. Three to five hundred dollars were paid for the loss of an arm or a leg. Uneducated as the laborers were, an amputation was the end of self-reliance and the beginning of descent into penury.

The midwife, called since her marriage "Magerou," the genitive form of Mageras, was eager to help her sick countrymen. When she heard of someone's illness, she relayed advice through her husband or others who came to his saloon. She often answered a knock on her door and opened it to find a sick man or boy. Long before the Greek men brought wives to America, they knew and respected Magerou.

The small cluster of Greek families grew, and Magerou was the matriarch. She was often the matchmaker, too. As the men married, she was there, smiling, helping to lay out the wedding feast while the men clasped hands and danced to old-country songs of courage under Turkish bondage. She was there to attend at the birth of children and there to administer folk cures. She spoke as she felt and used Greek curses and proverbs liberally. "Too much *Kyrie Eleison* wearies even God." "Better to have a wise enemy than a foolish friend."

Not only Greek, but Italian, Austrian, and Slavic women called Magerou at all hours. They preferred her to the company doctors. As the immigrants in American labor life became an increasing influence, industry was forced to improve living conditions; a new generation of medical school graduates came to the company towns with an interest, some with sympathy, for the immigrants. Although the young husbands quickly accepted the authority of these doctors, they could not persuade their wives to be delivered by them.

Life in the new country had affected the women immediately. The traditional sign of modesty for married village women, the wife or black head scarf, was out of place in America, an invitation to gaping. Husbands forbade them. Women wore them only about their houses and yards. They wore hats to church and to town. Hats, the symbol of educated town and city women of Greece, were now theirs. The appearance of the immigrant mothers changed drastically, but not their ideas. Modesty impelled them to ask the midwife, not American men doctors, to attend them.

Magerou, then, ruled over the birth of children, the proper realm of midwives. She did not lose a mother or child in her long years of practice. If she detected an abnormal pregnancy, she insisted that a doctor be called and took the lesser role of assistant.

Cleanliness was a compulsion with her. Early each morning she performed a ritual of washing herself, combing her hair into a bun at the top of her head, and dressing in clean cottons to be ready for any call. She was continually mopping and airing her house: "Soap and water are too cheap in America to be dirty." The water pumps, at easy access even in camps like Snaketown and Ragtown, were a marvel to her. There was no longer the arduous work of bringing water from the village well, often only a thin stream.

Regularly pregnant herself, Magerou took care of her women patients with the efficiency of a contemporary obstetrician. While olive oil and baby blankets were kept warm in coal stove ovens, she boiled cloths, kept water hot, cut her fingernails, scrubbed her arms and hands well, and after observing American doctors using alcohol and rubber gloves, she added these to her accoutrements.

Women clamored for Magerou. Small though she was, her voice carried through the neighborhoods, exhorting, shouting, "Scream! Push! You've got a baby in there, not a pea in a pod!" Once the baby was born, Magerou gave her entire time to the newly delivered mother, the *lehóna*, and to the baby. She neither cooked nor took care of the rest of the family. From the backyard she chose the plumpest chicken, simmered broth, stood over the mother forcing her to wash and to dress in a clean housedress, combed her long hair, and twisted it into a knot. For the first time in her life, the woman knew what it was to be pampered. The autocratic young husbands were reduced to errand boys.

"Bring plenty of butter. The lehóna needs butter for strength! Send a ton of coal. The lehóna mustn't catch cold! Go to J. C. Penney and buy a robe. The lehóna must be warm!" A legion of immigrant mothers wore J. C. Penney robes made of blankets stamped with Indian designs.

When the mother and baby were taken to church, the mother to be "cleansed" of the Biblical forty days' uncleanliness, the baby to be blessed as Christ was, Magerou's duties were fulfilled.

The early twenties were the days of her greatest activity. Still new in America, the immigrants depended on folk cures. Some of these had a physiological basis; others were unexplainable, and the victims or their relatives' faith in them produced psychological healing. The Evil Eye was a common complaint. A child would suddenly fall into lassitude. Unexplained fevers brought on convulsions; or the child whined, cried, and was sleepless. Someone with the Evil Eye had looked on the child with envy. Magerou used several prescriptions: three pinches of *liváni* (powdered resin, an incense burned on Saturdays to purify houses for the Sabbath) in water, or three drops of holy water, or three symbolic spittings—all accompanied by the Lord's Prayer. Three, the holy number representing the Trinity, was of prime importance.

Hot red wine and powdered cloves, tea and whiskey, mustard plasters on the chest, back, and soles of the feet cured pneumonia and bronchial infections. Olive oil softened burned skin. For *soúfra* (rickets) Magerou burned a bay leaf with a blessed candle leaving only the stem. On three different moonless nights, she touched each joint with the stem.

Bleeding was a favorite remedy of the midwife's and she used it for almost every ailment, especially infections. In America there was no need to search in ponds for leeches; drugstores sold them. For respiratory infections, Magerou applied *vendoúzis*. She heated the inside of water glasses with a tuft of burning cotton and placed them on the patient's back. The heat and pressure inside the glass drew up the flesh. If the patient were very ill, Magerou cut crosses in the swelled flesh to drain off the "bad" blood. To cure jaundice she made a small cut with a razor blade in the thin string of flesh connecting the inside of the upper lip with the tissue above the teeth. For abdominal pain attributed to a spleen that had grown and "traveled," Magerou nicked the skin on the abdomen drawing black blood and forcing the spleen to "go backwards."

To stop bleeding Magerou used a small amount of soap or the scrapings of the inside of a leather belt on the wound, then applied pressure and a bandage. One of her most successful cures was called *pakia* for backache presumably from pressure on the kidneys. The patient lay face down. Magerou clutched the flesh at the small of the back and deftly lifted. A small crack was heard, and the backache was gone.

For colds and influenzas the midwife used *vizikánti*, a powdered Spanish fly that produced blisters on the skin. With a quick twist of her fingers, Magerou broke the blisters and the "uncleanness" in the body broke out.

The midwife was noted for setting bones. She mixed powdered resin and egg white with clean sheared wool and bound this over the set bones with cloth. Her son, Tony, was once thrown off a horse in front of the Magna post office. While six people held him, his mother set the broken arm and applied her cast. Magerou used no anesthetics except whiskey. Whatever whiskey was left over, she poured on her hair to make it strong and to take away headaches.

Two men owed their legs to her. A Greek baker in Garfield had mashed his knee; the surgeon decided to amputate. The baker left the doctor's office and went to Magerou. She used her remedies and "in a week the baker was walking about." A justice of the peace had crushed his leg at Mercur and sought the midwife's help rather than submit to an amputation. Again she was able to save a leg.

In the second and third decade of the century, Greek brides came in increasing numbers. Magerou's name was known by all. Babies were brought to her from distances after doctors had despaired of them. Sometimes she traveled to families; she spent four months with one Nevada family whose mother had died. During these years the Mageras family moved several times, to Murray, Tooele, and again to Magna. Wherever she went, patients followed.

The Magna Greek Town became established on the western side of the town. All of the houses had gardens, and the mothers delighted in the plentiful irrigation water that ran down the alleys of the back yards. Magerou spent her spare time tending her garden. The canning of fruit and vegetables, unknown in Greece and only just now being introduced there because of the prohibitive expense of bottles and caps, was another joy to her. Magerou prepared well for her large family. When making *hilopétes*, thin egg noodles cut in small squares, she began by breaking thirty dozen eggs.

As the immigrants lived longer in America, they began to call in the local doctors. Also Magerou found that what she had been doing was called "practicing medicine without a license." She began assisting doctors in deliveries, more often than being in charge herself. At times babies were born before the doctor arrived, and he had only to sign the birth certificate. Several doctors delivered the babies and left Magerou to cut the cord and to finish the process. Among the doctors she worked for were Drs. Russell Owens, George McBride, T. C. Weggeland, Stephen Netolicky, Dean A. Moffat, Phillips M. Chase, Burton Musser, and, much later, Owen Reese. They called her "Mamma" or "Grandma" and understood her ungrammatical, malapropian version English.

The large number of births among the immigrant people coincided with an increasing prejudice against these "unassimilable aliens" as newspapers called them. The anti-immigrant propaganda of the World War I years and the early twenties' campaigns against the South European immigrants by newspapers, the American Legion, and the Ku Klux Klan completely turned the isolate Greeks inward.

Hostility exploded into night raids through Magna's Greek Town, crosses burning on the foothills of the Oquirrh Mountains, and Klan marches from the hilltop graveyard down through Main Street. The immigrant mothers became afraid to call in American doctors. Whisperings became hysterical fears: the doctors could be Klan members themselves. Many women returned to Magerou. For those who remained faithful to their doctors, Magerou, instinctively protective of them, minimized the importance of the Klan, even after a group of young Greeks followed the marchers to the town park and tore off their robes. "Leading citizens" were exposed.

The Klan's influence waned as their excesses grew. Slowly relationships were restored. Children of Klan members and those of immigrants formed lasting friendships during the Depression years. For the majority of Greek mothers, however, the pattern set by their Greek Town enclave and the events of those years was never altered; their husbands, children, and Magerou were their only tenuous link with non-Greek life.

Magerou's life, in contrast, was not diminished by the prejudice she found in America. She had faith in time's solution to problems. The many pictures of her show a smiling, serene woman appearing much younger than she was. The Mideastern *ach* and hand-wringing against fate had barely brushed her nature. She was stoic over the deaths of her own infants and family tragedies. She endured without knowing that she did. The liturgical feast days of her church gave her life order and happiness.

The Mageras family celebrated each holiday twice. Magerou was Greek Orthodox, her husband Roman Catholic. The children born in Greece were baptized in the Greek Orthodox church. The children born in America were baptized in the Catholic church. The Greek Orthodox church in Salt Lake City was consecrated in 1905, but the eighteen miles of travel were a hardship. The household observed both the Julian Calendar of the Eastern Orthodox and the Gregorian Calendar of the Roman Catholics.

The traditional lamb of the Greeks was followed by the roasted pig of Austrian Christmases and Easters. A few weeks before New Year's, the family planted wheat in a coffee can. According to Austrian folklore, if the wheat was up by New Year's Day, a good year would follow. Candles were lighted around the can of green shoots and placed on the dinner table.

On Greek Easters, Nick Mageras butchered lambs at his daughter's farm for many Greek families. The lambs were put on spits and barbecued in a long row. The feast of *Agape* (Christian Love) was celebrated at the Klekas farm for several decades.

Soon the generation Magerou brought to life was beginning to marry. Another world war began. Many of her grandsons were soldiers and sailors. In 1946 her husband died at the age of eighty-three. Magerou continued going wherever she was called. She was actively working until her late seventies.

She died in 1950 at the age of eighty-three. Her progeny includes seven children[10] and enough grandchildren, great-grandchildren and great-great-grandchildren to form, it has been said, a village. At all gatherings of the remnants of the first two Greek generations in America, anecdotes about Magerou are told. She was the most important member of Utah's Greek immigrant community and a symbol of the color and uniqueness of Greek immigrant life.

Alice Merrill Horne. Photo courtesy of the Utah State Historical Society.

ALICE MERRILL HORNE
Art Promoter and Early Utah Legislator

Harriet Horne Arrington

Harriet Arrington, a University of Utah graduate in education, has taught school in Utah and Georgia. An adjunct to her education has been attending art exhibits with her family, especially her grandmother, Alice Merrill Horne. Alice exhibited Utah artists' works in business and art facilities, Intermountain centers, and schools. As her oldest granddaughter, Harriet developed an intimacy with her grandmother from her earliest youth when they talked of art, Utah history, and family lore, and she met many of the artists Alice promoted. That bond of insight and affection was strengthened in 1948 when Alice, age eighty, composed her memoirs. Each week she boarded the bus from downtown Salt Lake City to deliver that week's hand-written chapter to Harriet to type. The activity became a catalyst for Harriet's writing the biographies of Alice and other notable women. Harriet admits, "I have discovered a fascination with exploring and composing the essence of people's lives through writing biography." Devoted to Utah art, Harriet helped coordinate several exhibits for Utah women artists at the Museum of Fine Arts at the University of Utah and chaired that exhibit when it was held at the Springville Museum of Art in 1987. Harriet is included in Who's Who of American Women *and* Who's Who in the American West. *In this essay, a revised version of an article which appeared in the* Utah Historical Quarterly *58 (summer 1990), Harriet shares a glimpse of her grandmother—"a glimpse," as she says, "I don't think others had."*

Alice Smith Merrill Horne, the second woman elected to the Utah House of Representatives, was born in a log cabin in Fillmore, Utah, on January 2, 1868.[1] Her father was Clarence Merrill, a pioneer farmer and operator of the Cove Creek and Fillmore telegraph stations. Her mother, Bathsheba Smith Merrill (often called Kate), was the daughter of George A. and Bathsheba Smith. Kate was the mother of fourteen and active in Millard County theatrical circles. Alice was the third daughter and fourth child in the large family. Her father had two other wives, with whom he also had children. He married one wife shortly before Alice's birth and the other when Alice was eleven.

Alice was always proud of being born in Fillmore, once the territorial capital of Utah. Displayed in the Old State House there is a portrait of Alice Horne by artist Florence E. Ware. In her adult years Alice recalled that during the family's occasional five-day wagon trips from Fillmore to Salt Lake City, a round-trip distance of three hundred miles, her father introduced her to the beauty of flowers and trees and the bounties of nature, including wild things such as snakes, lizards, chipmunks, and a buck or a doe with her fawn.[2] He pointed out the colors in the sunset and sang in his fine bass voice "Roll on Silver Moon" as night settled in. All the while, her mother would be bedding them down in the wagon and entertaining them with favorite stories from the Bible, LDS history, and the Arabian Nights. Alice recalled lying on her back in the wagon watching the stars appear one by one, waiting, anticipating, and then naming the Great Bear (Big Dipper), the Little Bear, and the Lady in the Chair. These outdoor experiences were heightened by summers spent on one of her father's farms.

Alice's mother was manually dexterous, creative, and talented with the needle and at drafting patterns and sewing. Alice profited from her mother's instruction and became skilled and proficient in designing and crafting clothes.

Alice, called Allie when she was young, started school after her sixth birthday, in a rock schoolhouse in Fillmore, still standing today. Well into her later years she could still recite poems she learned there: "Woodman Spare That Tree," "Tolling of the Bells," "The Village Smithy," and others they practiced in resounding tones in her classes.

Twice a year leaders of the LDS Church held stake conferences in

Fillmore. Alice remembered the long walk out to the main road to greet the incoming officials. Her grandfather, George A. Smith, a cousin of the Prophet Joseph Smith, an apostle and first counselor to Brigham Young, and official historian of the LDS Church (1854-1876), was one of the visiting authorities. Her grandmother, Bathsheba Bigler Smith, accompanied him. The welcoming songs and hurrahs of the community provided a cheerful reception for these leaders. Well aware of the esteem afforded her grandparents, Allie remembered the exciting ride back into town in their carriage.[3] In 1871, when Allie was three, her family spent nearly a year with George A. and Bathsheba Smith while the Merrills' new brick home in Fillmore was being constructed. At times like these the Merrills savored the well furnished home and headquarters of the church historian's office, the library, and the more formal activities of Salt Lake City.

In 1875, when Alice was seven, Clarence Merrill hastened to his home with telegraphed news that Bathsheba Merrill's father, George A. Smith, had died at his Salt Lake City home in his wife Bathsheba's arms. The following year, after a visit to Fillmore by her widowed grandmother, Allie was taken to Salt Lake City to live with her. Bathsheba Smith, a close friend of Emma Smith, wife of LDS Prophet Joseph Smith, while living in Nauvoo, Illinois, and a member of the original group of eighteen that formed the LDS Relief Society in Nauvoo, was a leader of LDS women in Salt Lake City. She had made the motion in a women's meeting of leading sisters that eventually led to the legislative proposal to grant women the right to vote in Utah Territory in 1870.[4] As a result of the lobbying of Bathsheba and other women leaders, the Utah legislature followed the Wyoming legislature in granting women suffrage in February 1870. Because Utah elections were held in May, Utah women were the first in the nation to vote. Congressional passage of the Edmunds-Tucker Act in 1887 rescinded female suffrage in Utah Territory. However, Utah's Constitutional Convention restored women suffrage in 1896, when Utah became a state—long before the 1920 ratification of the Nineteenth Amendment which granted the vote to all registered women, even in states that had not yet permitted it.

Alice's grandmother, Bathsheba Smith, with whom she lived intermittently after age eight, was also an officiator in the Salt Lake

Endowment House and later in the Salt Lake Temple. Named a counselor to Zina D. H. Young, general president of the Relief Society in 1888, Bathsheba Smith was called to the position of general president of the Relief Society in 1901 after the death of Zina Young.

As her grandmother's companion, Allie was reared in a home and environment where the important LDS women of the territory—Eliza R. Snow, Zina D. H. Young, Sarah M. Kimball, Emmeline B. Wells, Susa Young Gates, Emily Tanner Richards, and others—often met and discussed the religious, political, business, literary, artistic, and educational affairs of Utah Territory. Bathsheba's large hand-carpeted "keeping room" became their unofficial meetinghouse. In these groups Allie formed early alliances with the elite of the territory. She absorbed the art of leadership, independent action, and organizational ability while developing a taste for usefulness and competence in social, political, and cultural affairs.

In addition to her regular association with her grandmother and the intermittent visits of her mother and sisters, Allie also visited persons her own age in Brigham Young's Lion House and Beehive House, just across the street from her grandmother's home, and in the nearby homes of various church and territorial leaders.

Allie's grandfather, having been church historian and Speaker of the House of Representatives of the territory, had made his home a repository for LDS church historical and territorial archival materials. Thus, Allie's new home was replete with books, magazines, and manuscripts that she enjoyed.

Another positive element in this site change for Alice was exposure to art. Interested in painting, Grandmother Bathsheba had taken drawing and painting lessons from William W. Majors, a prominent Nauvoo artist and teacher, when she was in Nauvoo in the 1840s. She often showed Alice her sketchbook—one still exists in private hands—with her exquisitely rendered copies of classical subjects and some original creations. She encouraged Allie in her own artistic endeavors, allowing her to use her paints, which were imported from England, as well as giving her access to the pictures George A. Smith had brought back from Europe and the Near East illustrating the architecture and works of art in those regions. All of these sources helped provide the "seed-time" of development in art appreciation for Alice as she studied these pictures and also advanced her reading skills from the printing on the cards.

Alice's training in the Thirteenth Ward School, perhaps the finest elementary school in Salt Lake City at the time, also contributed to her scholastic training and understanding. When fourteen years old, having graduated from the ward school, Allie enrolled in the University of Deseret for what can best be regarded as high school and college training. She completed work for a teaching certificate and a degree in pedagogy in 1887. Her literary talent and theatrical interest are indicated by the fact that she organized a Shakespearean Society at the university and read an essay on Ophelia and Lady Macbeth at the commencement exercises. At the university she also studied art with George M. Ottinger, a Mormon convert from Pennsylvania and a versatile and well-trained artist. Alice continued her association and friendship with Ottinger in the years that followed, and he encouraged her to make the promotion and production of art one of her principal lifetime commitments.

Allie, by now more formally called Alice, taught at the Washington School in Salt Lake City. In 1890 she married George Henry Horne, a local banker and son of pioneer leader Joseph Horne and his wife Mary Shepherd Horne. George had been a member of the Shakespearean Society Allie had organized in 1885. Within a year of their marriage, George and Alice became parents of a daughter, Mary.

In 1893 George and Alice traveled to the Columbian Exposition in Chicago and then went on to New York City to visit with George's brother, Albert. Alice represented Utah on the Liberal Arts Committee of the world fair and published a book of Utah art and poetry to illustrate Utah's developing culture. She carried it with her on the train to be displayed at the exposition. This trip was a catalyst to many programs developed by Alice over her lifetime.

In 1894, soon after their return to Utah, George was called to serve as a missionary for the LDS Church. Alice realized George had decided to accept the call when she saw him chopping a two-year supply of wood for her. While he labored in the southern states for two years, Alice supported him and their young daughter by resuming her teaching at the Washington School. She also studied art and painting under J. T. Harwood, Mary Teasdel, and John Hafen, all prominent Utah artists recently returned from studying art in Paris, France. She was an enthusiastic member of Utah's vibrant art colony. One of her closest friends was Harriet ("Hattie") Richards Harwood, the wife of J. T. Harwood and herself an artist almost as prominent as her husband.

Alice's political career began in 1894 while she was teaching at Washington School and her husband was on his mission.[5] The twenty-six-year-old Alice was indignant that the Salt Lake City public school system had instigated a new art program from the beginning grades through high school called the Augsburg system of drawing. The text used was *Drawing Simplified* by D. R. Augsburg, a member of the art staff at the University of Utah during 1892-94 and art supervisor of the Salt Lake City schools.[6] The Augsburg system spelled out a mechanical form of art instruction, dividing the subject into three branches: representative drawing, constructive drawing, and decorative drawing. It neglected the essential development of aesthetic principles acquired by artists as they study art.[7] Alice regarded the system as foolish—not at all what the practicing artists she knew had used when they studied art. She challenged Professor Augsburg, and after some prodding from her, he finally said, "Mrs. Horne, if you can fool the public, fool 'em."[8] She next attempted to persuade Jesse F. Millspaugh, superintendent of the Salt Lake City schools, to replace the Augsburg system, but he just laughed at her. Deciding that political action offered the only remedy, she persuaded her friend Oscar W. Moyle, a former classmate at the University of Deseret and a respected attorney, to run for the Salt Lake City Board of Education. He agreed to run but told her, "I shan't do a thing to secure the nomination."[9] So it was up to Alice. Each day after school she called at three homes in the neighborhood urging voters to attend the upcoming primary and to vote for Moyle. She also arranged for attractive ballots to be printed which the citizens could use in voting for her candidate. At the crowded primary convention everything went according to Alice's plan with nominating and seconding speeches for Moyle. Although a popular person was nominated to oppose him, Moyle was elected by a large majority. True to his promise to Alice, he engineered the demise of the Augsburg system and provided in its stead a good course in drawing with J. Leo Fairbanks, a Utah impressionist trained in Paris, as art supervisor.

In the meantime, George H. Horne had returned from his mission, taken a business course at the newly established LDS Business College, and after a year of study secured a position as cashier for the State Bank of Utah, to which he was connected for most of the rest of his business life.

In 1898 the thirty-two-year-old Alice continued to encourage greater production of good art in the schools and in the community. One way to do this was to create a state program. "Poverty is a poor excuse for ugliness," she wrote, "and wealth can never get rich enough to purchase good taste. But God has created gifts, and men work so that we're not without poets, painters, sculptors, architects, craftsmen, gardeners and homemakers. So long as talent and industry unite there will be art— original, spontaneous, inspirational—the kind that lives."[10] In another writing she quoted a statement by Ralph Waldo Emerson—"The art of America will come out of the West, amidst the feet of a brave and earnest people"—and speculated that Emerson meant the Mormon pioneers and their posterity. "I had seen enough of large cities," Alice wrote, "to know that art could not go along with people who did not live with it."[11]

Spurred on by the success of Sarah Anderson, who had been elected to the first Utah House of Representatives,[12] Alice agreed to allow the Democratic party to nominate her for representative of Salt Lake's Eighth District. She was elected by a comfortable plurality and served one term, 1898-1900.

Here is Alice's own account of her election in 1898 as a woman legislator:

> About this time, the Democratic party decided to put a woman on the legislative ticket of Salt Lake County. Some highly intelligent women sought the prized position. When things were at a whiteheat, Mr. David C. Dunbar arose, saying "Gentlemen, I know a good looking young woman who works like hell, who will run like a deer, and her name is Alice Merrill Horne!"
>
> The highest vote for a legislator gave me the nomination in the convention. All of the mining towns gave me their entire support. So much, I reflected with beating heart, for hand-made clothes!

Some of the women called me "the doll!" They were intelligent; I knew I was not so smart. There was Dr. Ellen Ferguson, so brilliant, but down-at-the heel.[13] I should like to dress her in the Victorian style! Aah, I reflected, if I could only sew myself brains. But I set myself to think what could be accomplished at the legislature.

However, the *Salt Lake Tribune*, the Republican sheet, sizing up its Democratic opponents said: "Mrs. Alice Merrill Horne is a woman of attainments but not the kind to be made a legislator. Should the Democrat be elected, in the midst of her compeers she would shine like a white diamond on the bosom of an African Princess."

When the votes were counted, this woman candidate for the legislature led the ticket with a thousand votes to spare![14]

Alice's principal object in running for the legislature was to establish a state agency that would hold an annual art exhibition and make annual purchases of paintings to begin a permanent collection of art. With the assistance of George Ottinger, she had prepared a bill to accomplish this purpose even before she decided to run for the House. After taking the oath of office, she went to the Speaker of the House, William M. Roylance of Provo, and asked him to assign her to the Education, Art, and Public Health Committees. The Education Committee was already filled, he told her, but she was prepared to argue a little. "Mr. Speaker, I am the only woman in the House. Surely a woman should be on the Education Committee. And besides I am a teacher."[15] Finally, she agreed to an appointment to the Rules Committee, and at her request he also appointed her to the Public Health and Art committees.

The Rules Committee met first, as Alice knew it would, to adopt the rules under which House business would be conducted. As that meeting got under way, Alice arose to say that she had an art measure to present and proposed that because of their close alliance, Education and Art be made one and the same committee. There was a second and the motion passed unanimously. She was now on the Education and Art Committee. Her first goal achieved, she went on to say that one important matter to be brought up during this session was the use of the land grant offered by the federal government for the establishment of the University of Utah. Alice moved that the House establish a University Land-Site Committee. A second was forthcoming and the motion prevailed. Alice was named chair of that committee. She now offered a third motion that no smoking be permitted in the House or cloak room. The men agreed only grudgingly. After a little campaigning by Alice, the Senate adopted the same rules.

Alice had said nothing about her scheming via the Rules Committee, but someone else talked and the next morning's paper had a note on the back page under the heading "Her Little Game," reciting how she had been at first denied and then had won a place on the Education Committee, now called Education and Art.[16]

One of the controversies in Salt Lake City during her tenure in the legislature was whether tubercular teachers should be employed in the public school system, especially in the lower grades. Alice had spoken at a school mass meeting in favor of requiring the Board of Health to insist that only teachers who were "safe" be employed. The morning paper carried a cartoon, "Mrs. Horne Sweeping the Microbes from the School Room," in which she looked very ladylike but was active with a broom.[17] Her proposed measure was not popular with everyone, but the richest man in her district, W. S. McCornick, a leading banker in the state and prominent non-Mormon, supported her. McCornick's comment was: "You are right, Mrs. Horne. Don't fear criticism but stand by your guns. I see you are elected to the State Legislature. Get your law going and keep only one thing in mind—the good and welfare of the people."[18] Alice's husband had great respect for McCornick and told his wife that she need not fear if such sound men as McCornick approved of her efforts. So, in her words, "I stuck to my guns." She wrote to the Salt Lake Medical Association asking if they considered tuberculosis infectious. They answered that the opinion on the subject was divided. Alice's equivalent in the Senate, Dr. Martha Hughes Cannon, the only woman in the upper house, prepared and introduced a measure providing the first rules and regulations for contagious diseases. Alice sponsored the bill in the House.[19]

At a public reception held shortly after the legislature had begun its deliberations, Gov. Heber M. Wells, whose wife had died, invited

Mrs. Horne to stand by him in the receiving line. Officers from Fort Douglas attended this reception. Alice's memoir describes one episode:

> A very clever young officer, groomed snappily and rather handsome, stepped up to me and addressed me, speaking so clearly that all could hear. "Mrs. Horne, you would be surprised to know how little I care for your noble efforts to ban those teachers who have lung trouble from earning a living by teaching in your public schools."
>
> I kept smiling and everyone stopped, awaiting my reply. I did not hesitate, but took my turn. I replied, "You might be even more astonished to know how little other person's opinions matter to me on such questions as Public Health."
>
> There was a general laugh. "Serves you right," said his fellow officers. "This should teach you to be good."[20]

Some opposition to Dr. Cannon's public health bill surfaced in the legislature, but the two women shepherded the measure through their respective houses.[21] Alice wrote:

> As the Public Health Measure lay before the Senate waiting the final vote, Mrs. Cannon and I went about scattering flowers on the desks of the senators, press, messengers, and employees of the Upper House. This gave David O. Rideout a fine opportunity to recite poetry; he quoted from Longfellow: "The hand that scatters flowers." Soon there was the roll call in the Senate Chamber. The Bill passed! Up we went to the Lower House on the third floor and repeated the work of distributing our flowers with the same results. Then the Governor promptly signed. How happy Mrs. Cannon was with that great accomplishment![22]

Alice waited until the University Land-Site bill was signed by the governor before bringing up her art bill. Four persons expressed opposition. She described her critical maneuvers. On the bill's third reading, "Representative Albert A. Law moved to strike out the Enacting Clause.

I rushed to my desk, picked up a bunch of yellow jonquils—the Women's Suffrage colors—and tossed them on his desk. The men recognized the portent of the yellow flowers and laughed." No one seconded Law's motion. Horne and Cannon "repeated the little act we put on for her Public Health Bill. Lovely flowers were laid on each desk." Then John Fisher from Davis County told her, "If it will make no financial difference, I shall not vote for your bill. Would you care greatly?" She replied, "I should die." He changed his mind and voted for the bill. Nathan Tanner, a representative from Weber County whose main interest was bridges, also proposed to vote against the art bill. "Representative Tanner, this is just a bridge I am asking for. Here we are on the desert side—we can get a bridge over that stream to that green meadow—there are starving flocks," she told him. He, too, was swayed and changed his vote. When the final objector to her measure cited the greater need to control the grasshopper "menace," she asked him: "If I were to tell you how to kill off the grasshoppers, will you vote for it?" She told him of her interest in zoology at the university and how professor Orson Howard had told her "to gather up the eggs [grasshopper or cricket] and boil them." He also voted for the measure.[23]

Cannon and Horne had agreed that they would not speak a word on the floor of the House and Senate but, instead, would speak to each member individually. Inevitably, they had missed their contacts with one or two men. Alice was approached in the House by "that raw-boned, wall-eyed Doc King who came to her whispering, 'Mrs. Horne, you are needed in the Senate Chamber. They are ready to vote on the Art Bill and Senator [Aquilla] Nebeker says you have not spoken to him about it. He declares he will kill it. You will have to come down and tell Senator Nebeker that you sent him the roses—a $15 bunch. Every other senator knows that Senator [David H.] Peery was the donor, and there is danger that Quill will find out.' "[24]

Alice went quickly to the Senate chamber and stood in front of Senator Nebeker, on whose desk was a large vase of roses. "Do you like the roses?" she asked. When he wanted to know if she had sent them, she replied, "You must answer my question first. Roses purchased in the dead of winter. Can't you say you like them?" He confessed sulkily, "I'm bought."

Alice returned to her own desk in time to hear the voting start in the House. A note dropped on her desk stated, "The Art Bill passed the Senate unanimously." In the House, four representatives voted against it, but the remainder, either to please Alice or "to bring a more beautiful life to the people of Utah," as she expressed it, voted for it. Governor Wells, once again, signed it quickly, with the declaration: "This art Bill assures that Utah is the first state in the Union to provide a state institution for the encouragement of the fine arts. So far as we know, it is the direct result of equal suffrage: I congratulate you, Mrs. Horne." He handed Alice the pen.[25]

The bill that Alice had written out in her own hand and sent to the printer at her own expense to provide copies for both houses was now the law of Utah.[26] Her recollections express thanks to the many who "did a service to Utah worthy of remembrance."[27]

Horne and Cannon had initially decided that they would concentrate their efforts on passage of their three bills — Public Health, Art, and University Land-Site Selection — and would not give speeches on other bills that were brought up for consideration. But three other measures introduced near the end of the session induced Alice to "take the floor." The first bill was designed to make theft of one sheep or one cow or steer an act of grand larceny instead of petty larceny. Alice recalled this episode in her personal history. Marcus Shepherd, "A rather brilliant speaker, . . . joked about turning a five-dollar sheep theft into grand larceny instead of petty larceny and moved to strike out the Enacting Clause. The whole assembly was laughing at [his quips]." When Alice took the floor she told of growing up in Fillmore. Starting out in a log cabin with a small acreage, her father built a two-story brick house, planted an orchard, and grew fruits and vegetables that he sold in Pioche, Nevada. Eventually he sold the house and orchard, bought a "band of horses and cows," and moved to a ranch near Marysvale, Piute County. The ranch had wide meadows and long timothy grass on which the cattle grew fat. To raise oats for his horses, he bought a sulky plow, hitched up a favorite, old Billy, and with the Merrill children following like seagulls, opened up a long furrow in what he had considered to be virgin soil. She continued:

But what greeted our eyes? What was planted there? A

steer's skull? Yes, verily! We children gathered up what had been
sown of bleached bones, cows' horns, short horns, long horns. . . .
All afternoon we gathered horned skulls from the vast cemetery
of unmarked, unsung graves!

Gentlemen, when it is such an easy thing to cover in a
shallow grave the evidence that would convict a cattle rustler or
a sheep stealer, don't you think that when one sheep's skull or
one steer's head is found as proof of theft, that such proof is sufficient to establish more than a suspicion that somewhere that
cattle thief has a whole graveyard of heads of horned stock?[28]

The legislators grinned, nodded, and proceeded to pass the bill. The
daily paper the next day referred to the incident with the headline: "Mrs.
Alice Merrill Horne Makes her Maiden Speech on Sheep-Stealing."[29]

A second bill that prompted Alice to conduct an unanticipated
campaign in its favor was a Fish and Game Bill introduced by Salt Lake
Rep. John Sharp. With some nostalgia for her childhood in Millard and
Piute Counties, Alice retained a lifelong interest in the streams and
wildlife of Utah and favored regulations that would protect them. As
debate on the Sharp Bill progressed, she became furious. Rep. Heber
Bennion said he could see no reason why deer should be protected;
they ate his sheep's grass and the grass of other men's sheep. James
Betts of Payson even objected to robins—they ate up his cherries.
Instead of being protected they should be shot. Alice described her
response:

I took to the floor, declaring that I had been elected to
protect the fish and game. As fast as proposed sections of the
measure were voted down, I straightway introduced substitute
motions that repaired the damage or restored what was lost.
Some Representatives who were at first indifferent soon enthu-
siastically joined those fighting for Utah's wildlife. We had to
work fast. When the smoke of the battle cleared, a fairly good
measure had been salvaged. Mr. Sharp came to me and said, "Mrs.
Horne, I thank you for your fine work. You know more about
fish and game than two-thirds of the men here. Had I known

your interest before, I should have put the proposed measure in your hands before its introduction in the House.[30]

The day before the introduction of new bills was scheduled to be prohibited, Professor William M. Stewart of the Normal School at the University of Utah approached Alice about introducing a free scholarship bill he had prepared. It provided for 200 tuition-free scholarships to be given for four years of college training. Stewart told her, "I have noticed that you women stick to your pet measure, and I believe if you will undertake this free scholarship bill you will somehow coax it through." She took up professor Stewart's measure and soon had it through the House. That evening, when she thought her legislative work was finished, she learned that the Senate, angered by the House's refusal to pass forty Senate bills, had stricken the enacting clauses from forty House bills, among them the free scholarship bill. She quickly went into action, demanding of Senate President Aquilla Nebeker:

> Have the Alfalfas [rural representatives] killed my Free Scholarship Bill, Mr. President? This is a great error which must be rectified before it is too late. The Utah schools are forced to import, every year, many teachers for lack of Utah instructors. The two-year free scholarship courses do not allow aspiring teachers sufficient time to fill college requirements. It would be better statesmanship to give our own young people the opportunity to take four-year courses. I tell you our teachers need a sounder foundation. You alfalfas should remember that your own bright young people could be shining in lights in the far-off settlements if these four-year free scholarships were made available. We would not only stop importing teachers, but could furnish teachers for surrounding states.[31]

Swayed by her words, Nebeker said that if Abel John Evans, the senator from Lehi, reintroduced the bill he would not object. Alice approached Evans at once, saying, "You know me as an Alfalfa, bred and born. Why should I, why should my measure, be treated as an enemy of the cowcounties when it was drawn in their interest?" Evans chuckled, "Mrs.

Horne, you are good-looking and I will bring it up." The bill was soon passed and sent on to Governor Wells who remarked, "I am signing this Four-year Free Scholarship Bill, remembering the gifts of our young people as well as recognizing what women's suffrage has done and is doing for education, also to preserve the culture of Utah." The entire episode took "just thirty-six minutes," Alice remembered.[32]

In 1900, pregnant with her third child, she chose not to run for reelection. She never again held any statewide elective office, although she did serve as Salt Lake County chair of the Democratic party, helped organize and served as second president of the Daughters of the Utah Pioneers, helped organize and served as regent of the Daughters of the Revolution, and was chair of the Utah branch of the National Peace Society. She also served as a member of the General Board of the LDS Relief Society during 1902-16 and was invited to give two addresses at the 1904 International Congress of Women in Berlin—one on her service as a legislator and the other on art in Utah. She also found time to author two books: *Devotees and Their Shrines* (1914) and *Columbus, Westward Ho* (1921).

Alice continued her own career as a creative artist until she decided that it was interfering with her career as the mother of six children. Nevertheless, she devoted much energy to exhibiting and promoting Utah art and artists. She sponsored more than thirty-five permanent exhibits in Utah's schools, each dedicated to a Utah artist. Many of these paintings were paid for by the contributions of children as their legacy to the schools. Her concept was that "Utah has always kept the art's finer ideals . . . and [Utahns] are an art-loving people."[33] Alice Merrill Horne died in Salt Lake City at the age of eighty, on October 7, 1948.

When the Salt Lake Council of Women established their Hall of Fame in 1934, Horne was one of the first to be inducted. Posthumously, in 1954, one of the Heritage Halls at Brigham Young University was named for her.[34] Perhaps the greatest tribute to her, however, was given at her funeral by Minerva Teichert, one of the many local artists she had encouraged. Teichert mentioned the dozens of artists that Alice had helped. "Always was this great woman looking after the welfare of the artists, hoping they would be able to 'make a go of it' financially and still grow in spirit. Few people are so forgetful of self. Sometimes she'd lose patience with those she thought worldly. . . . Sometimes she forgot on what a pinnacle she stood. We couldn't crane our necks high enough to get her lofty viewpoint. I have eaten with her, wept and prayed with her. I have . . . dreamed with her. How great were her dreams!"[35]

Whatever her other successes, Alice was always proud of her work as a legislator. The Utah Institute of Fine Arts created by her bill held state-sponsored art exhibitions and acquired prize-winning paintings to begin a state-owned collection, called the Alice Art Collection. It contains at present some 1,200 paintings valued at more than $2 million. Since the art bill's preamble stipulated an intention to "advance the interests of the fine arts, including literature and music," the act was later used to establish the WPA Orchestra, which became the Utah Symphony. The University Land-Site Selection Committee, chaired by her, selected and located the University of Utah at its prominent site on the hill overlooking Salt Lake City, and Alice was always regarded as a special friend of the university. In 1921, twenty-two years after the adjournment of the Third Legislature, she asked Elbert D. Thomas, then a professor of political science and secretary of the University of Utah, how many students had received free scholarships under her bill. By then, he told her, more than 8,000 students had used the scholarships and Utah was sending teachers to several adjoining states and the program had been discontinued.

That Alice's spunk did not desert her after her service as legislator could be demonstrated in many incidents, of which two will suffice here.

The first relates to her campaign to clear Salt Lake City's air of smoke coming from coal and wood fires, smelters, railroads, and assorted backyard bonfires. She organized the Smokeless Fuel Federation and the Women's Chamber of Commerce in Salt Lake City, but she and her friends received no support from the Salt Lake newspapers, which refused to publish reports of their activities. Determined to make them carry a story, she and two friends set up a coal cookstove on the corner of Main Street and South Temple, near the Brigham Young Monument, and proceeded to bake rolls and pies, attracting a considerable crowd and disrupting traffic. The women used smokeless coal—coal from which the oil and gas had been removed. Alice reported: "My friends and I wore white dresses and white gloves. We would pick up lumps of coal and I even wiped off the inside of a stove lid with a lace handkerchief with nary a smudge. Needless to say we got columns of publicity that next day."[36]

In 1936 she entered another campaign when the mayor, city council, and planning commission of Salt Lake City announced their plan to widen State Street. This would have required the razing of Eagle Gate, a famous landmark that Alice and some friends in the Daughters of the Utah Pioneers thought best to be preserved. The women held their protest meeting and determined to stand as a solid phalanx to prevent anyone from tearing down the celebrated archway. A cordon of women surrounded each of the pillars. Said Alice, "We simply must prevent the continued despoliation by politicians of our pioneer atmosphere in Salt Lake City. We must save our landmarks."[37] Deluged with appeals from many prominent individuals and organizations the State Road Commission abandoned its plans. Indeed, the chair of the Utah Highway Commission insisted that they had never intended to destroy the landmark.[38]

A daughter of early pioneers, Alice Merrill Horne fought to bring health, beauty, and culture to Utah's urban and rural communities. As an art connoisseur, artist, teacher, writer, organizer, preservationist, and legislator, she was determined, even aggressive, in pursuing worthwhile educational, artistic, and humanitarian goals. She was refined but could be militant, kind but also forceful, gentle but always determined.

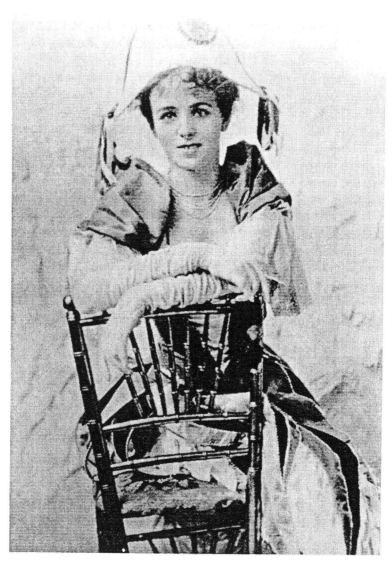

Maude Adams. Photo courtesy of the Utah State Historical Society.

MAUDE ADAMS
No Other Actress Can Take Her Place

Rachelle Pace Castor

Rachelle Castor is an early childhood educator. With her husband, Douglas, she practices her craft on their three sons. Writing is an ongoing endeavor. She particularly enjoys working with children's literature and women in history. Her interest in history and her love of the performing arts made an exploration of the life of Maude Adams a logical choice for her. She hoped to discover what kind of impact Adams's Utah roots had on her career as an actress and "found studying Maude Adams to be delightful and her childhood to be especially fascinating."

During the late 1800s and early 1900s Maude Adams was considered by many to be the most talented actress in American theater. In the cover story for the December 1906 issue of *Human Life*, Hugh C. Weir stated that Maude Adams "has been termed at once the most serious and the most lightsome woman on the American stage." Another writer avowing Adams's talent, referred to an organ in Europe the tones of which could shatter glass. "Maude Adams," he wrote, "had tones that did exactly that to ones heart."[1]

Her mother, Asenath Ann (Annie) Adams, was the daughter of first generation Mormons who had been part of the Nauvoo exodus to Salt Lake City. Annie was born in a log cabin at Little Cottonwood three weeks after her parents finished trekking across the plains. Annie claimed the constant motion of the pioneer exodus gave her a lifelong desire to keep on the move.

When Annie was eight years old she was chosen to play children's parts by Brigham Young's wife, Emmeline, who managed Young's Salt Lake Theatre. The theater seated 1,500, was lighted with oil burners, and was described by Mr. Walter Prichard Eaton as "the most remarkable playhouse in America. Remarkable first because it was built at all, and by rare good luck had absolutely perfect acoustics."[2]

Annie's description makes the demanding schedule the actors were expected to follow seem grueling. The performers learned a new play almost daily and performed nearly every night, all without pay. Eventually a group of actors, including Annie, informed Brigham Young that they could not continue performing without some compensation. After much debate, Young relented.

Maude's father, James Kiskadden, was not a Mormon but an Irishman who had traveled to Salt Lake presumably to work as a cashier in his uncle's bank. He attended the theater often and sat in a red velvet box kept for "Gentile" theatergoers. It was here that he first saw Annie and fell in love with her. Although James had little more to do with the theater other than being a patron, he possessed a natural stage presence. It was said that he had the face of a poet and that when James Kiskadden came into a room it was as if there was no one else there.

Annie and James married in Salt Lake City in 1869. They became the parents of twin boys who died shortly after birth.[3] On November 11, 1872, Annie gave birth to Maude Ewing Adams Kiskadden. Maude became their pride and joy. She proved to be courageous, responsible, and determined—much like her mother's side of the family whereas her comedic talent seemed to come from her Irish father. She had large blue eyes, wavy ashen brown hair and was described as being elfish in her mannerisms. She was tiny as a child which was why she was billed in her youth as "Little Maude Adams," "Maudie," "La Petite Maude," or simply "Little Maude." She remained petite as an adult.

Maude was about nine months old when she made her impromptu theatrical debut. After Maude's birth Annie returned to the Salt Lake Theatre and would keep Maude, who liked to sleep during the day and play at night, backstage during mother's performances.

On the occasion of Maude's debut, Annie was performing in *The Lost Baby*, in which a young child was to be brought out on a silver platter. Phil Margettes, a blacksmith who acted part-time at the Salt Lake Theatre, had insisted on realism and refused to use a doll in place of a real child. At the moment of its entrance cue the child who had been cast for the part was throwing a tantrum and Mr. Margettes grabbed Maude as a last minute stand-in. She was to play the part of a sleeping baby, but instead sat up and looked about in awe at the audience. Despite the unexpected script change, her debut was a success. When she reached stardom easterners and westerners both claimed Maude as their own, but there is no disputing that her first appearance was in Salt Lake City.

Maude was fond of Salt Lake and said, "My childhood had been guarded by the kindly Wasatch Range, and the Rockies were friends from my beginning."[4] She often played in her grandfather's fields, which, according to her friend Phyllis Robbins, was the same land that is now Salt Lake's Liberty Park.[5] She believed Salt Lake City had benefited her character. Maude had a gentle, courteous way and when complimented on her kindness to strangers she would say, "It was not kindness; it was Salt Lakeness."[6] In later years she reminisced about her childhood home:

> Apart from the life in the theater there are two cities that hold very dear memories. One, in a lovely valley protected by friendly mountains is always "home." The people of the valley have gentle manners, as if their spirits moved with dignity. Their forebears suffered great hardness in the search for their haven, but those who survived found peace and plenty in the beautiful valley of Salt Lake. And their children have inherited the gentleness that comes from having endured hardness. The memory of them, the thought of them, and their lovely valley is an anchor in a changing, roving life.[7]

Maude's roving life started early. When she was four, her family moved to San Francisco. Her father dealt in mining machinery and her mother continued her acting. It was here that Maude's childhood career was launched. Her first auditioned part was to be a replacement for an actress who was not doing well as "Little Schneider" in *Fritz*. Maude's mother knew it would be difficult to convince her husband to allow Maude to perform, as he had expressed some concern that Maude might make a fool of herself. But when Maude promised in her four-year-old voice that she would not embarrass him, he laughed and consented. Her mother points out that after Maude got the part, it was he who nearly made a fool of himself bragging over his daughter.

From the onset of her theatrical career Maude chose Adams for her stage name, as a courtesy to her father, who initially objected to her pursuit of a stage career. However, she was known for a number of years by her given name and often signed her childhood letters "M. E. Kiss," short for Maude Ewing Kiskadden.

While living in San Francisco, Maude and her father created many memories together. They would take long walks while he told her clever stories of how the West was won. He was also her greatest ally. On one occasion when her mother insisted that she wear a hat that was "all the rage," a hat that Maude disliked, her father hid it so that Maude could wear an old favorite.

San Francisco proved to have many opportunities for Maude to perform. For a time she and her mother traveled with a theatrical "barn storming" troupe, which played in rough mining towns. Maude believed then, as she did throughout her life, that people from all walks of life should have a chance to see the theater.

Perhaps stemming from her first performance on the silver platter, Maude always demanded realism in her work. One of her roles at age five required her to fetch a pitcher of beer. The traditional substitute was cold tea but Maude refused to carry a counterfeit when beer was available. She won her point to the great satisfaction of the actors.

The public raved about Maude even though the early plays were often poorly written melodramas. One critic said of her, "Little Maude Adams is a remarkable child. She is free from the parrot-like delivery and stilted gestures of most infant actresses. She is as natural as can be wished, or expected."[8] Another called her "the reigning child actress of the Pacific Slope."[9]

By the time she was six she was involved in every aspect of her career including business arrangements and did not hesitate to refuse a role if it paid too little. She applied her own make-up and was concerned to do it just right. Once she asked her mother what she thought of her eye makeup: "Have I put on too much? Do I look fast?"[10]

The "little" actress was often cast as a boy, to which she did not object except for her longing to wear feminine attire. One night before a show she begged her mother relentlessly for a chance to look female. Maude prevailed and "Little Boy Blue" wore a skirt that night.

Fashion was important to Maude throughout her life. As a child she wrote about her fashion dreams in third person, a writing style she often used as a girl. "Several ladies in black silk gowns with beautifully dressed gray hair sat about the drawing-room in bleak austerity. Nevertheless, they were much admired and it was then decided that some day she would have a black silk dress and a purple silk dress and, of course, a brown silk; and for very gay occasions perhaps two gray silks, one lighter and one darker. And it would be so nice when she had gray hair to wear them with."[11]

Her childhood dream to wear beautiful gowns came true, however, her preferred color changed to a shade much like the gray-green of sage brush. As an adult she once made quite an impact on the fashion world. The San Francisco *Chronicle* carried a column describing Maude's influence in December of 1902.

> In the play *Quality Street* by J. M. Barrie Miss Adams carried a muff of snowy lamb's wool so huge that it reached from her waist down to her knees. Women were delighted with this muff. They said: "It not only keeps her hands warm, but all the lower part of her as well. It is very picturesque to carry a muff so enormous. . . ." Miss Adams thinks the big muffs are delightful. "Yes, it is true," she said, "that I made them the fashion. That is why I like them so much. Have you ever planted a seed and had a fine tree grow from it? If you have, your affection for your tree is unspeakably great—the rest of the world can't understand it. Well, I have that kind of an affection for the big muff, and may its shadow never grow less."[12]

Maude performed in a variety of plays as a child. She was "Adrienne" in *A Celebrated Case*, "Dolores" in *Across the Continent*, "Susy" in *Out to Nurse,* and "Alice" in *Kit, the Arkansas Traveler.* Other childhood parts included *The Octoroon,* in which she took the part of a mulatto boy who speaks Black English. She portrayed "Christine," the granddaughter of a blind man, in *The Romance of a Poor Young Man.* In *Nights in a Bar-Room* she played the part of "Little Mary Morgan" who is hit in the head with a flying liquor glass. Before she dies from the injury her father vows that he will sober up, which he does by the end of the play. Some familiar roles included "Oliver" in *Oliver Twist,* "Little Adele" in *Jane Eyre,* and "Little Eva" in *Uncle Tom's Cabin.* All in all Maude appeared in over twenty-five plays as a child.

In 1879, when Maude was seven, she and her mother traveled to Salt Lake for a visit and made joint appearances in *A Woman of the People* and *Little Susie.* When Maude was nine, her parents decided she could no longer put off a formal education and she was sent back to Salt Lake City to stay with her grandmother and attend the Collegiate Institute, a Presbyterian school. The school principal wrote that she was "an excellent scholar—brilliant in dramatic recitations—with a total ignorance of her power—a simple, beautiful, artless schoolgirl."[13]

She was in Salt Lake for less than a year when she received news that her father had died. Maude remained in Salt Lake for a time, but as her mother grew lonely she eventually sent for Maude to join her. By the time Maude returned to San Francisco she was eleven years old. She refers to the period following her father's death as the saddest in her life.

Other things had changed for Maude. She was no longer "Little Maude" and no longer satisfied with her performances. Maude called this the "betwixt-and-between" time. It was not just a time of grief and change, it also proved to be a time of training.

Annie had always seen herself as the actress of the family and had never seriously considered a theater career for Maude. It was not until a friend reminded her that it was her duty to plan a life for her daughter that Annie decided to give up her own pursuits so that she could give full attention to Maude's career. Some believe that the genius of Maude Adams was directly linked to her mother's profound dedication to her daughter. Annie saw to it that Maude had instruction in music, voice, and dance. Maude also apprenticed in a company touring small communities in the California area. Although there were few parts for her during this "betwixt-and-between" time, Maude worked hard, continuing to perfect her craft, even when times were lean.

By the age of fifteen Maude had grown shy, self-conscious, and unassuming, but had developed a deep desire to play tragic roles. Her mother pointed out that she could not possibly play a tragic part with a small, straight nose like hers. Maude had little reason to take offense since their noses were identical.

While performing for a year with the San Francisco-based Alcazar company, she met Charles Frohman, an up-and-coming New York producer, who would later have major impact on her career. It was Annie who arranged an interview with Frohman so that she and Maude could meet with him. Maude was terrified at the prospect of meeting someone of such great importance, but the results of the interview were favorable. Frohman told them Maude must drop her western "r" and let him know when they were in New York.

When the mother-daughter team finally did make their way east, there was a long waiting period until a part in a play became available. Maude's first eastern role was in Boston. She was given the role of "Jessie Deane" (nicknamed Little Red Ridinghood) in E. H. Sothern's *Lord Chumley* in Boston. It was performed in the Hollis Street Theater, where she acted alongside the talented Miss Belle Archer. Belle became Maude's mentor, and they shared a lifelong friendship.

At sixteen a long-time dream was fulfilled when Maude was invited to join Charles Frohman's Traveling Stock Company. Frohman was pleased to note that she had indeed dropped the western "r." One of her parts with Frohman was "Nell" in *Paradise Lost*. After two years with Frohman she left to become actor John Drew's leading lady. She stayed with the Drew company for the next five seasons. However, she remained professionally involved with Frohman for almost three decades even though she worked primarily for other producers.

In the East the "betwixt-and-between" came to an abrupt end as Maude met with great and immediate success. Before her twenty-fifth birthday she was heading her own company which provided the lion's share of productions at the Empire Theatre in New York. From 1897 through 1934 she took part in dozens of productions involving herself in every aspect of the theater from staging and scenery, to sound, costumes, and lighting. Her electrical consultant, Bassett Jones, claimed she was the finest production artist in the country. One of her greatest accomplishments was in stage lighting. Maude had always found the available lighting of the time, starting back with the oil burners of her childhood, to be antiquated. Consequently, when Maude felt she needed a change from her rigorous pace after a serious illness, her friends suggested she try something in motion pictures. Realizing it would involve lighting she embraced the new project with enthusiasm. For two years she worked at the General Electric Laboratories experimenting with color lamps for movies. She invented a high-powered incandescent lamp that later made colored movies possible, but she was given no credit for her contribution. She was deeply disappointed by this injustice and her lawyer advised her to sue, believing she could settle out of court for a half million dollars. She refused to pursue litigation and later noted in her diary that she thought herself an "idiot" for her decision. She was not beyond making public claim, however. When she saw her invention being used she would say, "Those are my lamps."[14]

During Maude's years with her own company she acted in and produced a variety of plays, including her hoped-for tragedies. Her public loved her as "Juliet" in *Romeo and Juliet*, despite many negative reviews. She also performed in *Twelfth Night* and *The Merchant of Venice*. She was particularly memorable in *L'Aiglon*, authored by Edmund Rostand, who is most famous for his *Cyrano de Bergerac*. In *L'Aiglon* Maude played the "Duke of Reichstadt," son of Napoleon II. Her slight build proved perfect for the delicate young man she portrayed. Although her performance in *L'Aiglon* was one of her best known, it was Sir James M. Barrie's plays that made her a star.

Barrie's plays ran consecutively for a number of years at the Empire Theatre in New York, with Maude performing in all of them, including *The Little Minister, Quality Street, What Every Woman Knows, The Legend of Leonora, A Kiss for Cinderella,* and *Peter Pan.* Barrie wrote *Peter Pan* hoping Maude would play the lead. Barrie and Miss Adams seemed to have a deep understanding of one another as is evident in Maude's description of their relationship. "So much of Barrie's life is second nature to me that I have to remind myself that other people do not know it so well; and much of it is so intimate that it is hard to touch with a sense of the delicacy it demands."[15] However, Maude strongly denied any romantic involvement with Barrie or with anyone during her life. The theater was her first and only love.

Maude's role as "Peter" in *Peter Pan* had a great influence on American theatergoers. Fans, especially children, would attend the performance night after night until every word was memorized. Louise Boynton in the December 1906 issue of *The Century* magazine writes:

> New York needed Peter Pan. The play came at one of those discouraged moments when the public mind was occupied to an almost morbid degree with huge and vexing problems, and with things that were going wrong. . . . At such a moment came Peter Pan, created in the mind of a man of insight and gentleness, embodied by a woman beautiful in life and thought, with the soul of an artist, and the heart of a child. . . . Playing Peter Pan is not acting a role. It is embodying a living thought. It is expressing the life-force in the simplest, most beautiful way by teaching us to look at life from the child's point of view. . . . Realities that seemed formidable are found not to be real at all, and all sorts of lovely illusions are dreams that may come true.[16]

Maude writes of her own feelings about the play. "It was not only that *Peter* was the most delightful of all the plays, but it opened a new world to me, the beautiful world of children. My childhood and girlhood had been spent with older people, and children had always been rather terrifying to me. When one met the eyes of the little things, it was like facing the Day of Judgment. Children remained an enigma to me until, when I was a woman grown, Peter gave me open sesame; for whether I understood children or not, they understood Peter."[17]

It was not just Peter Pan that tied Maude so endearingly to the Empire Theatre. She had contributed more to the success of the Empire than any other performer. In 1943, for the Empire's 50th birthday celebration, a bronze plaque was mounted in the theater with the names of its most beloved contributors. Maude's name was at the top of the list.

In 1915, at age 43, Maude entered one of her most difficult years. Charles Frohman died on the passenger liner *Lusitania* when it was torpedoed on May 7, and soon after, John W. Alexander, Maude's costume designer, died. Then Allen Fawcett, Maude's stage manager also passed away. Her most difficult challenge came when her mother became very ill. With this news Maude closed the Empire Theatre and returned to Salt Lake City to be with her mother, who died in March 1916.

There was little reprieve when in 1917 Maude finished her season in New York on May 5 and boarded the midnight train to Boston to begin the World War I war work classes. Joining with others, she learned cooking, marketing, and gardening. This was an example of her remarkable drive to make things better, not only in the theater but in all areas of life. One of her dearest ambitions was to educate women about society's needs, hoping to inspire more responsibility in public affairs.

She volunteered at the Y.W.C.A. during the summer of 1918, where she stayed busy nearly round the clock putting forth her usual best effort. So as not to waste any time, she would use her spare minutes to fold napkins or arrange flowers. One Sunday after serving 1,000 meals, she was so exhausted she and a friend lay on the floor and indulged on plum preserves.

She did some entertainment touring during the war, and described those times as difficult, but she made things brighter with her contagious humor. Reminiscing with a friend, she wrote, "Do you remember those horrible buns with an infinitesimal bit of ham in their middle that we lived on day after day in tourist coaches from six in the morning till we reached the next one at night? Then we learned that Mr. McAdoo [a fellow traveling mate] was lolling in a private car. How contemptuous we were of him!"[18]

Maude made a concerted effort throughout her life to give to charity. She contributed to many benefits, not only for the recovering soldiers and others helping with the war, but also for earthquake and flood victims. She also appeared at fund-raisers to help build new college theaters, including one for the famous Yale Repertory Theater. Often she would send tickets for blocks of seats to poorer districts so that all children could see *Peter Pan*.

It was those children and perhaps the child in every war-time soldier that were most comforted by Maude Adams's portrayal of "Peter." The cynic Alexander Woollcott, a *New York Times* critic and friend to

Maude, wrote a letter to her from war-ravaged France in October of 1918 that describes the poignant longing of a past performance of *Peter Pan*.

> When, as all of us do sometimes, I get very tired of shells and shell-holes, tired of an endless wilderness of crumbled homes, tired of mud, mud, mud, I like to shut my eyes and listen to the music that used to usher Peter in through the high nursery window, to see Nibs dancing the pillow-dance in the firelight, to wait while Miss Thing comes down the silver stairway to that absurdly perky strain. All that dear music has been with me through more than a year of exile. . . . I need scarcely have reported all this to you, had it not occurred to me insistently the other day that you ought to know the war chroniclers are omitting something salient, when they merely tell you how brave our soldiers have been. Indeed, they are brave. . . .
>
> But what I want you to know is that the fiercest of them is a good deal like Michael slaying a pirate or two. I knew that, the other day, as I stumbled at dawn over an exhausted doughboy who had come out of the line and gone to sleep in his tracks with his face, that has yet to meet a razor, pillowed on his gas-mask. I wished, then, that you were here and that I could introduce you to him. I know him so well. I know that his first-aid kit is gone because he has used it to staunch some other fellow's "wounds in the rain" —a rain, lady, of shrapnel. I know that for his buddie, as he calls his pal, he would gladly lay down his life. I know that the last time he fought for three days and nights with nothing to eat, he didn't complain. You, yourself, at the first glance, would see that he can't be much more than seventeen. And you would see for yourself, what I'm rambling along in an effort to tell you, that the American soldier—I mean the plain, unadorned infantryman—would make his strongest appeal of all to Wendy.[19]

More than any other "fan," Woollcott seems to wrenchingly tag the complicated social atmosphere that Americans found themselves in during the "war to end all wars." Somehow Maude Adams's "Peter" was a piercing comment if not a reassurance to those like Woollcott, caught between childhood and the horrors of the twentieth century.

Another performance loved by her audiences was *Joan of Arc*. It was played at a Harvard open-air amphitheater large enough for the extravagant production which included grazing sheep, charging stallions (over 200 horses in all), and a cast of over 1,400 that played to an audience of 15,000. Realizing she would need to stay atop a horse and being true to her spirit of excellence she practiced many hours to perfect her horseback riding. She did have a problem with the given name of her practice horse, one Tuberculosis, so she called him Dan.[20]

Later in her career, after the season would close for the summer, she would travel to different places for rejuvenation. One summer it was to Switzerland, another to Vienna, and one to Trinity College in Dublin. She spent an entire year in France learning to speak the language. Her final holiday was to Egypt.

After retirement she still wanted to work. In 1937, at age 65, she headed the drama department at Stephens College, Columbia, Missouri, a junior college for girls.

As she did in her younger years, she set about to produce her best work expending much energy even though her health was poor. She reported being somewhat troubled by her students' concern that changing their diction to a more pleasant enunciation was "unnatural" or "pretense" while at the same time the girls delighted in curling their naturally straight hair. She was confident that her teaching methods would prevail. And they did, as reported in an article in the *New York Times Magazine* on November 7, 1937. Eunice Fuller Barnard wrote, "Under Miss Adams's inspiration almost every department in the college is working literally night and day on [the show] *Chantecler*. Three evenings a week two hundred girls meet with the singing instructor to do breathing exercises. And at odd hours from dormitory to dormitory sounds of "bah, bah, bah" and "boo, boo, boo" startle the passer-by."[21]

She ended her teaching at Stephens College in 1950 at the age of 78 but continued to work by devoting a great deal of time to writing. It was a frustration for her that no matter how determined she was to organize her papers, she never seemed to manage it. She wrote to her friend Phyllis Robbins: "I am sifting, sifting, sifting. There were at one time four copies of the Articles. . . . Now they are one copy all together and fighting as to which is the more important page. . . . In moments of desperation it seems impossible; in hopeful seconds, I can now and then see light."[22]

Her last years were quiet, spent in a cottage just outside of Tanersville, New York. The cottage was placed back from the road among peonies and apple trees. She loved to watch the deer come to nibble. This setting was very much to her liking because it made her feel like working on her writing.[23]

Maude had a shyness and modesty that prevailed through her highly successful career, a career which was her life, her love. At one time she wrote, "No man knows another, and everyman is ever another to himself. It is one of the many blessings of life in the theatre that we are always so delightfully busy being someone else, that we scarcely spare a moment to know ourselves. That doubtful pleasure can always be deferred. And what a mercy! If we really knew ourselves, how could we endure it?"[24]

In 1953 Maude Adams died of a heart attack at the age of 81. It was said at the time of her passing, "We have no other actress who can take her place in the theatre."[25] She was buried at the Cenacle Convent at Ronkonkoma, Long Island, in a private cemetery.

Maude Adams's influence began in Salt Lake City and was felt across the country during her lifetime. Remarkably, even her passing did not erase her ability to charm and thrill audiences even decades later. Many moviegoers will remember a film about a young writer who is so bewitched by a picture of a haunting beauty that he finds a way to travel through time to find this fascinating creature. The novel *Bid Time Return* by Richard Matheson and the film *Somewhere in Time* were inspired by a photo that Matheson saw hanging in the Virginia City Opera House — a photo of Maude Adams.[26]

Kuniko Muramatsu Terasawa in the early 1920s, shortly after her arrival in America. Photo courtesy of Haruko T. Moriyasu.

Caricature of Kuniko Terasawa, 1987, by Susumu Nemoto, cartoonist for *Asahi Evening News*, 1951–1966. Courtesy of Haruko T. Moriyasu.

KUNIKO MURAMATSU TERASAWA
Typesetter, Journalist, Publisher

Haruko T. Moriyasu

Haruko Moriyasu is currently the director of the Asian American studies program at the University of Utah, where she teaches for both the ethnic studies program and theater department. The daughter of Japanese immigrants to Salt Lake City, she grew up with the family newspaper, The Utah Nippo, *a Japanese language publication that served thousands in the Mountain West. She first wrote about her mother's contributions to the paper, and through it to an entire region, only ten years ago as the result of a conference at the University of Utah. She is currently expanding this delightful insight into Kuniko's personal and professional life into a book for publication in both America and Japan.*

At age ninety-four, for the first time in some sixty years, she put on a kimono she had made as a young woman and exclaimed, "How can Japanese women wear anything as uncomfortable as this!"[1] This Meiji Japanese woman was outwardly American, most comfortable in the sneakers, pants, and shirts she generally wore in the final years of her life. The inner person was still the Japanese woman, courteous and respectful of others, strong willed yet humble.

Kuniko Muramatsu Terasawa was born in Shimoina (now Iida City), Nagano Prefecture, Japan, on July 8, 1896, the 29th year of the Meiji Period, to Kintaro and Kiu Muramatsu, a well-to-do farmer and landowner. She was the second child in the family of four, three girls and a boy, and given the name Kuni (country, nation), a name with strong meaning for a woman. When a baby was born in her family, the custom was to write appropriate names on pieces of paper and place them on the *kamidana*, a high shelf reserved for the family gods. A child would then be lifted up to reach the shelf and to select one of the papers. The name written on the paper became the baby's name. The strength symbolic in the ideographic character was exemplified in the strong willed Kuni. When she came to the United States in 1922, a person who studied the meaning of names told her that she should add "ko" to her name, "Kuniko," to soften the effect of the name. The addition of the ideograph "ko" (child) would change the name to mean "nation's child or child of nation or country." She was born in an era of major changes in Japan and her attitudes and philosophy of life were shaped by the events and actions of the leaders from that time.

The period of the Meiji Restoration resulted in changes in Japanese attitudes toward women—their roles in the family, their education, and their participation in the community. In the family, their role was eventually based on the twin ideals of "good wife, wise mother," *ryo-sai kenbo*, which later became a guiding principle in the basic education of women.[2] In education, a system of universities, middle schools, and primary schools was established for both men and women. Education was mandatory for all children with initially four, and later six, years compulsory for everyone.[3] In 1899, a law was passed mandating the establishment of at least one higher school for women in each prefecture. This increased the number of post elementary schools for women but narrowed the focus of their education to represent their defined role in the family. Women's education was not to be academically equal to that of middle-class men.[4] In the community, women were limited in political and economic participation; however, the recognition of women's productivity and the designation of the home as a "public place" gave them a greater role in the community. This period was also to bring about a change in women's roles from one of responsibilities as wives to one that encompassed their roles as mothers through the influence of reformist and feminist women active in Japan in the early twentieth century.[5]

As a woman born and educated during this period of major changes in Japan, Kuni received both the six years of compulsory elementary school and the high school education. Upon graduation in March 1913 (the eleventh graduating class of her high school), she requested that she be allowed to continue her education. She became one of the first women from her village to go to a post secondary school in Tokyo, opening the way for her younger sister and other women from her village to seek a higher education in Tokyo. Philosophically, she viewed education as a vital investment in herself. She, therefore, convinced her father that she should be allowed to use her dowry for an education that would be equivalent to a college degree today, even though her mother constantly reminded her that too much education would make her less desirable for marriage. She graduated from Tokyo Kyoritsu Joshi Shokugyo Gakko (Tokyo Kyoritsu Women's Vocational School, currently Tokyo Kyoritsu Women's University).

While attending the school, she was challenged by the fact that one of her teachers had difficulty in passing the demanding Ministry of Education examination for teachers. She studied for the examination during the summer, then took and passed the test on her first attempt. With this achievement she returned to Iida with a license to teach sewing and needlework at the Iida Fuetsu Women's High School, from which she had graduated. Her philosophy for a strong education led her to advise her daughters and other young women that a strong education was an investment: "Money and material things can be stolen or taken away but an education will go with you to your grave."

Kuniko was generally modest about her accomplishments; however, she often referred to two that seemed to be of particular importance to her. The success with the Ministry of Education examination was one. The other was being chosen to embroider a set of silk handkerchiefs that was annually presented to the empress. She had the honor of doing so each year she was in attendance at the Tokyo school. Her work was also selected to be a part of the Japanese display at a World's Fair in the United States, circa 1918. Ironically, she did not think she had sufficient artistic ability to succeed in a career in design. She did have a sense of composition and technical ability that her creations in silk were exquisite in detail and perfection. These abilities served her well when she took on the responsibilities of publishing a newspaper. She also did not labor over her work; therefore, her embroideries and other creative efforts were clean and meticulous in appearance. The needlework she produced, especially the silk embroidery and the kimonos, continue to be treasured by members of her immediate and extended family.

Kuniko's opportunity to come to the United States occurred in 1921, when she heard about a potential marriage prospect while talking to a fellow teacher. Marriages in Japan were arranged by match-makers who acted to bring two people together who would be considered compatible. The colleague had been approached by a match-maker concerning a marriage with a forty-year-old man who published a newspaper in the U.S. The woman was reluctant to accept because she was afraid to make the trip across the ocean. Kuniko became interested in taking the woman's place. She had previously had several opportunities and offers of marriage to local men. None had been of interest to her. By the time she heard of the opportunity in America, she was 25 years old and had reached an age at which women became less desirable as marriage partners. Her status as an "old maid" had negative ramifications for her and her siblings who were also of marriageable age. In Japan, it is customary for children in a family to be married in order of age—the oldest first, then younger children in declining order. An older unmarried sister remaining in the home would create difficulties for the younger siblings. Kuniko concluded, "Living in Japan without marrying at my age would be worse than living in America." She also thought that she could be of greater help to the man in the United States than to any of the possible prospects in Japan.

Kuniko had been interested in going abroad to Paris to study and to become a fashion designer but had not done so because languages—English and French—had been difficult for her to master. However, going to America as the wife of someone who had been in the United States for almost twenty years and apparently had done well was a different situation. Her older sister had recently emigrated to Brazil. This also helped her to make her decision and to gain permission from her father, who would have preferred to have all of his children living close by. Unfortunately, her sister had passed away shortly after reaching Brazil. Had this news reached Japan before Kuniko had left for the United States, she most probably would not have been permitted to leave.

The man, Uneo Terasawa, whom she eventually married, was from a neighboring village, Yamabuki, and was also from a farming and landowning background. He was the oldest of five children. His father had been an influential village headman (mayor), who in taking responsibility for the debts of another person had lost most of his own property and his position. Uneo had gone to the U.S. in order to support his family and to earn sufficient money so that he could eventually return to Japan and go into politics. He had established himself in Salt Lake City, Utah, first as a farmer, then as the publisher of *The Utah Nippo*, a Japanese language newspaper, and finally as a community leader. His return to Japan in 1921 was his first trip back since he had left in 1905. He had returned to be reunited with his father and brother and, at his father's suggestion, to find a bride. At age forty, finding a young bride might have been difficult; however, his short stature and youthful appearance gave him hope of finding a suitable young woman.

Kuniko Muramatsu and Uneo Terasawa, a man fifteen years her senior, were married in December 1921. The age difference did not create a problem for her as there was considerable difference in her parents' ages and the idea was not new to her. She arrived in the United States with her husband in January 1922, following an eighteen day ocean voyage that included a brief stop in Hawaii. The couple visited San Francisco for two days then boarded the Union Pacific train for Salt Lake City.

During her early years in Salt Lake City, Kuniko's major role was that of the Meiji ideals for women: "good wife, wise mother." She also exemplified the Meiji ideals of endurance, frugality, modesty, courage, literacy, hard work, and productivity. She took the position of being an *"ennoshita no chikaramochi,"* literally, the foundation that supports the house, figuratively, the person who does the disagreeable work that is never recognized but necessary to do. Initially she had very little to do with the publication of *The Utah Nippo*. Her major role was that of a homemaker, providing a strong moral foundation for her children, and a hostess for the many visitors her husband entertained. She became well known for her culinary abilities based on one incident when she had an unexpected guest for dinner. Using only the tofu she had, she proceeded to prepare several dishes. The guest immediately proclaimed her excellence as a chef and her reputation was established. Her expertise with the needle was also well known, and she was often called upon to sew kimonos and western dresses for others.

Kuniko's husband was a typical Japanese man who defined husband and wife roles along patriarchal lines. However, children, as members of his family, were expected to participate in a variety of activities considered to be important for their education and development. The two daughters, Kazuko and Haruko, were regularly included in a variety of social, recreational, and even some business activities. During the depression of the 1930s, fishing trips were taken to "get away from creditors." Kuniko learned to bait a hook with nightcrawlers by rolling them in the dirt first, as she did not like to touch them and she could not wait for someone else to do it for her. As with the worms, in recognition of the need to be able to function independently, she learned to do many things that she had not had to do before and that had not been a part of her culture. Her mentors were Japanese women who had lived in the United States for many years and who had experienced the hardships of being transplanted into the same, foreign environment. Mrs. Gen Nishiyama became a close friend and, until she returned to Japan following her husband's death, was a major source of support. Haruye Masaoka, a widow with a large family, was another source of support and information.

In April 1939, Kuniko's life was suddenly changed. She had been a homemaker who had occasionally helped at the newspaper and who had devoted most of her time to her two daughters and to community service. During a twelve-day business trip to Nevada, Uneo caught a cold that developed into pneumonia when he went on to Ogden to help the widow of a friend. When he returned home, he was so ill, he could not get out of the car without help. He passed away on April 24, after a short stay in the hospital. Following his death, the continuation of the newspaper was in question. Kuniko had to make the decision of returning to Japan, where she would be supported by her younger brother, or remaining in Utah and continuing the paper. A group of seventeen of Uneo Terasawa's friends and colleagues convened to discuss the fate of the paper. At the meeting, Kuniko expressed her intention to comply with the wishes of her late husband to have the paper continue to serve the Japanese community of the intermountain area.

In a short article appearing in the May 5, 1939 issue of *The Utah Nippo*, she stated:

> To the very end, Terasawa's resolve was to continue the publication of *The Utah Nippo*. Even though I may have to face a great deal of hardship, I cannot disregard the death of my late husband as if it were someone else's concern and return to Japan. Regardless of the extent to which I may have to depend on those of you who have been supporters and those who have been subscribers, if at all possible, I would like to continue to publish the paper.
>
> As a vehicle serving the Intermountain Area that you all believe to be essential, to even think of leaving the newspaper and ending its publication is too lacking in consideration of my late husband's wishes.
>
> Mrs. Abiko is courageously publishing a major newspaper (*Nichi Bei Times*, in San Francisco); however, while it is a responsibility that may seem improbable for someone like me to take on, if you empathize with my views and will be willing to help, I am prepared to continue the paper according to the wishes of my late husband until I die.[6]

With this statement, Kuniko Terasawa became the publisher of the paper her husband had started in 1914. She continued to publish it until her death in 1991. Her philosophy had always been that a person could do anything or at least try to do anything that another human being had done. With this conviction she took over the publication of the newspaper that included picking and setting type, printing, writing articles, and serving as the president of the corporation. The responsibilities for the publication of the newspaper was generally covered by the existing staff. However, the diverse aspects of managing the corporation and keeping in contact with the subscribers and advertisers were jobs that Kuniko had to take over. This required acquiring a skill she had not learned: the ability to drive a car.

Initially, she hired college students to drive her on long trips. However, Kuniko disliked being dependent on others for mobility. Therefore, during the summer of 1939, she spent one week with an instructor, Harry M. Eda, a friend of her husband who came in from Helper, to teach her how to drive. She took the test for her driver's license and then went on a business trip. She had learned to drive forward but had difficulty backing up, and she would only make right turns. She would drive into a farmyard but would often need someone to back the car out if she did not have enough space to turn around. Because she was small, her head visible just above the window, she was difficult to see while she was driving the car. She and the car became well known in the area. Whenever "the car without the driver" was seen, the people knew that Mrs. Terasawa had arrived. The business trips became a source of additional information for the subscribers and presented opportunities for networking within the area. Her daughters were sometimes left alone under the watchful eyes of the neighbors, but Kuniko often took them with her during the summers. They accompanied her to the neighboring states to share experiences and to broaden their outlook on life.

The immediate period following the death of her husband was difficult. There had been few resources and a number of debts that needed to be repaid. Her husband's hospital bills were paid in large part with monies saved for her daughters from gifts they had received for Christmas, New Year, and other special occasions. Also she had the traditional monetary offerings from mourners who had attended her husband's funeral that she planned to use in whatever way necessary. While people had pledged support for the continuation of the newspaper, the amount of supporting funds was minimal. Kuniko asked the seventeen community people who had met to determine the newspaper's future to find additional subscribers to ensure continuation of the paper. Her resolve, in the face of all the difficulties, eventually helped her to succeed. She once again became something of a role model for other Japanese women. An additional incentive was her determination to remain in the United States. She was not going to return to Japan to become dependent on her brother; this would have been an intolerable position.

The fifty-two years of *The Utah Nippo* under her leadership were periods of change in the status of the newspaper as well as of the Japanese American people in the United States. One of the first changes to occur in the newspaper was the addition of an English section. By 1939, many of the Nisei, second generation Japanese Americans, had come of age and had a need for a vehicle that would publicize their activities and give them a voice in the community. Mike M. Masaoka, a Nisei leader in Salt Lake City, approached Kuniko shortly after she became the publisher about including an English section in *The Utah Nippo*. She agreed to the proposal on a trial basis. One-half of page four, the "back page" of the newspaper, was designated for this purpose. In the beginning, due to the lack of general support sufficient to cover the cost of typesetting, the English section was not able to continue on a regular basis, and publication was suspended for a period. Eventually, however, the section was to become a permanent addition. Starting with the August 31, 1942 edition, it became a medium of communication for the dissemination of news for the Nisei generation. This addition was particularly important as World War II had begun, and 120,000 Japanese had been relocated from the West Coast, two-thirds of whom were American-born citizens.

During the start-up phase of the English section, material for publication was solicited from the area Nisei. Published articles included editorials, feature articles, and a variety of news items about community activities and happenings important to Nisei in Utah, Idaho, western Wyoming, and eastern Nevada. A calendar of events, meeting announcements for community organizations, social, religious, and sports activities, Nisei achievements, personal sketches, and vital statistical information were also printed. Although most of the news was of local interest, news from the ten relocation camps was an important inclusion during the war years as the paper was distributed to those sites as well.

Within hours following the Japanese bombing of Pearl Harbor and the beginning of World War II, Issei (immigrant Japanese) community leaders and businessmen were detained and eventually taken to federal detention centers in Kentucky, Montana, New Mexico, Louisiana, and Texas. Kuniko Terasawa, as publisher of *The Utah Nippo*, would also have been a prime candidate for detention. However, she had only been a publisher for eighteen months, and since her activities in the community were in support of her husband, she was not detained. She was later told by Mike M. Masaoka, a leader of the local chapter of the Japanese American Citizen's League, that she did not have to worry about the possibility of detention. The newspaper, on the other hand, was closed from December 11, 1941 to February 28, 1942. The FBI arrived on the morning of December 11 and waited while one of the employees who lived on the premises packed his belongings. They then nailed the doors closed, handed the employee the hammer, and effectively terminated the publication of the newspaper indefinitely. Kuniko was also questioned in her home by the FBI during this interval. Her conclusion after the interview was that she was considered to be a relatively insignificant person. With two young daughters and little previous history of community leadership involvement, she was just not important enough to detain. Judging from the comment made by Mike M. Masaoka, there may also have been testimony in her favor to prevent detention.

While the Japanese language newspapers on the West Coast had been closed for the duration of the war, the two papers in Colorado continued publication under the jurisdiction of the Alien Property Custodian. After two months of inaction and the need for employees to have a means of support, a request for clarification of the status of *The Utah Nippo* was made. The newspaper was given permission to resume publication on February 25, 1942 as a privately operated newspaper under the leadership of Kuniko Terasawa. However, publication was resumed under the condition that only translations of news appearing in the American English newspapers could be used. Kuniko would occasionally report on such incidents as visits made by wives to detention centers where their husbands—community leaders and businessmen—were being held. When articles of this nature or articles reporting news that was not previously printed in English language newspapers appeared in the Japanese section of *The Utah Nippo*, a letter would come from the censors threatening closure if such reporting continued. Thus the paper was permitted to publish under private entrepreneurship during the war years but under extremely limited conditions and under heavy censorship.

The increased number of subscriptions and bulk distribution of the newspaper to the ten camps—10,000 copies per publication—required a change in equipment. A hand-fed, totally inadequate, antique press had been the only equipment used to publish the paper. A self-feeding press and folder were added and the space occupied by the paper increased to two floors. The number of employees increased from three to nine, all men, working under the leadership of a woman. This was an unusual arrangement for Japanese men. However, because Kuniko was not a dominating employer, she was able to maintain a satisfactory relationship with her employees.

As the war ended, Japanese government representatives and private citizens began to arrive in the U.S. Kuniko was to take part in another facet of her husband's activities. The newspaper became the local contact for visitors from Japan. As publisher, she was not only on hand to greet them, but often helped to schedule their itinerary and acted as their host. In eight millimeter films and slides taken of this period, she can be seen greeting then Crown Prince Akihito, talking with Diet member Kaju Nakamura, meeting and, in some cases, picnicking with diplomats and their families. She also helped travelers from Japan in small ways such as providing them with box lunches, *obento*, and helping them to get to their destination. She was generous in extending aid. She would tell those to whom she was giving aid that there was no need to repay the favor directly to her and that repayment would occur when they in turn helped someone else. She maintained that one should always remember what others have done for you but forget what you have done for others. She never gave thought to the returns that she herself might gain. However, in many cases, the friendships she developed with the people she helped continued throughout her life and often brought her unexpected rewards and recognition.

She generally supported and sometimes initiated community activities, taking little credit. In many situations, even though she may have taken the initial lead, she played the traditional role of the Japanese woman. Once an activity was under way, male community leaders would be found in the forefront and Kuniko would support from the background, allowing others to take credit for the work she had initiated and accomplished. She was again the *ennoshita no chikaramochi*.

When the Salt Lake Council of Women decided to establish the Peace Garden in Jordan Park in the late 1940s, she was one of the early supporters of the development. *The Utah Nippo* spearheaded the effort to raise funds for the Japanese sector of the gardens and helped to raise $10,000 to cover the costs. Even though the garden was being built in Salt Lake City, the construction of the Japanese garden was supported by

Japanese Americans from the entire intermountain area and from subscribers in other areas of the country. Additionally, the combined efforts of the people involved in the project resulted in donations of three stone lanterns and other items from individuals in Japan. The garden was at one time a "must see" focal point for all visitors from Japan.

During the 1950s when President Dwight D. Eisenhower first established the Sister Cities Program, Tamotsu Murayama, a resident of Tokyo and a columnist for *The Japan Times*, approached Kuniko with the idea of establishing a sister city relationship between Salt Lake City and Matsumoto. His parents had emigrated to the U.S. from Matsumoto City in mountainous Nagano Prefecture. He thought that the two cities were indeed like sister cities, and this idea, coupled with his close ties to the Japanese Americans in Salt Lake City, gave rise to his interest in the program. Again, Kuniko supported the effort, helping to fund the preliminary costs of getting the program established. She actively supported the project and eventually was awarded an honorary citizenship of Matsumoto. She and *The Utah Nippo* continue to be of interest in Matsumoto City. The City requested artifacts from the newspaper which have been placed on permanent display in the Matsumoto City library. A complete set of existing newspaper files is stored in the library and one bank (twenty-six cases) of Japanese type, regular as well as headline type, is on display. Microfilm of the papers are available for the use of the general public. A *Utah Nippo* study group has been formed to research material published in the paper.

In 1966, at the age of seventy, Kuniko Terasawa was once again at a crossroads. She had stated in 1939 that she would die with the paper; however, semi-retired and with four employees still working on the newspaper, a decision to continue or to close was being forced on her. The Salt Lake County plan to build the Salt Palace on the two blocks on which most of Japan Town existed was to decimate the Japanese community and force the businesses on the two blocks to move to other locations or to close permanently. Very few of the entrepreneurs owned the properties on which they conducted their businesses. Uneo Terasawa had rented the space on a handshake agreement with the owners of the building at the outset and the Utah Nippo Corporation had no more control of the space than the other businesses.

In April 1966, a single flyer announcing the pending move and demolition was passed around the two block area. The flyer did not get around the block to South Temple. As a result, in early May when the demolition contractors appeared to break the building down, the newspaper employees were still working. They did not realize what was going on until things began to fall from the ceiling. Kazuko, who worked with her mother on the paper, immediately went outside to ask what was going on. The building had been sold but the remaining tenant, the newspaper, had not been notified of the sale nor of the pending demolition. The contractor was surprised to find that the building was still occupied, and a separate agreement was made to delay demolition until plans could be made. Demolition did proceed on an adjacent building that caused debris to continue to fall, and the employees joked that cooking pots needed to be worn for protection.

The decision to move to another location or to cease publication now had to be made. The employees' wishes were to continue working for at least another four years until they could retire. Kuniko decided that she would prefer to go on working for as long as possible. Her comment at the time was, "Two weeks are all I need to do what I want to do in the garden and then what can I do!" She and her daughters decided to take whatever resources they had, find a site and build a small building that would hold the necessary equipment and type. One of the employees owned a lot adjacent to his home that he offered as a possible location. Plans were drawn and the ground was broken in early June. The building was compact and efficient. By the middle of July, the structure was completed and the move accomplished. The paper resumed publication not for just four years but as Kuniko had promised in 1939 until her demise twenty-five years later in 1991, at the age of ninety-five. She and the paper outlasted the two employees who had expressed the desire to continue working. She had taken on the picking and setting of type and had become the sole person working on the Japanese portion of the newspaper. Kazuko edited the English section and was responsible for the printing of the paper.

Although a woman who sought little recognition and who did things because it was necessary and right, Kuniko Terasawa became well known both in the United States and in Japan. She was honored locally by both the Japanese American community and the larger community. In 1967, the Japanese government awarded her the "Order of the Sacred Treasure, 5th Class," a medal for service to the Japanese community. In 1987, the Japanese branch of the Avon company awarded her the Avon Grand Award as an outstanding Japanese woman. Avon has established a scholarship for non-traditional students at the University of Utah in her name. She was the first Japanese woman living outside of Japan to be so honored. She appeared on television news programs and had extensive coverage in the print media in the United States and in Japan. She was amused by the publicity she received late in life, saying, "If you live long enough you will get notoriety; unfortunately my husband, who would have enjoyed the acclaim died too early."

Kuniko Terasawa played many roles in her long, productive life. She was a teacher, an expert with a needle, a homemaker, a publisher, a typesetter, a mother and grandmother. In sum, she was a "Jill-of-all-trades" who attempted and succeeded in most things that she found necessary to do. Her broad range of interests that she passed on to her daughters and grandson kept her absorbed in what she considered to be productive activities. Her involvement in the newspaper occupied a great deal of her time; however, opportunities for recreation and activities with her family and friends were also important. A picnic, trips to the National Parks as well as to canyons close to Salt Lake City — Big and Little Cottonwood, the High Uintas, and Millcreek — were on the agenda for summer recreation. During the 1970s she would take the travel time to teach her only grandson, Mikio, old Japanese children's songs that many have forgotten. She found ways to keep him entertained at home and on the road and always had time to spend with him enabling him to grow up understanding Japanese as well as English. She has passed on an important cultural history and an important family tie. These trips were also memorable for the friends, young and old, who shared the occasions. Whenever outings occur today, references are still made to memories of her cooking *sukiyaki*, a regular menu item, over a camp stove.

Kuniko Terasawa's indomitable spirit was evident even late in life. On a trip to Japan in 1985, at age eighty-nine, she visited Expo '85, a high-tech world exposition site, and Tokyo Disneyland. She amazed everyone as she kept pace with her sixteen-year-old grandson as they toured both sites. She was still eager to learn and experience new things, to try anything at least once; and she was not going to be left out of sharing activities with her family. At one stop at Expo, she rode a large Ferris wheel type of conveyance, eighty-five meters in diameter. At the very top, when the wheel stopped to load more passengers, her two nephews who accompanied her became uncomfortable at that height; but as usual, Kuniko took it in stride.

At age eighty-nine, instead of using a shovel to remove a tomato plant, she played tug-of-war with a well-established plant at the end of the season. She lost! She broke her wrist and had to go to a physician to have it taken care of. She observed that he probably thought she was a lost cause. She had rarely had reason to see a doctor before, and she was determined never to see a physician or enter a hospital until she died and needed a death certificate.

She was not concerned about her own mortality; however, one of the most difficult things for her to accept late in life, was the death of a man whose marrige she and her husband had arranged in 1936. At the time of his death, she was the typesetter that she deprecatingly laughed about, saying, "Who would have thought that I, who had been trained to be a seamstress and teacher, would end up being a *katsuji kozo*, a type setter." While she would not admit it, writing the man's obituary and setting the type seemed to be an ordeal for her and she avoided the task for as long as she could.

Kuniko slowed down considerably in the final years of her life. However, she remained active until her passing on August 2, 1991, at the age of ninety-five. She had joined her family and friends on a picnic on the 24th of July in Millcreek Canyon. For the next week, she continued her usual activity of going to the newspaper office and dining with her family. On the day before her death, she went to Haruko's home for dinner as usual; however, this time she had difficulty climbing stairs and even more difficulty going back down after dinner to return to her own home. She had to be helped by both her daughter and her grandson. Kuniko's last words as she got in the car that night were: "When a human being can no longer move under her own power that's the end."

Ivy Baker Priest. Photo courtesy of the Utah State Historical Society.

IVY BAKER PRIEST
Treasurer of the United States

Stanford J. Layton

Stanford J. Layton was raised in Layton, Utah. He completed a bachelor's degree at Iowa State University, served two years in the United States Army, and then returned to Utah for a master's and a doctoral degree from the University of Utah, where he also taught full time for a year. His specialty is the twentieth-century United States with a concentration in political history. Since 1973 he has directed the publications program at the Utah State Historical Society which includes responsibility as managing editor of the Utah Historical Quarterly. *To identify a Utah woman of significance, he returned to his roots. As a boy growing up in Davis County, he took special pride in knowing that a woman from his own county had just been appointed treasurer of the United States.*

"She was a real lady," reflected an acquaintance of Ivy Baker Priest recently, "someone you would always remember."[1] Indeed, for thousands of Utahns who ever had a greenback in their purses or pockets during the Eisenhower years, she was the native daughter known then and remembered since for her distinctive signature on the face of those bills. She was, after all, the treasurer of the United States—only the second woman to hold that title and the first Utah woman appointed to such a high-level office.

Ivy was born in Kimberly, Utah, on September 7, 1905, the first child of Clara Fearnley and Orange Decatur Baker. The child thrived from the beginning. However, Kimberly was not so lucky. That picturesque little central Utah mining community would disappear a few years later, its modest precious metals vein having been exhausted by hard-rock miners who then moved on to other beckonings.[2] But for the future treasurer of the world's richest country, being born atop a gold-silver-lead-copper mine was wonderfully symbolic.

Not that the Baker family ever had much money itself. After a brief sojourn in Grass Creek, near Coalville, the Bakers settled in Bingham, a few miles southwest of Salt Lake City. Orange D. Baker was a miner and machinist who seemed to miss more than his fair share of work from on-the-job accidents and company layoffs. For a time the financial pinch became so tight that the Bakers opened their home to boarders. Young but energetic and willing, Ivy worked hard in the kitchen and dining room before and after school to help the family through those hard times. For her, it was a grand adventure.

In fact, growing up was just one long adventure for this precocious child. She was tall, athletic, and extroverted and therefore something of a leader among her peers. She more than held her own with the most daring of kids in the rough and tumble games of Bingham—jumping from one moving tramcar to another, swinging from the edge of cable-borne ore buckets, and shinnying up the town's many railroad trestles. Her heads-up coaching of her younger brothers in a Fourth of July greased pole climb caught the eye of Congressman E. O. Leatherwood. "Smart girl, you've got, Mrs. Baker," he assured Ivy's mother as he gave the proud girl a politician's hug. "She ought to go into politics."[3]

Indeed, in retrospect, it seems unlikely that Ivy Baker would have ever pursued a career other than politics. Even as a youngster she was gregarious and goal-oriented. Additionally, she had the advantage of a wonderful role model as she grew up—an upbeat, community-involved, and proud mother who involved her in grass-roots politics at an early age. When Clara Baker decided it was high time that Bingham should have sidewalks to spare pedestrians the irritation of walking through the mud—and housekeepers the travail of cleaning it off shoes and floors— none of the town fathers was willing to listen. But after striking an alliance with the town doctor, whom she promised to support in his bid for mayor, she worked diligently to mobilize the women of the community, even helping some to establish citizenship so they could register to vote. Her enthusiastic ten-year-old daughter was kept busy throughout the campaign as an errand girl and babysitter. On election day their hard work paid off, and the good doctor was elected. "I felt as elated as a kingmaker," Ivy later wrote. Bingham soon got its sidewalks, and Clara Baker ever after had a reserved seat on the platform when politicians came to town to make a speech.

In high school Ivy proved herself a diligent student and popular classmate. She was elected to the student council, worked on the student newspaper, served as captain of the debate team, and landed a leading role in the school play. At this point in her life she was already showing a number of personality traits essential to a successful political career. She was confident and full of good humor, being careful not to take herself too seriously or to be unduly bothered by life's little embarrassments. Additionally, she held a certain reverence for hard work. Most important, however, was a characteristic she inherited from her mother. "She knew and liked people," Ivy once said of her. That simple assertion could have easily served as her own epitaph many years later.

After graduating from high school, Ivy hoped to enroll at the University of Utah and pursue a law degree. When her father sadly announced that he could not afford that, her life took a remarkably different turn.[4] Dissatisfied with her job selling tickets at a local theater, she became increasingly receptive to the advances of handsome Harry Hicks. They had met in California the previous summer while she was visiting friends, and he had come to Utah to look her up. The youthful romance blossomed; they were soon married and headed for a new life in North Carolina. But signs of trouble surfaced almost immediately. Harry was not inclined to hold a steady job, was impetuous and sulky, and disdained the thought of having children. After four frustrating years the couple divorced. Ivy returned to Bingham disappointed but not defeated. The experience strengthened her resolve never again to depend on someone else to shape her life. "It was sink or swim on my own," she reflected. Fortunately, with her strength of character and the support of an admiring family, she hardly missed another stroke.

Ivy's return to Utah coincided with the stock market crash. The depression that followed was particularly severe in Utah and especially so within the mining communities. To complicate matters, Orange D. suffered another of his periodic accidents. This time he was hit by a car and suffered a fractured skull. After a lengthy convalescence from that injury he was diagnosed as suffering from silicosis. With mounting medical bills and no breadwinner, the family was forced to mortgage its home and to accept LDS church welfare for a time. Ivy found work as a telephone operator but soon moved to a better paying job as a salesclerk first in Salt Lake City, then in California, then in Salt Lake City again. Bit by bit, hard times eased, though Orange D. was never able to return to work.

The year 1932 was a propitious one for Ivy. First, it marked her plunge into politics beginning with her election as a delegate to the state Republican convention and followed by her elevation to the post of voting district vice-chairman. Second, it witnessed a remarkable blind date with Roy Priest, a short, balding man twenty-one years older than Ivy. He greeted her with a smile "that just warmed up the room," as she described it. Their courtship ran for three years which included Ivy's unsuccessful campaign for election to the state legislature. ("I didn't know whether I was supposed to be winning a bride or an election," Roy later joked.) They were married on December 7, 1935.

Mr. and Mrs. Priest moved to Salt Lake City, where their first child, Patricia Ann, was born. From there they relocated to Bountiful. The sixteen years they spent there can only be described as idyllic. Roy made a comfortable living as a traveling salesman, and Ivy enjoyed her roles as mother and homemaker. The family grew. After Patricia came Peggy Louise, then Nancy Ellen, then Roy Jr. The Priests' one great period of sadness came with the death of fifteen-month-old Peggy Louise, the victim of a congenital heart condition.

Although Ivy had again involved herself in politics—as an officer in the Utah Legislative Council, a nonpartisan women's group—it was not until after the baby's death that she sought a significant responsibility, in part to combat her despondency. Special encouragement came from her concerned mother, who admonished her to get busy with her god-given talents. "To waste them is a great sin," she counselled in her hackneyed English accent. "It's yer trust, and if ye don't use yer talents, ye fail yourself and ye fail God." It was like a mother goose coaxing her gosling to water. Ivy first sought and gained election to the Republican State Central Committee, then in 1943 to the Republican National Committee. She was a tireless party campaign worker in 1946. As a delegate to the national convention in 1948 she supported Dewey's nomination for president, then returned home and campaigned hard for him in his unsuccessful bid for election.

By 1950 Ivy Baker Priest was a well-known name and trusted personality among the Republican party faithful in the state. Not surprisingly, they turned to her as their candidate for congress from the first district that year. Initially reluctant for want of a campaign chest, she soon consented. The race that ensued was noteworthy for featuring two women candidates — a rarity for that time and the only such congressional contest in the nation that year. It was also remarkable for its civility, even though both candidates waged an energetic campaign that featured several face-to-face debates. Early returns on election day put Ivy in the lead, and she continued to hold that position throughout the entire day. Only after midnight, when votes from the northern cities of Davis County came in heavily for Reva Beck Bosone, did the margin turn in favor of the incumbent. Ivy lost by 10,000 votes, but she gained greatly in terms of name recognition and had obviously enjoyed the experience.[5]

The year 1952 was even more eventful. Ivy attended the Republican national convention in Chicago as the only member of the Utah delegation not firm for Taft. She had met Eisenhower earlier that year. "When he smiled and firmly gripped my hand," she later wrote, "I felt as if I'd known him all my life, and a sense of confidence and optimism swept through me." The avuncular Ike must have had reciprocal tinges; shortly after his nomination on the first ballot his campaign director called Ivy and asked her to direct the women's division of the Republican National Committee. Still in grief over the sudden death of her mother, whose stroke had forced her to leave the convention early, she assented. For Ivy Baker Priest, electoral politics was always balm for the soul.

During the hot summer months and into the fall, Ivy worked tirelessly on Eisenhower's campaign. Her schedule can only be described as hectic, flying from one speech appointment to another, making time for radio debates and interviews, organizing grass-roots volunteer groups, raising funds, and paying bills, accompanying the presidential and vice-presidential candidates when asked, helping to formulate strategy, and serving as an ambassador of good will. She was well suited by experience or temperament for all these roles, and the entire campaign was enormously gratifying to her. It was the right time for Eisenhower, but he could not have sailed into the White House without the help of dedicated workers like Ivy. The number of women voting in the 1952 presidential election increased 40 percent over 1948; 52 percent of them marked their ballots for Ike.

Ivy stayed in the East for a month after the election, tying up loose ends, writing thank-you notes, and preparing a final report to the president-elect. She then flew to New York to present the report to him, and it was there that he offered her the job as U.S. treasurer. Although surprised almost to the point of fainting, she accepted on the spot. Within three months the Priests had relocated to Washington, and Ivy was sworn in as the thirtieth treasurer of the United States.

The position of treasurer is not to be confused with the secretary of the treasury. It is not a cabinet-level, policy-making position; but depending on the personality of the appointee and the attitude of the administration, it can be highly visible. Such was to be the case here. The new president recognized that he had an energetic, charismatic, and willing emissary in Ivy Baker Priest. During her eight years at the treasury she proved to be a careful and capable administrator who handled her day-to-day duties efficiently; but perhaps her greatest contribution was in making speeches, attending socials, supporting all manner of state affairs where the presence of a gracious woman was especially needed, and campaigning always for Republican candidates and platforms.[6]

It was a job tailor-made for the personality and talents of this extraordinary woman. Tall and trim at 5' 8 ½" and 140 pounds, dark complexioned, and well poised, she moved easily among these roles and audiences. She wrote her own speeches and always preached the feel-good doctrine of the Eisenhower years in outlining administration objectives: maintaining a sound and stable dollar, cutting expenses, reducing taxes, encouraging greater production while maintaining free markets, and protecting the savings and pensions of old Americans while preserving opportunities for young ones.[7] Her audiences ranged in size "from fifty to fifty thousand persons" and covered the social spectrum from the Commonwealth Club of San Francisco to the most modest neighborhood clubs.

During each major campaign throughout her Washington years, Ivy assumed yeoman duty. As an attractive woman with good name recognition, she was much in demand by candidates around the nation. Typical was the campaign of 1954 which she described as follows: "Sometimes alone, at times accompanied by my secretary, Grayce Abajian, I flew from coast to coast. We would touch down in North Carolina for a day, move on to Alabama where I would shake hands with sixteen hundred ladies at a nonpartisan reception, and then fly on to Tampa to stump for Bill Cramer, candidate for Congress. Then I would head west on a twenty-state swing to the coast—a merry-go-round of riding sound trucks, handshaking, speeches, and autographs."[8]

The pace was even more hectic in 1956 with Ivy pushing herself to the point of physical collapse. She spent most of the final week of that campaign in bed and under a doctor's care. Immediately after the election, she began another strenuous drive, this one as chair of the 1957 Easter Seals campaign. She again exceeded the bounds of physical endurance, and the result was the same. This time she listened to her physician: either slow down or die.

In addition to her administrative, political, and civic responsibilities, Ivy also had a family to worry about. As with the rest of her roles, she handled this one with confidence, care, and commitment. Hers was a picture-book nuclear family, albeit a bit atypical due to its high-profile mother. For the first two years, Roy managed to straddle the continent and the demands of businessman, husband, and father. Following a nonparalytic stroke in 1954, he retired from furniture sales and became a full-time family man. The children thrived. Pat married a young naval officer in a high-society wedding, Nancy took dancing and drama lessons and grew into a young beauty who represented the United States at the International Debutante Ball, and Roy Jr. basked in the limelight of his famous mother and an occasional handshake from President Eisenhower.

Ivy Baker Priest served as U.S. treasurer during the entire eight years of the Eisenhower administration. She retained a busy schedule of speeches and honorary duties through her last day in office. Whether breaking ground for a youth center swimming pool in her beloved Bountiful or touring U.S. military bases to promote savings bonds, she was a smiling and gracious agent of good will. Honors and recognition continued to come her way, including being named "Mother-in-Law of the Year" in April 1959. But she also knew sadness; in June 1959 her devoted husband died of a heart attack at age seventy-five.[9]

It was natural that Ivy would not retire when she left the office of treasurer in 1960. At age fifty-four and free from the demands of family life, she could not walk away from a life of politics and public service that she had always loved. Moving to California, she married Beverly Hills real estate man Sidney Stevens in the summer of 1961 and assisted him with his business. But the challenges of a political campaign and the lure of office continued to call her. In the summer of 1965 she announced her plans to seek election as California state treasurer.

The year-long campaign that followed was vintage Ivy. Changing her name back to Priest for purposes of public recognition, which was a very substantial 22 percent at the outset, she continued to build on her reputation as an experienced money manager. "I think I can safely say that I have handled more money than any woman in the history of the world," she assured her listeners. To keep the press interested, she used such gimmicks as wearing a hat spiked with $1 bills while announcing her candidacy and attempting to throw a silver dollar across the Sacramento River; when the coin plopped in the water a few feet from shore she was ready with the tag line, "A dollar doesn't go very far these days." Her energy, style, and charisma impressed the voters, and on election day she was victorious.[10]

As state treasurer Ivy did not have great latitude in matters of policy, the duties of that office having been strictly proscribed by law. She was able to achieve the consolidation of state bond sales within the treasurer's office, which improved the efficiency of that process, and she oversaw the investment of state monies with great success. For the most part, however, she provided administrative leadership for the office, made speeches in support of the Reagan administration, and took on a large number of civic responsibilities and honorary functions. She served as trustee for the National Society for Crippled Children and Adults, director of the California Easter Seal Society, member of the International Soroptimist Club, director of the Greater Los Angeles Safety Council, and member of the Business and Professional Women's Club.[11]

The year 1970 was another good one for Republicans in California, and Ivy was a person of stature among the voters. Her reelection was assured. Just as she had served eight years as the thirtieth treasurer of the United States, so would she serve eight years as the twenty-fifth treasurer of the state of California. But fate took a harsh turn for her during this final term. First came the death of her son, Roy Jr., in 1971 as the result of a boating accident. This was followed by her husband's death the following year. Then came news that she was suffering from cancer. Although she fought the disease valiantly and was able to finish her second term, she could not consider additional service. Returning to her apartment complex at 10700 Santa Monica Boulevard in Westwood, she was frequently seen by her neighbors, for whom she always had a smile and friendly greeting, as she strolled down the walks and around the fountain for a little exercise. Her big white Lincoln, with its distinctive "IVY 107" license plates, spent more and more time in the carport.[12]

Ivy Baker Priest died June 23, 1975. Her public and charitable service spanned a third of a century, won her the admiration of a nation, and defined a legacy of achievement truly extraordinary for a woman of that era. Although the dollar bills that once bore her signature have long since disappeared from circulation, her name is secure in the annals of history.

Esther Rosenblatt Landa, newly elected national president of the National Council of Jewish Women, delivering her acceptance speech at the closing banquet of the convention in San Francisco. Photo courtesy of Esther Landa.

ESTHER ROSENBLATT LANDA
Her Price Is Far above Rubies

Robert A. Goldberg

Dr. Robert Goldberg has been a professor of history at the University of Utah since 1980. His teaching and research field is twentieth-century America with a focus on the American West, social, and political history. He has won five teaching awards and is the author of four books: Hooded Empire: The Ku Klux Klan in Colorado; Back to the Soil: The Jewish Farmers of Clarion, Utah, and Their World; Grass Roots Resistance: Social Movements in Twentieth Century America; *and* Barry Goldwater. *He says, "Esther Landa was an easy choice for she is not only the leading woman of the Utah Jewish Community but has played a vital role in matters of education, politics, service, and women's rights in the larger city, state, and national arenas."*

When Jews the world over recognize the selflessness and courage of a woman, they often turn to Proverbs: 31 to recite the following verses:

> A woman of valor who can find?
> For her price is far above rubies . . .
> Strength and dignity are her clothing;
> And she laugheth at the time to come.
> She openeth her mouth with wisdom;
> And the law of kindness is on
>   her tongue.

Utah, too, has produced its Jewish women of valor. First among them is Esther Landa. For six decades she has volunteered herself to public service, answering the call of her community, people, and nation. In length and breadth of activities she has few rivals. The tasks of the volunteer are often thankless and unacknowledged. It is time to mark her contributions:

> Give her of the fruit of her hands;
> And let her works praise her in the gates.
> (Proverbs: 31)

Esther was born in Salt Lake City on December 25, 1912, the first-born of Simon and Sylvia Rosenblatt, long-time Utah residents. Esther's grandfather Nathan had left Poland in 1885 and journeyed to Denver before arriving in Salt Lake City four years later. Beginning as a horse-and-wagon peddler, he and his sons built up their business, the profitable Utah Junk Company, which developed into EIMCO, an international corporation. Simon, a leading businessman, provided well for his family, and Esther and her siblings Barbara and Bernard enjoyed comfort and security.

Much, however, was expected of Esther for her parents did not raise her for a life of leisure. While Simon's formal education ended when he left school at an early age to help in his father's business, he held her to high scholarly standards. Esther did not disappoint him. She attended public schools in Salt Lake City and twice skipped a half grade to graduate at age sixteen from East High School.[1]

A religious education was another Rosenblatt requirement. Simon Rosenblatt sent his oldest daughter to the religious school of Orthodox Congregation Montifiore, which his father Nathan had helped to found. This was a formative time for Esther. Her identity took shape as she absorbed the history and culture of the Jewish people. She also internalized values from the Five Books of Moses that would be her guiding lights: "If you ever were to read all my speeches, every speech is inspired by the same ideals, 'to do justice, to love mercy, to walk humbly with God.' "[2] Esther's mother and father reinforced these precepts in their daily lives. They encouraged their children to assume a responsibility to help those less fortunate than themselves. Both were actively involved as volunteers in Jewish groups and the wider community. For example, Simon was a member of the Zionist Society of America, the Rotary Club, Masons, and Shriners. Often, he left work to play the piano for the sick children confined to the Shriners' wing at the old St. Mark's hospital. Sylvia joined the Jewish Relief Society and the synagogue sisterhood. They instilled in Esther, by word and deed, a sense of service, an imperative "to give something back."[3]

Esther confronted few barriers growing up as a Jew in Mormon Utah. In fact, the handful of Salt Lake City Jews fit easily into this philo-Semitic world. The Mormons see Jews as Biblical brethren descended from Joseph, their mutual patriarch. A recent history of midwestern pogroms, an exodus across the Mississippi River into the western wilderness, and the settlement in a promised land with its own dead sea confirmed in Mormon minds a similar chosen destiny. Latter-day Saints are, as well, fervent zionists, predicting in accordance with ancient covenant and prophecy the eventual gathering of the Jews in Israel. Because conversion of the Jews was expected to occur only after their return, Mormon proselytizing efforts are inconsequential. Jews had long participated actively in Utah economic, social, and cultural affairs. A Jew, Simon Bamberger, would be elected governor of Utah just a few years after Esther's birth, continuing a tradition of service in state and local government. Esther fondly recalls her childhood as "the good life," free of any hint of anti-Semitism. She was active in school politics and well liked by her classmates. They remember her with affection as reflective, quiet, and the "smartest girl in the class."[4] Even though her closest friends were Jewish and her "tomboy" behavior acted to insulate her from schoolgirl cliques, she never felt "excluded."[5]

On graduation from East High in 1929, Esther Rosenblatt enrolled at Mills, a women's college in California. Her years there would prove life-shaping. Esther worked hard at her studies and earned a bachelor of arts degree and a Phi Beta Kappa key. Yet the influence of Mills went beyond the lessons of the classroom. Away from home for the first time, she encountered the "independent women" of the Mills faculty.[6] To Esther, they stood in sharp contrast to her mother, a "traditional" woman who never learned how to drive a car. "I had good female role models," she remembers. "You could be an achiever there."[7] This sense of personal efficacy was not solely academic. She credits her professors with nurturing her belief that individual activism can bring fundamental social and economic change.

When Esther left Mills in 1933, America was submerged in the Great Depression. Thousands of banks had failed, businesses across the nation had gone bankrupt, and nearly twenty-five percent of American workers were unemployed. Such circumstances further exacerbated women's already-restricted opportunities in the work place. "It wasn't fashionable then," declared Esther, "for a woman to go into business. We had a family business, but I wasn't encouraged to join."[8] Although cushioned by her family's resources and never experiencing hard times, she had few options. She remembers, "You had a BA, you had a Phi Beta Kappa key, you graduated with honors, but unless you could type, forget it."[9] Thus, Esther enrolled in a business college in Salt Lake City to learn the requisite secretarial skills to compete in the market place. Also during the thirties, convinced that the educational process was never completed, Esther Rosenblatt returned to Mills College to earn her master of arts degree in English literature.[10]

Networking through her Mills College connections, she parlayed her new skills into opportunities. Esther did public relations work for her alma mater and then moved east to seek, as she jokingly put it, "fame and fortune."[11] She worked at Bennington College in Vermont and later as an account executive for a New York City public relations firm.

In light of future loyalties, it is curious that during the depression Esther voted Republican and opposed President Franklin Roosevelt and his New Deal. Perhaps her successes in the work place strengthened her commitment to political conservatism. Surely, they firmed her belief in self reliance and individual responsibility, values instilled in her as a child. Family and socio-economic status also influenced political choice. Her parents were spared the trauma of the depression and had maintained their allegiance to the Republican party. Only later would Esther Rosenblatt turn to the Democratic party and become one of its most determined partisans.

The coming of World War II summoned Esther, as it did millions of Americans, to national service. She resigned her position in New York

City soon after the bombing of Pearl Harbor and went to Washington, D.C., where she worked as a mail sorter, stenographer, and then information specialist for the Office of Production Management, which later became the Office of War Information. Although "not the dating kind," Esther began seeing Jerry Landa, whom she had met previously through her Mills College connections.[12] Landa, from Texas and in the millinery business, was now serving with the Army Air Corps. They married in September 1943, shortly before Jerry's unit was shipped overseas. The couple's first child, Carol, was born in August of the following year.[13]

With the war's end, the Landas resumed their life together. Jerry Landa's firm sent him to Tulsa, Oklahoma. "Not really interested in sewing, cooking, and housekeeping," Esther looked for an outlet for her energies.[14] With the support of her husband, she found it in community service and became active in the League of Women Voters, the American Association of University Women, and the Tulsa County Public Health Association's drive to fund tuberculosis research.[15]

These diverse activities did not distract her from a commitment to Jewish causes. For Esther and American Jewry there have been three significant facts of life since World War II—the holocaust, the rebirth of Israel, and assimilation. Between 1939 and 1945, one-third of the world's Jewish population was butchered. The loss of the six million vitally shaped Jewish social, cultural, and religious perceptions. On the ashes of the holocaust the Jewish future was rebuilt. Jewish men and women reified the promise of "next year in Jerusalem" when they hoisted a star of David over the city in 1948. After a quest of almost two millennia, a homeland and haven had been restored in the land of Israel. Triumph in the American golden land, meanwhile, has presented Jews their greatest dilemma. The passing of the immigrant generation and the acculturation and assimilation of later generations have profoundly shaped the Jewish experience.

In the face of these challenges, Esther Landa acted and her Jewish identity strengthened. The memory of the holocaust, as for many Jews, was deeply etched in her mind. She was determined to combat any recurrence of the anti-Semitism that spawned it. Landa later remarked: "That's why we don't keep still now. If we have something to say, we say it."[16] She continued her work with Hadassah, a Jewish women's philanthropic organization, and the United Jewish Appeal. She also assumed a leadership position in the National Council of Jewish Women (NCJW), a group founded in 1893 to foster social action and community service on educational, welfare, child care, and women's issues. NCJW also set as key priorities the enhancement of Jewish life in America and support for the state of Israel. In this vein, perhaps it was President Harry Truman's strong commitment to Israel that moved Esther finally into the Democratic party fold.[17]

The death of Simon Rosenblatt in 1948 led the Landas to relocate to Salt Lake City to be closer to family. Jerry joined the city's business community as manager of a chain of millinery stores and later owned a wholesale house of his own. The Landas now counted a second child, Howard, born in Tulsa, with a third, Terry Ellen, soon to make her appearance. Returning to her home town, Esther not only resumed her volunteer work but accelerated it. She was involved in the Anti-Defamation League, Hadassah (becoming chapter president), the National Council of Jewish Women, and the Salt Lake Jewish Welfare Fund. She joined the Synagogue B'nai Israel sisterhood and in 1948 chaired the women's campaign for Israel. Esther did not neglect other concerns. She became a member and later president of the League of Women Voters. For two years, she served as the vice president of the Salt Lake area United Fund.[18]

In 1958, Esther Landa decided to run for a position on the Salt Lake City school board. Operating out of her basement, she conducted a successful campaign that made her only the second woman in the community's history to secure the post.[19] On the board she worked hard to convince members to seek federal dollars to bolster schools. Items high on her agenda were increasing aid to inner city schools, decreasing class size, raising teacher salaries, and expanding the program of adult education. The fight against racial and religious bigotry and discrimination was also given high priority. As she later summed up her goals: "Equal education for all."[20] Voters rewarded her efforts with two more four-year terms and then elected her twice to the Utah State Board of Education (1970 and 1972). Related to these efforts, Esther was a co-founder of the Utah Head Start Program, designed to prepare preschoolers for primary education, and vice-chair of the Community Action Program, a War on Poverty agency. Such activities, along with her other service projects would garner Esther the Utah State Bar's Liberty Bell Award (1963), the American Association of University Women Award (1965), and the Civil Rights Worker of the Year Award from the National Association for the Advancement of Colored People (1968).[21]

Esther Landa made one bid for political office, running for nomination as a state senator in the Democratic primary in 1964. In her campaign, she advocated consumer protection laws, women's rights, educational reform, support of the civil rights movement, and opposition to political extremism. Apparently, these positions proved too progressive for Utah Democrats and she was defeated.[22]

The women's rights plank in her platform was more than a reflection of a changing national agenda. It also indicated Esther's enhanced focus on a theme that has animated her life. In response to women's raised consciousness of their second-class citizenship, John Kennedy established in 1961 the President's Commission on the Status of Women. He charged the commissioners to examine the economic, social, and legal position of American women and make recommendations that would redress disparities and foster equal treatment. The commissioners' report recommended that women be allowed equal access to educational institutions and that they receive opportunities similar to those granted men in hiring, job training, and promotion. In light of women's multiple roles, commission members invited businesses to offer their employees paid maternity leaves and the government to expand child care services and supports. The report concluded with a call to women to enter politics and end their invisibility in government.

In the federal wake, state forums were created to discuss the problems of women at the local level. In 1962, Esther Landa helped organize and served as co-director of the University of Utah's state-wide conference on the changing role of women in a changing society. Two years later she directed a second meeting of Utah women. At the conferences, women drew attention to inequalities in economic, educational, and political spheres. Reviews of state statutes prompted calls for repeal of laws limiting women's property, legal, and economic rights. Such gatherings did more than generate a series of recommendations. They legitimized women's complaints of sexual inequality and raised the salience of the issue. A body of evidence now existed to substantiate claims of discrimination, to clarify targets, and to set a future course. From these bases networks of feminists grew to absorb women in labor unions, professions, private industry, the media, and universities. On common interests and through friendships, feminists erected in the states and through the nation the scaffolding critical to the construction of a women's movement.[23]

As the Director of Women's Programs in the University of Utah's Division of Continuing Education (1964–1969), Esther Landa was in a position to advance an equal rights agenda. To facilitate learning, she introduced special classes in the humanities for women. She also was instrumental in organizing management institutes for business women. Even more important was her role in chairing a faculty-community committee to survey educational opportunities at the university. In a wide-ranging investigation, the committee studied the status of women on campus, spotlighting disparities in curriculum, athletics, student aid, and faculty hiring and salary. One result of her committee's work was the creation of the University of Utah Women's Resource Center designed to enhance the educational experiences of women and men by providing programs, counseling referral, and information. Through these activities the center seeks to foster a better understanding of women's issues among the student body, faculty, staff, and the wider community.[24]

Critical life-changing events in the early 1970s led Esther Landa to shift her energies to activities beyond Utah's borders. Husband Jerry, who had long supported her service work, died in May 1971. The Landa children were now grown and had begun lives of their own. The end of her term on the state board of education in 1974 left her free to consider national opportunities. She found her calling as president of the National Council of Jewish Women. The NCJW, the oldest Jewish women's volunteer organization in the United States, enrolled over 100,000 members in 200 communities. Esther's election as president in 1975 and reelection two years later were the culmination of twenty-nine years of NCJW service in local, district, regional, and national leadership positions. Still, it was remarkable that someone from so small a Jewish community as Salt Lake City could rise to lead so prestigious an organization. Clearly, it testified to the high esteem in which members held her.[25]

President Landa wasted little time in enunciating her aims. In her acceptance speech she reminded members that as Jews they had a special obligation to respect the "infinite value, dignity, and sanctity of life." Translating this into concrete issues, she called attention to the central concerns of the times: the threat of nuclear war, overpopulation, pollution, and hunger. Esther recommitted the organization to justice for children and service to the aging. Women's rights, which she described as "a movement toward human liberation," meant support for displaced homemakers, an expansion of child care options, prevention of domestic violence, and an end to stereotyping and tokenism. She did not neglect the international scene and asserted American Jewry's common fate with Soviet Jews and the people of Israel.[26]

She was no figurehead president. Esther moved quickly to restore the fiscal health of NCJW by fixing a moratorium on spending and assigning greater emphasis to fundraising. Eager to keep in touch with the local chapters and maintain contacts around the world, she traveled 100,000 miles and gave scores of speeches during her presidency. Her message was always consistent and reached back to the words of the Biblical prophets that she had learned as a child. For example, in a talk in Johannesburg, South Africa, she eloquently declared not only the mission of her organization but the meaning of being a Jew: "We are commanded to redeem the captive, care for the poor, bury the dead, visit the sick, educate the young. Every institution in the Jewish community is predicated upon these values. . . . To give is to show our humaneness — to give of our feelings, deeds, time, money — to give beyond ourselves — that is the authentically Jewish experience."[27]

She reiterated, as well, the mission of her generation in the face of the challenges of its time: "It will profit us little to support Israel in the present, if we are not building a basis for the future of Israel. How can we build that foundation without support for our Jewish educational institutions, our synagogues, our schools. . . . If we in the Diaspora are not strong we will not have the means to support Israel in the future. And how do we remain strong? Only through the strength of our local communities."[28]

While her efforts as NCJW president had an unquestionable women's rights emphasis, Esther was even more directly involved on other fronts in the battle for equality. Esther was a strong advocate of ratification of the Equal Rights Amendment (ERA), lobbying the Utah State Legislature unsuccessfully for passage. In the face of the counter-attack on the Supreme Court's Roe v. Wade decision, she assumed a determined pro-choice stand. Planned Parenthood, Utahns for Choice, and the Women's Equity Action League counted her as a member. None of this made Esther, in her words, "a flaming feminist." Rather she was someone who simply believed that women should have the "same choices and opportunities that men have."[29]

In recognition of her prominence and activities on the state and national levels, Esther Landa was invited in 1977 to chair the Utah conference on women's issues. The meeting, preliminary to a national gathering in Houston, Texas, of delegates from the fifty states, was an event in the United Nations proclaimed International Women's Year. At Houston, delegates would set forth America's positions on women's rights, health, and economic and educational opportunities. Landa expected the Utah gathering to be a quiet affair attended by a few hundred women who would reaffirm support for equal opportunities, choice, and the ERA. That expectation was quickly shattered as more than 13,000 conservative women flooded the convention and under the direction of their male leaders methodically voted down every resolution in support of equal rights. Only in their opposition to pornography could liberals and conservatives find common ground. Despite the ideological chasm between them, Landa won the respect of the conservatives. Fair minded and even tempered, her leadership kept the proceedings from degenerating into a free-for-all of bitter name-calling and recrimination. The affair disturbed Landa: "It brought out in the open the latent prejudices of right-wing Utahns toward feminists, minorities, and any who don't hold their views. . . . It really broke the hearts and spirits of many." Still, her democratic instincts were assuaged. The results, she believed, reflected what the majority thinks and feels, "whether we like it or not."[30]

Esther was not elected by the Utah women to represent them at Houston but, because of her national reputation, she gained a seat as a delegate at large. In Houston, she stood in the majority and a progressive platform was approved. Esther basked in the victory because she saw it as a defining moment: "It was a great meeting because . . . it was cultural pluralism, intellectual pluralism, all the good things about our country were there and all different points of view were represented."[31]

In 1980, Esther Landa attended the United Nations second conference of the International Women's Decade in Copenhagen, Denmark, as a member of the U.S. delegation. She expected the gathering to focus on such issues as education, health, female infanticide, domestic violence, and poverty. Instead, she and Jewish feminists were stunned when the conference was "hijacked" by supporters of the Palestine Liberation Organization who advocated a U.N. resolution which equated Zionism with racism.[32] Ideological difference mutated into personal vendetta. According to Letty Cottin Pogrebin, who also attended the conference, Jewish women "were isolated, excoriated, and tyrannized." Her Jewish consciousness was raised: "So this is what it means to be a Jew in the world."[33] Esther Landa confirmed Pogrebin: "Everyone of us who was there was irrevocably changed by the experience—we were obsessed by it—some of us even suffered psychic trauma." Rather than immobilizing Esther, the experience further energized her. She called, for example, for a "tripling" of efforts to save Soviet Jews: "We must focus on the emigration issue like never before. We must turn the spotlight on those in prison, on the Refusniks, on the harassment they are suffering."[34] Also reconfirmed in her mind was the paramount need to safeguard the security of Israel.

After an assignment on President Jimmy Carter's Committee for a National Agenda for the Eighties, Esther again made Utah her base for activism. Although in her seventies, she showed no sign of slowing down. During the 1980s, she participated in Utahns against the Nuclear Arms Race, an educational group that warned of the dangers of nuclear war. For Esther, peace work was the legacy one generation leaves to another: "Yes, we believe that the Lord is the giver of peace. Peace will not be handed to us on a silver platter. We must work for it. . . . For the sake of my children and grandchildren—and their children—and all of you and your families—those here on earth now and those yet to come."[35] She continued to be active in feminist causes and served in the Utah Domestic Violence Council, Equal Rights Coalition of Utah, National Organization for Women, Salt Lake Council of Women, Utah Women's Forum, Women's Legal Defense Fund, and Women's Equity

Action League. In speeches she scolded America for ignoring the gender gap in salaries, the rise of pink collar ghettoes that kept women confined to low paying, dead-end jobs, the plight of single parents, the inadequacy of day care facilities, and the feminization of poverty. It was time, she insisted, "to make the slogan 'life, liberty, and the pursuit of happiness' a reality for all of us."[36]

The growing danger from extremists roused Esther as well, causing her to sound the alarm and reiterate her vision of the national purpose: "We should," she contended, "be committed to the *idea* of America, which is not blind patriotism or nationalism, but that we are an open, pluralistic democracy . . . that groups with different interests and different points of view should negotiate with one another in the market place of ideas and play politics under the accepted rules of the game."[37] Politically, Esther remains a strong liberal and a fierce Democrat. She has been continuously active in local and national campaigns and is especially determined to see women win their rightful share of seats in government.

Even with this plethora of activities, Esther still devotes herself to the Utah Jewish community, which absorbs her energies in a variety of organizations. She is in the vanguard of defenders of the state of Israel yet tuned to local concerns of anti-Semitism, assimilation, and project funding. Of particular interest to her are the needs of the Russian Jews and she is deeply involved in immigration and resettlement matters.

Esther Landa, now in her eighties and slowed somewhat by arthritis, is not content to rest on a lifetime of achievement. This self-described "widow, mother, grandmother, busybody, buttinsky" remains focused on her still unfinished agenda.[38] Racism and sexism still haunt America and while the national consciousness has been raised, she fears that "we're losing a lot of the gains that we made."[39] If young professional and business women have made strides, she insists that there has been "little progress" for those in service industries.[40] Esther shares the common concern of American Jewry for the continuity of Jewish life in America and hopes her grandchildren will embody the basic principles which have guided her life: "to do justice, to love mercy, to walk humbly with God." Her eye is also fixed on the Middle East, where Israel and its neighbors are entering a new era of negotiations that may prove as dangerous as their time of war. Still, she is infused with a powerful sense of purpose that convinces her that women and men will respond to reason and bring necessary change. Esther asks only that people recognize their common humanity: "Don't stereotype me as a woman. Don't stereotype me as a Jew. Just talk to me as Esther."[41]

Helen Zeese Papanikolas. Photo courtesy of Helen Z.
Papanikolas.

18

HELEN ZEESE PAPANIKOLAS
A Unique Voice in America

Miriam B. Murphy

This biography of Helen Zeese Papanikolas is Miriam Murphy's second contribution to this book, the first being her discussion of the life and poetry of Sarah Elizabeth Carmichael. This entry is also unique in that the subject is also a contributor; Papanikolas recorded the contributions of Georgia Lathouris Mageras, better known as Magerou, the Greek midwife. Papanikolas is well known as Utah's premier ethnic historian and the nation's expert on Greek immigrants. Murphy outlines here the intellectual and emotional process which led Papanikolas to this field of study, where she, in turn, has led many others.

> For whatever one has said well goes forth with a voice that never dies.
>
> —Pindar

The biographer of Helen Zeese Papanikolas faces a daunting task. The subject herself has already related parts of her life in such a compelling way that retelling them from another point of view seems useless, at least until greater historical distance has been achieved. I propose, therefore, to draw heavily on Helen's published writings and to thrust the reader immediately into Greek community life in Utah in the second decade of the twentieth century.[1] It is crucial to understand the milieu

243

in which Helen was raised, for it alone can illuminate the character and accomplishments of the mature woman.

Born on June 29, 1917, in Cameron (presently Royal), Carbon County, Helen was the second child of Greek immigrants Emily Papachristos and George Zeese.[2] A few months after her birth the family moved to Helper—railroad hub of the adjacent coal mining camps—with its diverse population of Italian, Serb, Croat, Slovene, Greek, Irish, and Japanese immigrants as well as Americans (including Mormons and a few African Americans). The Zeeses lived in half of a two-family white frame house, one of several built by an Italian farmer, Joe Bonacci. Here Helen learned to recognize the different whistles of passenger and freight steam engines, jumped the rope on hard dirt in the backyard, listened as neighborhood women came to her mother's kitchen to have their dreams interpreted, and heard songs that her father and his friends sang of their Greek ancestors rebelling against the Turks.

While Helen was absorbing the rich folk traditions of Greek village life, she was also exposed to aspects of "American" culture through Sarah "Killarney" Reynolds, wife of an Irish railroad worker and "the most frequent visitor" to Emily Zeese's kitchen. Reynolds introduced the family to American cooking—lemon meringue pies, Parker House rolls, fruitcakes, raisin oatmeal cookies—which the children thought far superior to Greek honey and nut sweets. And it was Mrs. Reynolds, Helen recollects, "who told our mother to send us to the YMCA Sunday School . . . and about visiting days at the Helper grade school, about American customs, about cures for childhood illnesses." Reynolds even suggested giving Helen's older sister Panaghiota (named for the Virgin, the All-Holy) an American name—Josephine.[3] It seems clear that "Killarney" Reynolds was a key figure for Emily Zeese in the process of acculturating to the American way of life, since married Greek women had few opportunities to mingle with others outside of home and church.

Although Helen felt secure within her immediate environs, she wrote that "beyond, all kinds of danger lay waiting: German shepherd dogs with bared fangs, owned by railroad families to keep tramps away; big, white-haired, white-eyelashed American-Mormon boys; dark, angry-faced boys from Wop Town; and other vague dangers that roused fears in my stomach." When Mormon and Italian boys shouted epithets and mocked each other's religion, Mrs. Bonacci came out of the house waving her broom and scattered them with "her torrent of South-Italian dialect." Helen learned early to keep the cross her godfather had given her at baptism hidden inside her collar.[4]

Other events that would shape the future historian and chronicler of Greek American life began in the summer of 1922: "Twice in the hot, dusty summer that I turned five years of age, I stood with my silent mother and looked out the living room window. The first time a black hearse went by slowly, and a line of open touring cars followed. . . . Inside . . . sat black-dressed men and women holding . . . blue and white flags. I knew instinctively they were of us—Greeks—and that the flags were Greek. The second time we watched soldiers . . . marching down the road. . . . Unshaven miners looked on."[5]

Years later Helen would realize the full import of what she had seen. Striking miners, many of them Greek, had joined a nationwide coal strike and protested wage cuts they were forced to accept even though coal prices remained the same. In the ensuing violence a deputy sheriff and a Greek miner were killed, and "the National Guard and townspeople rampaged through Greek coffeehouses, boardinghouses, and stores."[6]

Of more immediate concern to the young girl, however, was the beginning of the school year, which she describes with her usual flair for the telling of detail:

> Two months later I trotted at my sister Jo's side to my first day of school. Our mother sent us early "to get a good start." All summer long in the Bonacci court I had heard about two black girls pouring kerosene near the school staircase and throwing a match on it; of an Italian mother dragging a teacher by the hair to the school yard and beating her for sending her daughter to the principal who had left welts on her back with a rubber hose; of that dangerous place called the lavatory where the most terrible of all four-letter words was scratched on the gray-painted windows and metal stalls; and of the monstrous thing called

recess where Americans and Mormons stood on one side of no
man's land and immigrant children on the other, shouting and
daring each other to cross over.

Inside the squat brick schoolhouse, I followed Jo down
the hall thundering with the footsteps and voices of children. Jo
pointed out my room. Two teachers with marcelled hair banged
on the desk and ordered us to take turns standing and giving our
names. The teachers then looked at each other and said either
"High" or "Low." My sister, as the daughter of a businessman,
had been put in the High the year before. Quaking, I said my
name and one of the teachers said, "Low." When the teachers
finished their pronouncements, we of the Low, mostly miners'
children, American girls in faded ginghams too short or too
long, immigrant girls in homemade dresses, and boys in old
bib overalls, were told to follow one of the teachers into another
room. There I broke into sobs at my disgrace. The teacher put
me in a closet and shut the door.

. . . It took me five years to work into the High.[7]

Although the children of immigrants quickly assimilated, Greek
immigrant parents strove to perpetuate the Greek language, culture,
and Orthodox religion in their offspring. Helen hid her Greek books in
the back of her desk at the elementary school, but the other children
knew where their Greek classmates went after school and taunted them.
Greek school was held in various Helper buildings, including the railroad chapel and a former butcher shop. In rooms that steamed in the
summer and chilled to the bone in the winter, the children "struggled
to learn a purist Greek" they never heard spoken. Sometimes Helen felt
angry about having to attend Greek school, especially when her best
friend, Helen Barboglio, the daughter of an Italian immigrant father
and an American mother, was free to play after school. "Of all aspects
of our culture, attending Greek school made us feel most different from
others," Helen wrote.[8]

But Greek Town and the YMCA provided safe havens for children like Helen Zeese. Greek Town, with its small houses surrounded by
vegetable gardens, sheds for coal and wood and laundry, rabbit hutches

and chicken coops, and outdoor ovens for baking bread, seemed a festive place when the Greek women held "bounteous open houses for their
husbands and sons on their name days." Helen remembers that there was
always a "warm, yeasty scent of baking bread . . . over Greek Town, and
mothers were quick to cut us large pieces and slather them with butter.
The admonition we heard from our mother daily came with the offering:
'Bread is holy! If you drop it, make the sign of the cross and kiss it before
eating. If it can't be eaten, bring it to me to burn. Never throw bread
in the garbage! Bread is holy!' "[9] This was but one of many proverbial
messages Greek parents repeated to their children.

When Helen and her sisters began attending the YMCA Sunday
School on the advice of Mrs. Reynolds, others soon began to send their
children. Here they learned Protestant hymns and of a blond, blue-eyed
"American Jesus" who presented a marked contrast to the "dark, grieving Christ" of Orthodoxy. The Y also provided a selection of books that
the youngsters could take home to read.[10]

As her father prospered in business he moved his family to a larger
home with a clear view of the railroad tracks that brought passenger cars
and their well dressed occupants close enough to see from a window of
the house and where Helen "learned the colors and insignia of all the
freight lines." Of greater significance to her development as a writer and
historian was the cultural imprinting that took place here:

> In this second Bonacci house I came to know that Easter
> was the most important day of the year, that every day led in-
> exorably to it. . . . Fasting began in earnest two weeks before
> Easter for us; other families fasted the traditional forty days
> . . . in memory of Christ's shedding his blood. Nothing that
> came from blooded animals was allowed: milk, eggs, cheese,
> yogurt. Many Greek families lived on beans, lentils, and greens;
> some mothers would not even use olive oil because it was holy.
> Our food was bread, pickled peppers, squid with rice, spinach
> with rice, beans with rice, lentil and bean soups, and for some-
> thing sweet, *halvah*, crushed sesame seeds mixed with honey
> to form a nougatlike confection. To still hunger between meals
> we munched on dried, salted chick peas. . . . I lived on peanut

butter sandwiches. My father and other Greek men did not fast as their families did. There was a vague dictate that men worked hard and needed meat, eggs, and cheese for strength.

Holy Week came and there was no playing at all, no listening to the new . . . radio or the hand-cranked Victrola. The green blinds were pulled down. Mourning sighed in the house. Outside Mormon children played and called to one another, and never was the chasm so wide and so deep between them and us than at Easter.[11]

As the somber events of Christ's last days were commemorated, Holy Week moved toward its liturgical conclusion just after midnight on Easter Sunday when in the darkened church the priest carried forward a candle and individuals lighted their own candles from it until "the church was ablaze with hundreds of swaying flames. Louder and louder the people sang the song of Resurrection. . . . Then we were home, the dining room crowded with unmarried men who lived in hotels. The joy in the house shimmered and would not die," Helen remembers.[12]

Darker memories came to the young girl when in 1924 the Castle Gate mine disaster claimed 172 lives, 50 of them Greek. And in 1925 a revived Ku Klux Klan burned a cross in the Helper rail yards and warned "White girls" not to work for Greeks. George Zeese quickly brought two of his cousins from Nevada as bodyguards to watch over his daughters.[13]

Neither the Klan nor economic hard times deterred George Zeese in his quest for financial stability and comfort for his family. He built a large brick house in a Helper neighborhood dotted with the homes of doctors, lawyers, and businessmen like himself. "We were climbing farther up the fabled ladder America provided immigrants," Helen wrote, leaving behind the privies, chicken coops, and outdoor ovens of her early childhood.[14]

By 1933, with a crippling coal strike in the Carbon County mines and the depression casting its darkest shadows, the family was living in Salt Lake City where George Zeese opened the first of an eventual eleven grocery stores in his Success Market chain. Helper's Greek Town lay a hundred miles southeast of the Utah capital, but for the teenage Helen at East High School it never faded from memory. Her formative years in Carbon County had already shaped her life in direct, tangible ways. Almost fifty years later she wrote:

> Today almost all of the Greek Town people are gone. The Greek language is heard less often. Proverbs are seldom used to instruct, to moralize. Bread is thrown into the garbage. The grandchildren of Ku Kluxers and immigrants have married each other. But the faces of those Greek Town mothers and fathers remain deep in my memory, not as they were in their feeble years but as they were in their short-lived era as young matriarchs and patriarchs. A literary critic has complained that the characters in the novels of the great Greek novelist Nikos Kazantzakis are bigger than life. That critic would have known better if he had lived in Greek Town.[15]

Through Helen's powerful, evocative writing—both nonfiction and fiction—those matriarchs and patriarchs of vanished Greek Towns continue to live in our histories and our hearts.

From a modest home on Thirteenth East (smaller than the one the family left in Helper), Helen began a typical adolescent/young adult quest to identify goals and fulfill dreams. Although the Zeeses lived across town from Salt Lake City's ethnic enclaves, they remained immersed in Greek tradition and lore. In differing ways both parents maintained age-old customs that dictated their responsibilities toward extended family members and social relationships within the Greek community. Helen and her sisters took an active part in a Greek girls' club, and Helen wrote skits for the club to perform on Mother's Day. But she soon found study and school work an effective excuse to offer her mother for missing club meetings and ceremonial name-day visits. Good grades—she received mostly A's—were a necessity for reasons other than personal and family pride: Helen's goal was to become a medical doctor. She had been inspired to seek a career in medicine by the example of the four mining town doctors in her Helper neighborhood.[16]

Although she enrolled at the University of Utah in the basic science classes she would need, Helen could not neglect the inner drive that led her toward literature and writing. She wrote well enough that Professor Sidney W. Angleman encouraged her to consider seriously a career in writing. Nevertheless, she had to follow her medical dream to its conclusion. It took her to Northwestern University in her junior year, but she felt homesick and dissecting even invertebrate animals made her queasy. She returned to the University of Utah, graduating in bacteriology in 1939, but nonacademic activities reflect her true destiny.

Yearbook photographs reveal Helen as a tall, slender, fashionably attired young woman with a serious, almost remote, expression that carefully limited what the camera was allowed to capture. It is, one cannot help but believe, the persona of the young writer not the young scientist that one sees. By the 1937–38 academic year Helen had worked her way up to associate editor of *Pen*, the University of Utah literary magazine. The editor that year was Richard Scowcroft, future novelist and assistant director of Stanford University's prestigious creative writing program. Serving as assistant editor was Dale L. Morgan, who would have a distinguished career as a historian of the West. It is doubtful that *Pen* ever had a more brilliant editorial trio at its helm.[17]

During her senior year Helen advanced to the post of *Pen* editor. Still, upon graduation, she felt obliged to use her new skills to serve the community. ("I wish I had focused on writing earlier," she would later remark.) With her degree in bacteriology she found employment as a medical technologist at the old Salt Lake County Hospital at 21st South and State Streets. Although her job left little free time for writing, it exposed her to situations and characters that fuel a writer's imagination. She would never forget, for example, the administrator who demanded and received sexual favors from an employee who, he knew, was too poor to risk losing her job. The hospital was a world unto itself, but one Helen would not remain in for long. On January 26, 1941, she married Nick E. Papanikolas of Magna, Utah, who had graduated from the University of Utah with a degree in business in 1939. They would have two children, Zeese and Thalia.

A superb cook and a meticulous housekeeper, having been well schooled by her mother, Helen fulfilled the role of wife and mother that both Greek and American tradition required. She and her sisters "tended each other's children" and also helped their mother with the dinners she provided for lonely soldiers stationed at Utah's military bases during World War II. But the sisters did not require their children to attend Greek school—a disappointment to Emily Zeese.[18]

Marriage and motherhood did not end Helen's compulsion to write. For her writing was and remains a virtual raison d'être, and she has often remarked that when a day passes without her writing something she feels disquieted and unfulfilled. By the end of the war she had completed the draft of a novel about three friends from a Greek village living in America. An excerpt from the work in progress appeared in the second issue of *Utah Humanities Review*, a quarterly launched in 1947 by the University of Utah. In this segment Alexandra, a young woman of Greek ancestry, watches her friends dancing to phonograph records—Frank Sinatra followed by traditional Greek music—and muses about her childhood and the immigrant men who came to the coal town: "They were strong, hard men who loved the feel of their hairy hands clutching a pick handle. They exulted in their bodies and each strove to fill the most cars of coal or lay the most rails to prove his giant strength." Given the impressive list of professors editing the *Utah Humanities Review*, Helen must have been encouraged by this early recognition of her as a writer of fiction.[19] When she saw a notice in the *Salt Lake Tribune* that Cecil Scott, senior editor for Macmillan, was in town to look at manuscripts, she went to see him. Scott was interested in the novel and offered her a contract. As she worked on the novel's revision, he came twice to see her and she traveled to New York. Scott was especially concerned about the last quarter of the novel, insisting that Helen "must take the characters beyond the bedroom door." Unable to provide the required detail about her characters' love relationships (undoubtedly tepid by 1990s standards), Helen agreed to a mutual abandonment of the contract with Macmillan. Devastated by her perceived failure, she "didn't try again for years." Nevertheless, she continued to fill notebooks with ideas for fictional characters and plots, creating a rich seedbed that would germinate decades later.

Meanwhile, Helen's literary career was about to take a long, productive, and impressive detour. In the conservative post–World War II era, before the Civil Rights movement of the 1960s began to challenge old notions of race and ethnicity, scholars like Helen were initiating a quiet revolution in the subject matter of history. In Utah a major factor in the creation of a more inclusive history was and continues to be the Utah State Historical Society and its magazine, the *Utah Historical Quarterly*. Helen made her debut as a historian in the April 1954 issue of the *Quarterly* with "The Greeks of Carbon County."[20] A remarkable piece of writing, it set out major themes that the author would pursue over the next three decades. Although it contains much factual detail and analysis, it has a different feel from the author's later historical works. In its reflective, almost meditative tone it is more like an essay. After all, it represented her first published attempt to come to terms with the often frightening past that had shaped her parents' and her own generation. Significantly, she was able to analyze tumultuous events with rare detachment and dignity. Since she was destined to lead a cadre of historians toward the discovery of their ethnic roots, this early achievement boded well for the course of Utah historiography in the last quarter of the twentieth century.

A decade later Helen's next research project took her to the immigrant camps of Bingham in the Oquirrh Mountains. Published in the fall 1965 issue of the *Utah Historical Quarterly*, "Life and Labor among the Immigrants of Bingham Canyon" paints a vivid picture of the most diverse community in Utah outside of Carbon County's coal camps.[21] Using newspapers, census reports, state records, and interviews, she demonstrated that Bingham's immigrants had much in common with those in Carbon County but that the town's geography—a long, narrow canyon with houses and businesses crowded together—made tolerance almost a necessity. Moreover, Helen discovered, Bingham's elite—doctors, lawyers, teachers, mine managers, and church leaders—tended to remain longer than their Carbon County peers, which gave them a vested interest in helping the immigrants solve their problems.

With two major essays on immigrant life well received, Helen embarked on an ambitious monograph-length history: *Toil and Rage in a New Land: The Greek Immigrants in Utah* was published as the spring issue of the *Utah Historical Quarterly* in 1970. It was a coup for a living writer to command an entire issue of the *UHQ*; only Dale L. Morgan had previously achieved it and no one since 1970. In a note about the author, editor Charles S. Peterson, who had recently appointed Helen to the

UHQ's first advisory board of editors, wrote: "In this issue of the *Quarterly*, Mrs. Papanikolas's happy facility for lucid and graceful expression, her intimate knowledge of the Greeks, and her valuable photographic collection come together in a most worthy contribution to the social history of the Intermountain West."[22]

Although *Toil and Rage* filled an entire issue of the *UHQ*, it by no means exhausted the topic. She subsequently wrote two folklore articles and a definitive study of the 1933 coal strike in Carbon County, which appeared in the early 1970s, and more articles, which have since been published, were in their formative stage.[23] For one thing, she was researching almost continuously. For several years her major goal was to interview as many Utah Greeks as possible. The immigrant generation was dying off, taking with it a vast store of memories about early life in Utah. Helen tracked these men and women down in their children's homes, in nursing care facilities, and in towns across the state and beyond.

Toil and Rage signaled the beginning of a new era in Utah historiography. Ethnic and racial groups that had previously been ignored or marginalized in histories of the state now became the subject of numerous studies. Additionally, Utah's industrial development—especially mines, mills, smelters, railroads, and factories—began to attract greater attention. Young scholars encouraged by Helen's pioneering work began writing theses and dissertations on Hispanics, African Americans, South Slavs, and Italians, extending the parameters of American Indian history and shifting the focus of mining history away from discovery and entrepreneurship to a more inclusive view that emphasized development, economics, and especially labor.[24]

As word of *Toil and Rage* spread beyond Utah's borders, scholars throughout the country as well as Greek Americans eager to read about their immigrant forebears created such a demand for copies that the publication was reprinted twice. With that exposure Helen became recognized as the leading authority on Greek immigrant life in the United States. She presented papers at national and international conferences and served as a consultant for television documentaries and other projects. Then, when the Utah American Revolution Bicentennial Commission agreed to fund a historical publication, Helen became the obvious choice to edit a multiauthor work devoted to the history of the state's major ethnic and racial groups.

The fourteen chapters of *The Peoples of Utah* (1976) provide in-depth views of diverse cultural and racial groups, including native Americans, northern and southern Europeans, Jews, Canadians, African Americans, the Chinese and Japanese, Middle Easterners, and Hispanics. *The Peoples of Utah* became a bestseller and the standard text at Utah universities and colleges for courses that had only recently begun to explore ethnic history. It, too, was reprinted.[25]

The Peoples of Utah Institute—named after Helen's book and of which Helen was a founder (1977) and the first president—located and identified artifacts associated with ethnic life, produced a major museum exhibit, and sponsored lectures and other programs. Concerned about the preservation of numerous documents and extensive interviews associated with these projects, Helen was instrumental in organizing the ethnic archives at the University of Utah. Her productivity continued virtually uninterrupted, despite time devoted to parents in failing health and her own eye problems.

However, Helen has begun to shift the burden of being the state's premier ethnic historian to a group of younger historians, many of whom she had directly nurtured. They have started teaching the university classes in ethnic history, traveling to give lectures in small towns, and responding to endless inquires from outside the state. Despite wanting to free herself from history, she had unwittingly, by her excellence, trapped herself in it. Someone always wanted one more article or lecture from her, and many works came from her typewriter (how happy she was when she had a word processor installed at home) in the decade following publication of *The Peoples of Utah*.

The major work of the 1980s was *Emily-George*, the biography of her parents, which she had written originally for family members, especially her parents' grandchildren and great-grandchildren whose lives were far removed from the grandparents' immigrant days in Carbon County. The work was destined for much wider circulation, however, when it was chosen by the University of Utah Press as volume 3 in the Utah Centennial Series edited by Charles S. Peterson. In his introduction to *Emily-George* he wrote:

[Helen] writes in elegant prose which reaches beyond conventional history in the intimacy of the view it presents but still retains the precision of statement so essential to good historical writing. Also apparent in her writing are pride in place of origin, awareness of cultural diversity, and a sense of the role played by her people and other ethnic groups in building Utah and the West. Long before women's history came to its own . . . realistic contributing women emerged in Papanikolas's work, adding another dimension to her presentation.[26]

Helen also penned major essays on Greek funeral customs, bootlegging, ethnic minorities in World War I, and a comparative study of Mormon and immigrant cultures.[27] The latter tackled a topic of particular interest to her and one that lay at the center of a novel she worked on for years. In an introduction to her essay "Ethnicity in Mormondom," Thomas G. Alexander summarized its thesis: Immigrant and Mormon cultures clashed not primarily because of political and economic differences but "in the differing attitudes toward familial relationships." For example, "Though adhering in principal to a patriarchal family, . . . [immigrant] families were really centered on the mother, who served as the glue which held the extended family together. Far from being sexually promiscuous, as the common mythology would dictate, ethnic families tended to be extremely conservative in their attitudes toward even such commonplaces as hand-holding before marriage." Moreover, the liturgical services of Orthodox and Catholic immigrants "seemed lacking in substance to the Mormons while the Mormons' lay religion seemed informal and cold to the immigrants. Under these conditions, conflicts were inevitable, and only intermarriage, acculturation, and increasing business contacts have helped to mitigate the conflict."[28]

If the novel based on these themes proved difficult to realize, Helen by now was a widely recognized writer. She had received numerous awards and accolades, including the Archbishop of the Americas Iakovos Saint Paul Medal (1972); the Brotherhood Award, National Conference of Christians and Jews, Utah Chapter (1978); and an Honorary Doctor of Humane Letters from the University of Utah (1984). Having written her peoples' history to the best of her ability she need feel no guilt at turning to those notebooks filled with dozens of characters and plots. She should not abandon her quest to write fiction now.

With a great sense of fulfillment, then, she greeted the publication in 1993 of a group of thirteen short stories to local and national acclaim. *Small Bird, Tell Me* captures the lives of the Greek immigrants in a way that only fiction can with its freedom to enter into men's and women's minds. As one review noted: "She carries literary dexterity and grace to its ultimate. . . . Being rooted in her people, she is able to probe deeply into their personal experiences and their foibles, with compassion and understanding."[29] More than five decades have passed since Professor Angleman advised her to pursue a literary career. She is pursuing it daily now. Sidney Angleman would be proud.

Notes

List of Abbreviations Used

BYU	Brigham Young University, Provo, Utah
DEN	*Deseret Evening News*, original name of the *Deseret News*
DN	*Deseret News*
DUP	Daughters of the Utah Pioneers
ECIF	*Early Church Information File*
FCS	Federal Census Schedules
HR	*Historical Record*
JH	*Journal History*
LDS	Church of Jesus Christ of Latter-day Saints
LDS/CHD	LDS Church Historical Department
LDS/FHL	LDS Family History Library
NA	National Archives
NAM	National Archives Microcopy
ROM	*Record of Members*
RS	Relief Society
SLC	Salt Lake City
SLCo	Salt Lake County
SLT	*Salt Lake Tribune*
U of U	University of Utah, Salt Lake City, Utah
UHQ	*Utah Historical Quarterly*
USHS	Utah State Historical Society
USU	Utah State University, Logan, Utah
WPA	Works Progress Administration

The materials cited from the Family History Library are available through its branches worldwide. No names are shortened if they are part of the title of another work.

Preface

1. John Livingston Lowes, *The Road to Xanadu*, Boston: Houghton Mifflin, 1964, xiv.

Chapter 1: Patty Bartlett Sessions

1. "Patty Sessions," *Woman's Exponent* 13, no. 7 (1 September 1884): 51, 63. All the information given on the life of the Sessions family until their exodus from Missouri is found in this reference. In all quotations from this and from Patty's diaries, spelling and punctuation have been retained as in the original.

2. Since by actual count of her diaries in the years between 1846 and 1866 she delivered 484 babies (223 girls, 207 boys, 25 miscarriages, and 29 not identified as to sex), and considering even omissions or errors, a figure near 4,000 seems unlikely. Of course, prior to 1846, Patty had practiced midwifery for thirty-four years, so how can we know for sure? See Quig Nielsen, "Patty Sessions delivered 3,977 babies as a midwife," in *Davis County Clipper*, 2 March 1992. He quotes from Kate B. Carter, ed., *Our Pioneer Heritage* (n.p., n.d.).

3. Perrigrine Sessions, *Reminiscences and Diaries, 1839–1886*, B-7 to B-12. A good part of this information is also included in the *Woman's Exponent* series.

4. The "Extermination Order" was not rescinded until June 25, 1976, when Missouri Governor Christopher S. Bond issued an executive order recognizing its legal invalidity.

5. *Woman's Exponent*, 13, no. 11 (1 November 1884); Perrigrine Sessions, B-15.

6. *Woman's Exponent* 13, no. 11 (1 November 1884).

7. Patty's diary, inserted page, following entry for 16 June 1860.

8. *Woman's Exponent* 13, no. 17 (1 February 1885).

9. Patty's diary entries, 21 March–8 July 1858.

10. Leslie T. Foy, *The City Bountiful*, Bountiful, Utah: Horizon, 1975, 48.

11. Perrigrine Sessions, B-54.

12. Perrigrine Sessions, B-63.

13. Phebe Carter Sessions (Patty's daughter-in-law), obituary of Patty Bartlett Sessions, *Woman's Exponent* 27, nos. 1 and 2, p. 6. *DN*, 20 December 1883, carried a news item about the school, "Patty Sessions School."

14. One of the pleasures of editing Patty's diaries has been the interaction with her

descendants, who followed along in the diaries as I read aloud from my transcription. Besides sharing the almost spiritual experience of working with the documents, there was much sharing of memories and family legends and of being introduced to other descendants, who own artifacts and tales of Patty.

15.   *Woman's Exponent* 27, nos. 1 and 2, p. 6.

16.   Patty's diary, 5 February 1847.

Chapter 2: Jane Manning James

1.   Research for this study benefited from the cooperation of private citizens and public officials in furnishing access to local records and assistance in using them. Particularly helpful were George Frodsham, deputy recorder for SLCo, who provided guidance in the use of early-day property records; Blaine M. Hofeling, who located a large number of nineteenth-century assessment rolls for SLC; Herman J. Hogensen, SLC recorder, and Mildred V. Higham, his deputy, who granted access to these rolls; and Weldon Nichols, office supervisor at the SLC Cemetery, and Marci Jackman, his assistant, who furnished aid in using the burial and death records held by their institution.

2.   The origins of the Manning family are discussed in David Hermon Van Hoosear's "Annals of Wilton," as compiled and published in the *Wilton* [Connecticut] *Bulletin*, 23 March 1939. References to the "Annals," as well as copies of the relevant articles were graciously furnished by Mrs. C. R. Merwin, administrative assistant of the Wilton Historical Society.

    The earliest information on the nativity of Mrs. James is furnished by a patriarchal blessing issued in 1844, which states that she was born May 11, 1818, the daughter of Isaac and Eliza Manning. An older and a younger sister received patriarchal blessings at this time, and their parents' names are also listed as Isaac and Eliza Manning. (Entries for "Jane Manning," "Angeline Manning," and "Sarah Stebbins," *ECIF*, LDS/FHL.) The Eliza mentioned in the blessings appears to refer to Eliza Treadwell, their stepmother at that time. (Further information on Eliza, see endnote 13.) Later LDS records offering variants of this information on nativity include the following: *JH*, 21 June 1847; Eighth Ward, Salt Lake Stake, *ROM*, early-1905, microfilm no. 7767, 24 and 27, LDS/CHD; and "Jane Elizabeth Manning James," Patriarchal Blessing File, LDS/CHD. As no exact date can be established for Mrs. James's birth, and the earliest records offer dates between 1818 and 1822, the year 1820 is offered as an approximation.

3.   "Life Sketch of Jane Elizabeth Manning James" (hereafer cited as "Life Sketch"), Wilford Woodruff MSS, LDS/CHD. This transcript of an oral reminiscence is dated 1893, but internal evidence indicates that it was later revised and updated. It refers to Lorenzo Snow and Joseph F. Smith as presidents of the LDS Church, positions that they did not assume until 1898 and 1901 respectively. It also states

that only two of her children were then living, but four of her children were alive in 1893; one of them died in 1893 and another in 1897.

Mrs. James refers in the "Life Sketch" to four brothers and sisters as members of the party that made the trek from Connecticut to Nauvoo. The 1820 FCS for Wilton lists the household of Isaac Manning as containing five members, a man and a woman between the ages of 26 and 44, and three youngsters—one boy and two girls—under 13. The 1830 census for Wilton lists Phyllis Manning as the head of a free Black household containing five members, a woman between the ages of 36 and 55, a young woman between 10 and 24, and three youngsters—one boy and two girls—under 10 (1820 FCS, Connecticut, Fairfield County, 297, and 1830 FCS, Connecticut, Fairfield County, 223, microfilm copies, LDS/FHL). Van Hoosear states that the couple had "eight or ten" children.

4.   Van Hoosear was a descendant of Ebenezer Abbott II and hence was acquainted with Blacks who had served the Abbott household. Slavery was abolished in Connecticut by gradual abolition acts of 1784 and 1797, the provisions of which provided for freeing slaves when they reached age 25. Isaac Manning's occupation is listed in the Asahel R. Betts account book, according to a letter from Mrs. G. R. Merwin, 19 June 1973.

5.   Van Hoosear. The 1840 FCS for Wilton lists the household of Cato Treadwell as containing seven members, a man between the ages of 55 and 100, a woman between 36 and 55, four youths—one boy and three girls—between 10 and 24, and one male under 10 (1840 FCS, NAM 704, Roll 21, 326). Treadwell itemized his assets in submitting a claim for a Revolutionary War pension. They included only a few personal items in addition to an "old log-house" located on land belonging to another man. He gave his occupation as a day laborer (Revolutionary War Pension and Bounty-Land Application Files, NAM 804, Roll 2411, "Cato Treadwell").

6.   In her "Life Sketch," Mrs. James states that she went to live with the Fitch family at the age of six. The 1830 and 1840 FCS for Wilton list a household headed by Joseph P. Fitch, but the household does not contain a young Black girl who might be identified as Jane Elizabeth Manning.

7.   Estate of Silas F. James, decd., no. 1204, Third District Court for SLCo, Probate Division, USA; "Notice," attached to Third Amended Complaint, sworn 6 April 1909, in the case of Sylvester James v. Ellen M. McLean, no. 10219, Third District Court for SLCo, Civil Division; and Jane James, "A Reminiscence of Joseph Smith," *Dialogue* 5, no. 2 (summer 1970): 128.

8.   "Life Sketch."

9.   *Times and Seasons*, 2 (15 September 1841), 544–45, and 3 (15 April 1842), 763–65.

10.   Clarance Merrill, "History of Albert Merrill with Some Information and Dates of His Ancestors...," 5–7, electrostatic copy of the handwritten original, LDS/CHD; and *Times and Seasons*, 3 (1 July 1842), 844–45, 4 (15 April 1843), 174–75, and

4 (15 August 1843), 302.

11. "Life Sketch." The Eighth Ward *ROM* as well as a letter from Mrs. James to John Taylor, 27 December 1884, state that she was baptized and confirmed into the church on October 14, 1843. This date is clearly in error, for the records of church members arriving in Nauvoo reveal that she and several relatives had received temple recommends (certifications from a bishop testifying to their standing within the church) on September 10, 1843. They could not have secured recommends without having been baptized into the church. As Mrs. James reported being a member of the church for about a year before her departure for Nauvoo, it appears that she was baptized in 1842, possibly on the October 14 date that she gave. The *ROM* also states that Mrs. James's brother, Isaac L. Manning, was baptized into the church by Albert Merrill in December of an undesignated year. As Merrill was not converted until December 1841, and the Mannings had left Connecticut by December 1843, it appears that Isaac L. Manning entered the church in December 1842, about two months after his sister had joined (*ROM, Nauvoo, 1839–46*, "Members Who Came to Nauvoo Since July 31, 1843," LDS/FHL, microfilm copy).

12. *Times and Seasons*, 4 (15 August 1843), 302.

13. "Life Sketch." Twelve years later in "A Reminiscence of Joseph Smith," Mrs. James provided a slightly different listing of the relatives who made up the party. The earlier account seems more reliable, as it identifies them by name. .

Van Hoosear states that Jane's stepfather, Cato Treadwell, also made the trek to Nauvoo. After hostilities forced the Mormons to flee Nauvoo, he returned to Connecticut and died in 1849. Meanwhile, he had acquired another wife, Eliza Mead, apparently while residing in Nauvoo. She died in Keokuk, Iowa, in 1861. Cato's remarriage led some of Mrs. James's contemporaries to conclude that her mother was Eliza rather than Phyllis. The Eighth Ward *ROM* originally listed Mrs. James's mother as "Filles Abbott," but later replaced this with "Eliza Mead." Likewise, in the transcript of Mrs. James's "Life Sketch," her mother is originally listed as "Phillis," but "Phillis" is crossed out and replaced by "Eliza." The "Life Sketch," as well as other records, provide no information on Phyllis after the family's arrival in Nauvoo.

Sylvester was born out of wedlock when Jane was about 18. According to later family gossip, the father was a White preacher. After Sylvester's birth Jane returned to the Fitch family while her mother kept the child. Sylvester was five or six years old when the family reached Nauvoo ("a fair chunk of a boy," according to Patriarch John Smith). The circumstances of Sylvester's birth were a matter that Mrs. James refused to discuss with even her closest friends, and she omitted all mention of the incident in accounts of her life (addendum of Elizabeth J. D. Roundy to "Life Sketch").

14. Merwin, letter of 19 June 1973.

15. "Life Sketch" and Jane E. James to John Taylor. For a discussion of the status

of free Negroes in the antebellum North, including restrictions on immigration from state to state, see Leon F. Litwack, *North of Slavery* (Chicago: University of Chicago Press, 1961), especially 66–74.

16. Ibid. Mrs. James's account of the loss of her wardrobe is confirmed by the following notice, which appeared in the *Nauvoo Neighbor* of December 6, 1843:

> LOST
>
> ABOUT six weeks ago a company of saints arrived in this place escorted by Elder Wandal [sic] who had in his charge a trunk belonging to Jane Elizabeth Manning:- Sister Manning was not here then but has since arrived and can obtain no intelligence of her trunk; it is presumed that some one has got it in mistake as there was a number of passengers arrived at the same time. The trunk is about three feet long and covered with a light red hair skin, with the exception of the back, on which there is some white. It is directed to 'Jane Elizabeth Manning, Nauvoo.' Whoever will give such information as shall lead to the discovery of the trunk will be handsomely rewarded by applying to this office.

17. "Life Sketch;" "A Reminiscence of Joseph Smith," 128; and Jane E. James to John Taylor. The "law of adoption" was a religious ordinance, which began in Nauvoo and spread during the trek to the Great Basin. Under the law of adoption, Mormon men and their families were linked formally (i.e., "sealed") into the households of leading figures of the church. The practice fell into disuse in the late nineteenth century and was officially discontinued in 1894 (see James R. Clark, ed., *Messages of the First Presidency*, vol. 3 [SLC: Bookcraft, 1966], 252–60).

    Joseph and Emma's intent in offering to adopt Jane into their household cannot be ascertained, given the lack of first-hand sources, but Jane afterwards interpreted the offer under the law of adoption. In renewing her request for adoption in a letter to Joseph F. Smith, a member of the first presidency, in 1890, Mrs. James explained that she had not understood the law of adoption at the time of the offer (Jane E. James to Joseph F. Smith, 7 February 1890, Joseph F. Smith MSS, LDS/CHD).

18. *DEN*, 17 April 1911, reprinted in Kate B. Carter, *The Story of the Negro Pioneer* (SLC: Utah Printing Company for the DUP, ca. 1965), 12–13.

19. Ibid. President Joseph F. Smith confirmed Isaac Manning's role in the burial of Joseph and Hyrum Smith. Following Manning's funeral the church president informed his ecclesiastical associates, "Brother Manning dug the first grave of the Prophet and Patriarch, and helped remove the bodies, perhaps, twice. The first time they were buried in the northwest room of the Nauvoo House, and were afterwards removed to the private burying ground of the old home, where his uncles, Don Carlos and Samuel were buried" (*JH*, 20 April 1911, 1–2).

20. *ROM, Nauvoo, 1839–46,* "Members Who Came to Nauvoo Since July 31, 1843." Isaac L. and Lucinda Manning are listed in this record as having been received as members on January 15, 1844, Jane E. Manning on January 25, 1844, Angeline Manning on March 4, 1844, and Anthony and Sarah Ann Stebbins on August 5, 1845. The *ECIF* reveals that Angeline and Jane Manning, together with Anthony and Sarah Stebbins, received blessings at the hands of Patriarch Hyrum Smith on March 4, 1844, several months before his death.

    Almost no information is available on those members of the family who did not migrate westward. It appears that they too left Nauvoo, as none are listed in the 1850 census of the community. Lucinda Manning, the wife of Isaac L. Manning, was residing in 1850 with a White family in Keokuk, Iowa, but neither her husband nor other family members were listed as residents of the town (1850 FCS, NAM 432, Roll 186, 412). In the early 1880s Isaac L. Manning, together with his younger brother Peter, was living in southeastern Michigan. Peter died in 1883 in Milford, Michigan, at the age of 61, while Isaac moved to SLC in 1893 at the age of 78 (Samuel B. Thompson to William M. Dudley, 25 July 1884, in Revolutionary War Pension and Bounty-Land Application Files, "Cato Treadwell").

21. "Life Sketch;" Eighth Ward, Salt Lake Stake, *ROM,* Early-1905, p. 84; and *JH,* 21 June 1847.

22. *JH,* 21 June 1847.

23. A list of the emigrants, arranged to "tens," "fifties," and "hundreds," can be found in *JH,* 21 June 1847. Details of the journey have been taken from the account contained in a record entitled *Emigration,* vol. 1, 1831–1848, LDS/CHD. These *Emigration* volumes are unpaginated, but are organized chronologically by company of emigrants.

24. "Life Sketch." This appears to be the famine of 1855–56; for a full description, see Leonard J. Arrington, *Great Basin Kingdom: An Economic History of the Latter-day Saints, 1850–1900* (Cambridge: Harvard University Press, 1958), 148–56.

25. The following reminiscence was found among the WPA Biographical Sketches (A1188) at the USHS. Nothing in the file indicates when, where, or by whom the information was given.

> Jane Elizabeth James came to Utah Sept. 22, 1847 and camped on the temple block fixing their wagons in a circle around them. First had a house built in the center of the block north of the Temple block for four years and then moved one-half a mile from Liberty Park and lived for sixteen years by the Theatre before they went down to live at Liberty Park. She used to go down and get milk off Isaac Chase's wife, Elizabeth. When she had not one thing in the house to eat and felt very bad at having to beg milk but had to do so for the sake of her little child. The mill was built by Isaac Chase and called the Chase Mill. Then i[t]

was sold to Brigham Young.

26. As quoted in Carter, 9–10.
27. 1850 FCS, SLCo, Utah Territory, 56, microfilm copy, LDS/FHL.
28. Carter, 34–35, furnishes several accounts of an African American named Isaac who served as Brigham Young's coachman. She designates him as one of the slaves originally owned by Thomas Bedford Graham. But the 1850, 1860, and 1870 federal censuses fail to list any slaves belonging to Graham or any African American named Isaac Graham. The only African American with the first name of Isaac in any of these censuses is Isaac James. Hence, Mrs. James's reference to her husband's employment by Brigham Young ("Life Sketch"), combined with the accounts in Carter, suggest that Isaac James worked as Brigham Young's coachman. Isaac and Jane James appear to have known Brigham Young from the Nauvoo period. In her "Life Sketch," James reported marrying to Isaac James after leaving Joseph Smith's household and said she remained with them until Brigham Young left Nauvoo.
29. Twenty-eight households in the First Ward held more property than did the Jameses, while eighteen held less, and three others held the same amount (data compiled from the SLC Assessment Rolls, 1856 volume, First Ward, held by the Office of the SLC Recorder, SLC-SLCo Building). It should be noted that these comparisons furnish only a rough index of relative wealth. They do not take into account the number of working family members, the number of persons that the head of a household supported, or those households that held no real or personal property—and hence were not entered on the rolls. The rolls, moreover, would not include property owned outside the city. In evaluating data for the period following 1860, it is important to recognize that the First Ward was predominantly rural and relatively underpopulated in comparison to other wards in the city. The wealth of its residents was but a fraction of those wards nearer the center of town, where the commercial and professional classes resided.
30. Mrs. James listed her children by name in her "Life Sketch," but misplaced punctuation in the revision of the sketch separated middle from first names and left the number of children unclear. Five Utah-born children are reported in one or more of the federal censuses of 1850, 1860, and 1870. One other child, Isaac, is listed in the SLC Cemetery's *Books of the Dead* as still-born on April 22, 1854. The 1860 census gives the family's Utah-born children as Mary Ann, age twelve, Miriam, eight, Ellen D., seven, Jesse J., four, and Vilate, one (George Olin Zabriskie, "Compilation of the Black Population from the 1860 Federal Census for Utah," subject files, under the classification of "Negroes," USHS).
31. Sixteen households within the ward owned more property than the Jameses, while eighteen owned less (SLC Assessment Rolls, 1860 volume, First Ward).
32. "Report of 1st Regiment, 2d Brigade, Nauvoo Legion, Dec. 27, 1861," in "Record of Orders, Returns, and Courts Martial &c. of 2nd Brigade, 1st Division, Nauvoo

Legion," 45, typescript copy, LDS/FHL.

33. SLCo Assessment Rolls, 1861–65 volumes, First Ward, microfilm copies. It should not be concluded from this description of the Jameses' property holdings that farming was the major source of their family income. The 1860 FCS and the 1869 SLC directory list Isaac James's occupation as laborer. Given the size of lots in early-day SLC, eight one-and-a-quarter acre lots comprising a ten-acre block, and the rural nature of the community, many households, whatever the occupation of their heads, cultivated garden plots and maintained domestic farm animals. Moreover, the changing character of Isaac James's personal property during the early 1860s indicates that he engaged in considerable barter or trade. This observation is reinforced by the 1863 tax list, located among the county assessment rolls, which reports that he paid his $6.95 levy in "Cont[r]aband Cash & Scrip."

34. Isaac James to Jane E. James, quit claim deed, recorded 23 May 1870, Book A-4, 4, Abstracts of Title Volumes, Office of the SLCo Recorder, SLC-SLCo Building. Isaac sold the remainder of the family property two years later to Feramorz Little for $200. Little was a prominent Mormon businessman and church leader who was later to serve as mayor of SLC (Isaac James to Feramorz Little, quit claim deed, recorded 17 May 1872).

35. Eighth Ward, Salt Lake Stake, *ROM*, early-1905, 24. This record indicates that her husband was Frank Perkins. Little is known of his origins, but it seems clear that he arrived in Utah as one of the slaves of Reuben Perkins, who settled in Bountiful, Davis County, as a farmer (Carter, 28; Zabriskie).

    The Eighth Ward RS Minute Books list contributors and their donations on a monthly basis throughout the 1870s and early 1880s. Mrs. James is first mentioned as "Sister Jane Perkins" in the August 20, 1874 entry for receipts. From this date to April 20, 1876, she is listed seven times as "Perkins" and twice (October 20 and November 20, 1875, the next to last entries during the period) as "James" (Eighth Ward, Salt Lake Stake, RS, *Minute Book A, 1867–77*, lib no. C3978, passim). In the only recorded property transaction that falls within the period, she signed herself as "Jane E. Perkins," and the recorder described her as "Jane Elizabeth Perkins, formerly Jane Elizabeth James" (Jane E. Perkins to E. M. Cort, lease, recorded 16 October 1874, Book B-8, 153, Abstracts of Title Volumes). Mrs. James's use of "Perkins" as her surname in business transactions that were a matter of public record demonstrates that her relationship with Frank Perkins was meant to be permanent.

36. "Petition for Sale of Real Estate," subscribed 19 February 1889, Estate of Silas F. James, decd., no. 1204, Third District Court for SLCo, Probate Division.

37. "Final Account and Petition for Final Settlement and Distribution," subscribed 5 April 1889; Isaac James to Jane Elizabeth James, quit claim deed, recorded 27 March 1889, Book B-24, p. 149, Abstracts of Title Volumes; Eighth Ward, Salt Lake Stake, *ROM*, early-1905, 84; "Isaac James," Patriarchal Blessing File; and

JH, 19 November 1891.

38. Jane E. James to Joseph F. Smith. Walker Lewis was one of the few African Americans to gain the priesthood in the early days of the church. A Black barber in Lowell, Massachusetts, he was ordained during the lifetime of Joseph Smith, either by William Smith, Joseph's younger brother, or by Parley P. Pratt (Newell G. Bringhurst, *Saints, Slaves, and Blacks: The Changing Place of Black People within Mormonism* [Westport, Conn.: Greenwood Press, 1981], 90–91, 103). Lewis had died in the mid-1850s, but James claimed, "he wished me to be sealed to him."

39. *JH,* 19 November 1891; and Zina D. H. Young to Joseph F. Smith, 15 January 1894, Zina D. H. Young MSS, LDS/CHD.

40. 1870 FCS, Eighth Ward, SLC, SLCo, Utah Territory, 10, microfilm copy, LDS/FHL. According to the census, taken after Mrs. James had moved from her First Ward homestead, her household included the following relatives: two sons, Silas and Jessie, ages 24 and 15, both working as "laborers;" two daughters, Ellen and Vilate, ages 18 and 11; and a granddaughter, Malvina, age one.

41. Feramorz Little to Jane E. James, quit claim deed, recorded 13 July 1871, Book A-2, 244, and Jane E. James to Feramorz Little, quit claim deed, recorded 3 July 1871, Book A-4, 4, Abstracts of Title Volumes.

42. Henrietta Bankhead, interview with the author, Murray, Utah, December 1972.

43. SLC Assessment Rolls, 1871–92 volumes, Eighth Ward.

44. The RS Eighth Ward Minute Books list not only the amount of individual contributions, but designate whether they took the form of cash or sundries. If the contributions were sundries, the records describe the items involved. Throughout the period 1870–1904 more than four-fifths of Mrs. James's contributions are listed as "cash" (Eighth Ward, Salt Lake Stake, RS, *Minute Book A; Minute Book C, 1879–85,* lib. no. C3980, *Minute Book 1882,* lib. no. C3981, *Receipt Book 1894–1902,* lib. no. C3982, and *Minute Book 1905–13,* lib. no. C3983R, LDS/CHD).

45. SLC Assessment Rolls, 1884 volume, Eighth Ward.

46. Jane Elizabeth Perkins to E. M. Cast, lease, recorded 16 October 1874, and Jane Elizabeth James to Erick M. Cast, lease, recorded 23 September 1879, Book B-8, 153 and 155, Abstracts of Title Volumes. Some idea of the slight value of this land can be gained from the terms of the original lease. In 1874 Mrs. James leased the property for $15 a year. In 1889 she sold it outright for $500 (W. A. Wiseman to Jane E. James, receipt of part purchase, recorded 11 February 1889, and Jane Elizabeth James to William A. Wiseman, warranty deed, recorded 24 May 1889, Book B-14, 149, Abstracts of Title Volumes).

47. 1880 FCS, Eighth Ward, SLC, SLCo, Utah Territory, p. 28, microfilm copy, LDS/FHL. This census listed Mrs. James's occupation as "laundress." The members of the household included Mrs. James and two grandchildren. One of these was Malvina Robinson, daughter of Miriam James Robinson, then deceased. Malvina had been listed as a member of Mrs. James's household in the 1870 census. The parentage of the other grandchild, Jessie James, age five months, is undetermined.

48. Robert W. Sloan, ed., *Utah Gazetteer and Directory 1884* (SLC: Herald Printing and Publishing Company, 1884); *Salt Lake City Directory 1885* (New York: U.S. Directory Publishing Company, n.d.); Lorenzo Stenhouse, ed., *Utah Gazetteer and Directory 1888* (n.p., n.d.); and R. J. Polk and Company, *Salt Lake City Directory*, 1893 and 1894–95 volumes (published annually in SLC since 1890, except for single volumes covering the years 1891–92 and 1894–95).

49. "Historical Sketch of the Relief Society for the Jubilee," dated 17 March 1892, in Eighth Ward, Salt Lake Stake, RS, *Minute Book 1882.*

50. Eighth Ward, Salt Lake Stake, *HR, 1856–75* (lib. no. A7384, LDS/CHD); and Eighth Ward, Salt Lake Stake, RS, *Minute Book A, 1867–77, Minute Book C, 1879–85. Minute Book 1892, Receipt Book 1894–1902*, and *Minute Book 1905–13.*

51. *DEN*, 17 April 1911; statement of Anna Shipp, in Carter, 9.

52. "A Reminiscence of Joseph Smith," 128–30.

53. For discussions of Joseph Smith's attitude toward slavery and race, see Lester E. Bush Jr., "Mormonism's Negro Doctrine: An Historical Overview," *Dialogue* 7 (spring 1973): 13–22; Stephen G. Taggart, *Mormonism's Negro Policy: Social and Historical Origins* (SLC: U of U Press, ca. 1970); Dennis L. Lythgoe, "Negro Slavery and Mormon Doctrine," *Western Humanities Review* 21 (autumn 1967): 329–30. Lythgoe, following William J. Mulder in his "The Mormons in American History" (Twenty-first Annual Reynolds Lecture, University of Utah, 14 January 1957), characterizes Joseph Smith as a "gradualist" on the slavery question. Smith's policy of compensated emancipation did place him to the right of William Lloyd Garrison and other abolitionists who advocated immediate and complete emancipation. Within the context of American politics in 1844, however, even gradual emancipation was a radical proposal. It had been only seven years, for instance, since Elijah P. Lovejoy had been murdered in Alton, Illinois, for his advocacy of abolition.

54. The fullest discussion on the development of Mormon racial policies during this period is Bringhurst, 144–64.

55. Endowments involve special temple ceremonies essential for exaltation in the hereafter. They may be performed for the Latter-day Saint as a sign of worthiness usually on such special occasions as entrance into marriage or departure on a mission. Completion of construction of a series of temples in the late nineteenth century attested to their importance in Mormon religious life.

56. Jane E. James to Joseph F. Smith, 7 February 1890 and 31 August 1903, Joseph F. Smith MSS, LDS/CHD; Wilford Woodruff Journals, 14 October 1894, LDS/CHD; "Excerpts from the Weekly Council Meetings of the Quorum of Twelve Apostles, Dealing with the Rights of Negroes in the Church, 1849–1940," entries for meetings of 22 August 1895 and 2 January 1902, George Albert Smith MSS, U of U. President Woodruff explained the denial in terms of "the *Law of God*" in his diary: "As *Cain killed Abel* All the seed of Cain would have to wait for redemption untill all the seed that Abel would have had that may come through

other men can be redeemed."

57. Jane E. James to John Taylor, 27 December 1884, LDS/CHD; Jane E. James to Joseph F. Smith, 7 February 1890, LDS/CHD; Zina D. H. Young to Joseph F. Smith, 15 January 1894, LDS/CHD; "Excerpts from the Weekly Council Meetings. . .," entry to meeting of 2 January 1902, George Albert Smith Papers, U of U.

58. Angus M. Cannon to Jane E. James, 16 June 1888, Angus M. Cannon Letterpress Copybooks, LDS/CHD.

59. Jane E. James to John Taylor, 27 December 1884, LDS/CHD.

60. In a letter of September 5, 1885, relating to temple ordinances for members of the church who were Black, Joseph E. Taylor, acting president of Salt Lake Stake, reported personal knowledge of several specific cases in which Blacks or mulattos had received their endowments (Taylor to John Taylor and George Q. Cannon, Joseph E. Taylor MSS, LDS/CHD). The hardening of the church position on temple ordinances culminated in a 1907 decision by the first presidency and council of twelve proscribing participation by anyone of Afro-American ancestry, no matter how remote (Bringhurst, 148).

61. "Excerpts from the Weekly Council Meetings," entry of 2 January 1902.

62. *DEN*, 21 April 1908.

63. Mary Ann Robinson, under date of 9 April 1871, and Mariam [*sic*] Williams, under date of 8 December 1874, *Books of the Dead.*

64. *DEN*, 4 March 1897.

65. Silas F. James, under date of 17 May 1872, and Jessie J. James, under date of 22 May 1894, *Books of the Dead.*

66. Data for this statistic were compiled from cemetery records, church membership lists, and census schedules for the families of Sylvester James, Miriam Williams, and Mary Ann Robinson. Even grimmer statistics might be compiled if information on her children's families were more complete, for Mrs. James in her "Life Sketch" states that only eight of her eighteen grandchildren were then living.

67. "Life Sketch;" "A Reminiscence of Joseph Smith," 128.

68. Eighth Ward, Salt Lake Stake, *ROM*, early-1905, part 2, 7; *DEN*, 17 April 1911; *Salt Lake City Directory*, 1894–95 to 1906 volumes; and 1900 FCS, Utah, vol. 4, sheet 81A, contained on NAM T623, Roll 1684.

69. "Findings of Fact and Conclusions of Law," in the case of James v. McLean, no. 10219, Third District Court for SLCo, Civil Division.

70. Ibid.

71. Eighth Ward, Salt Lake Stake, RS, *Record of Disbursements, 1908–15,* lib. no. 03984R, LDS/CHD. It is a testimony to Mrs. James's faith and generosity that in 1904–5, while she was receiving occasional aid from the Relief Society, she still made intermittent cash contributions to the organization (Eighth Ward, Salt Lake Stake, RS, *Minute Book 1905–13,* entries under "Receipts for the Year 1904" and "Receipts for the Year 1905").

72. Jane E. James to Marion [*sic*] Williams, quit claim deed, recorded 29 May 1872, Book A-2, 244, Joseph Williams, by Leonard G. Hardy, to Tacy A. Hardy, certificate of sale, recorded 9 February 1889, Book B-2, 36, and Jane Elizabeth James to Estella Elizabeth Williams, Joesphine Williams, and Lucretia Emeline Williams, warranty deed, recorded 8 January 1890, Book B-2, 217, Abstracts of Title Volumes.

73. This conclusion is drawn from the various complaints and the findings of fact filed in the case of James v. McLean, no. 10219, Third District Court for SLCo, Civil Division. The following property transactions tend to substantiate the conclusions of the court: Jane E. James to Ellen M. Wallace, warranty deed, recorded 5 June 1886, Wallace to James, lease, recorded 16 July 1886, Wallace and James to David Woodmansee, mortgage, recorded 1 October 1887, and Wallace and James to John A. Williams, mortgage, recorded 5 January 1888, Book A-10, 211, and Wallace to James, warranty deed, recorded 21 April 1888, Book A-10, 279, Abstracts of Title Volumes.

    The case of James v. McLean involved a disputed deed to Mrs. James's Eighth Ward homesite. Mrs. James had deeded the homesite for no financial consideration to her daughter Ellen in 1907, after having made a will in 1905 that left the property as a life estate to her brother Isaac L. Manning. Following Mrs. James's death and the reading of her will, her son Sylvester challenged the validity of the deed, charging that his sister Ellen had obtained it fraudulently. The court ruled for Sylvester, taking note of Mrs. James's infirm condition, Ellen's failure to claim the property before her mother's death, and her previous manipulations of her mother's property.

74. One of her great-granddaughters noted that she was "very particular and fussy" in preparing for church or other public occasions (Henrietta Bankhead, as quoted in Carter, 9).

75. "Life Sketch."

76. *DEN*, 21 April 1908.

77. A compilation of statistics for Utah's Black population, broken down by counties for the period 1850–1960, can be found in Margaret Judy Maag, "Discrimination against the Negro and Institutional Efforts to Eliminate It" (master's thesis, U of U, 1970), 103–4. The description of Black household structure in SLC is based on information and statistics gathered through a page by page examination of the 1870 FCS.

78. Compiled from the 1870 FCS, Utah Territory, SLCo. The families that are listed one after another and hence apparently lived side by side were those of Miles Litchford and Green Flake, residing in South Cottonwood, Samuel Chambers and Edward Lagrove (Leggroan), residing in Salt Lake City's First Ward, and Samuel Bankhead and James Valentine, residing in the city's Ninth Ward.

79. SLCo Assessment Rolls, 1872–78 volumes for SLC's Eighth Ward. The families were those of Samuel Chambers, Ned Lagrone (Leggroan), and Joseph Williams,

Mrs. James's son-in-law.

80.   SLCo Assessment Rolls, 1876–77 volumes for South Cottonwood and 1872–84 volumes for Union; 1880 FCS, Union, SLCo, Utah Territory, 19–20. The heads of families holding property in this area were Green and Abram Flake, Daniel Freeman, Miles Litchford, and George Stevens; the boarder holding property was Hark Wales.

81.   The only apparent area in which Utah institutionalized racial discrimination was through legislation outlawing mixed marriages. The territorial slave code of 1852 included a provision prohibiting sexual relations between Blacks and Whites, reflective of church leaders' fears of miscegenation (Lythgoe, 51–52; Bush, 23–25). In the 1880s, if not before, the church refused to solemnize marriages between Whites and Blacks, although permitting such unions between Whites and Polynesians (Joseph E. Taylor to John Taylor, 5 September and 5 November 1885, Joseph Taylor MSS, LDS/CHD; John Taylor and George Q. Cannon to Joseph E. Taylor, 7 September 1885, and John Taylor to Joseph E. Taylor, 20 November 1885, John Taylor Letterpress Copybooks, LDS/CHD). Utah's first marriage statute, enacted in 1888 by a predominantly Mormon legislature and a Gentile governor, prohibited marriages between Whites and Blacks and between Whites and "Mongolians" ("Mormon Legislation against Polygamy," untitled four-page sheet, LDS/CHD).

       Public hostility to miscegenation might suggest that Utah's Black population had no alternative to marrying among themselves. Census statistics, however, do not confirm this assumption. The 1880 census schedules for Salt Lake County reveal that eight of twenty-two "Black" families containing at least husband and wife involved interracial marriages. Six of the eight marriages involved Black or mulatto men and White women, one involved a Black man and an American Indian woman, and one involved a White man and a mulatto woman. It may be significant that six of the eight non-Black partners in these relationships were not native born, White Americans. Four of the six were English, one was Danish, and one was Indian.

82.   William Henry James to Sylvester Perkins, warranty deed, recorded October 30, 1893, Book B-9, 54, Abstracts of Title Volumes; Carter, 28–30; "Statement for Final Account and Petition for Distribution," estate of Sylvester James, decd., no. 11164, Third District Court for SLCo, Probate Division.

83.   1870 FCS, First Ward, SLC, SLCo, Utah Territory, 1 and 4.

84.   Feramorz Little to Ned Legroc (Leggroan), quit claim deed, recorded 27 May 1871, Book A-2, 244, and Ned and Susan Leggrove (Leggroan) to Herrmann Hill, warranty deed, recorded 18 November 1879, Book A-10, 31, Abstracts of Title Volumes; SLCo Assessment Rolls, 1872–80 volumes for SLC's Eighth Ward, 1878 volume for South Cottonwood, 1880–83 volumes for Butler; Carter, 20 and 50–51; and *Salt Lake City Directory*, 1908–20 volumes. The marriages united Esther Jane James and Henry Leggroan, and Nettie James and Louis Leggroan.

85. Compiled from the 1880 FCS, Utah Territory, SLCo. The compilation located 124 of the 133 Blacks supposedly listed in the schedules for SLCo.

86. Petition of 2 September 1892, signed by residents of SLC and members of the Afro-American Republican League of America in support of Irving A. Benton for United States Marshal, Appointment Papers, Utah, 1889–93, "I. A. Benton," Records of the Department of Justice (Record Group 60), NA; *DEN*, 13 and 23 August and 26 October 1895. References to the newspaper accounts were graciously furnished by Ms. Beverly Beeton.

87. J. Cecil Alter, *Early Utah Journalism* (SLC: USHS, 1938), 274; and *Salt Lake City Directory*, 1896–99 volumes.

88. The 1891–92 *Salt Lake City Directory* contains the first listing of a predominantly Black congregation, Methodist in affiliation. The congregation is listed in the directory during the remaining years of the nineteenth century, but the frequent changes in address and pastor suggest that it had yet to obtain a permanent structure and location for its services. The first predominantly Black Baptist congregation was formed in 1896 by a group of women who met in private homes. It was only after the turn of the century that this congregation secured a permanent site and building. The Methodist congregation was the locus of the African Methodist Episcopal Church, later Trinity Methodist Church, while the Baptist congregation became Calvary Baptist Church (Interview with Mignon Barker Richmond, SLC, December 1972).

89. Absence from the family household obscured the last twenty years of Isaac James's life. Prior to his departure both the FCS and the city directory listed his occupation as laborer. His oldest son, Sylvester, lived past the age of 80 and at the time of his death in 1920 owned realty and water rights valued at $2,500. In the late nineteenth century his occupation had been listed alternately as a farmer, gardener, and laborer (estate of Sylvester James, decd., no. 11164, Third District Court for SLCo, Probate Division). The second son, Silas, died in 1872 at age 25, owning five acres of land on the East Bench of SLC, the value of which was no more than a few hundred dollars. The 1870 FCS listed his occupation as laborer (estate of Silas F. James, decd., no. 1204, Third District Court for SLCo, Probate Division). The third son, Jessie, died in 1894 at age 37. Living at his mother's home most of his life, he apparently accumulated no property while working as a laborer and porter.

90. SLCo Assessment Rolls, 1872–78 volumes for SLC's Eighth Ward, 1876–77 volumes for South Cottonwood, and 1878–84 volumes for Union.

91. Most of the statistical interpretations in this paragraph are based on the geographical chart of Utah's Black population in Maag, 103–4. Personal compilations from the 1870 and 1880 FCS indicate that Utah's mining boom of the late 1860s and 1870s drew few Blacks to the mines. Only one Black in the 1870 census, and but two in the 1880 census, were described as miners. Park City had the largest number of Black residents of any mining town in the territory. They numbered

but six in 1880, and none were miners.

92. Since the research for this article was originally conducted, the 1900, 1910, and 1920 FCS have been opened to research, making a substantial body of additional data available for such a study.

93. Mrs. James's children appear to have been raised in the Mormon faith, if the experience of her youngest daughter is typical of that of other children in the family (obituary of Vilate Warner, *DEN*, 4 March 1897). Her oldest son, Sylvester, remained a member of the church until 1885, when he was excommunicated for "unchristianlike conduct," a vague charge that could cover a multitude of greater and lesser offenses. He never returned to the church (First Ward, Salt Lake Stake, *ROM*, early-1904, lib. no. 6578, 14, microfilm copy, LDS/CHD). Her youngest son, Jessie, was baptized into the church at an early age, but seems to have been inactive as a member until he was rebaptized less than a year before his death (Eighth Ward, Salt Lake Stake, *ROM*, early-1905, part 2, 9).

My impressions of an attrition in church membership, gained from research on the James family, have been reinforced by a discussion with William G. Hartley, associate professor of history and research historian at the Joseph Fielding Smith Institute for Church History at BYU, whose own study of early-day Black settlers has noted a similar decline in Mormon affiliation among their descendants.

Chapter 3: Mother M. Augusta (Anderson)

1. Minutes of the meeting of the Council of the Sisters of the Holy Cross, 13 May 1875. All references cited in these notes are in the Archives of the Sisters of the Holy Cross, Saint Mary's, Notre Dame, Indiana.

2. The *Encyclopedia Britannica*, 1951 edition, says that Sherman was "adopted" by the Ewings, but if so it was without a name change. Sherman's mother was still living at this time.

3. Quoted in Sister M. Emerentiana (Nowlan), unpublished chronicles, vol. 1 (n.d.), 215.

4. *Our Western Province*, vol. 5 of *Centenary Chronicles of the Sisters of the Holy Cross* (privately printed, n.d.), 2.

5. 20 June 1875.

6. 20 June 1875.

7. 12 July 1875.

8. The source ("Utah," archive box, Salt Lake City: Saint Mary-of-the-Wasatch, 1875–1969) says July 27, but that seems impossible in view of the fact that the building was in use by September 6.

9. *Our Western Province*, 2.

10. Flyer signed by Sister Augusta and quoted in many places. "Utah," archive box,

Salt Lake City: Holy Cross Hospital, 1875–1994; Narrative 1875–1939.

11.   "Commercial health insurance in this country began with a compulsory plan for merchant seamen in 1798. The first private insurance company to issue medical insurance was Massachusetts Health Insurance Company in 1847. But 1929 is usually thought of as the birth of health insurance in America. Because of the poor economic conditions of the depression, Baylor University Hospital in Dallas, Texas, saw a need to insure itself against its patients' inability to pay their bills. Baylor initiated a plan for schoolteachers, who paid 50 cents each month to cover 21 hospital days each year." Patricia A. Hamilton, *Health Care Consumerism* (St. Louis: C.V. Mosby, 1982), 40. Another account states that "the earliest form of health insurance, mutual benefit funds, may be traced back to the late medieval days and the guilds of skilled craftsmen. These funds were financed by the pooling of small weekly contributions. They paid cash 'sick benefits' to eligible members during periods of disability." But it skips from the medieval guilds to the periods following World Wars I and II. Herman Miles Somers and Anne Ramsay Somers, *Doctors, Patients, and Health Insurance: The Organization and Financing of Medical Care* (Washington, D.C.: Brookings Institution, 1961), 225–26. Another source also puts the start between the wars. "Modern health insurance was born," the Health Insurance Institute reports, "in the Great Depression of the 1930s as a means of helping people cope with the costs of health care, and of bringing financial relief to hospitals faced with empty beds and declining revenues." "Controlling Health Costs," in *National Health Issues* (Washington, D.C.: Congressional Quarterly), 28 January 1977.

12.   Bernice Maher Mooney, *The Salt of the Earth: The History of the Catholic Church in Utah, 1776–1987* (SLC: The Catholic Diocese of Salt Lake City, 1987), 67.

13.   Xeroxed copy of a clipping from a newspaper, not identified. The clipping is dated (with pen and ink) 20 January 1898. "Utah," archive box, Salt Lake City: Holy Cross Hospital, 1875–1994; Narrative, 1875–1939.

14.   St. Mary's in Park City, 1882 (closed 1933); St. Joseph's in Eureka, 1885 (closed 1941); and the school at Kearns-Saint Anne's Orphanage in Salt Lake City, 1891 (the Sisters of the Holy Cross withdrew in 1941 and were replaced by the Sisters of the Incarnate Word).

Chapter 4: Eliza Kirtley Royle

1.   Karen J. Blair, *The Clubwoman As Feminist: True Womanhood Redefined, 1868–1914* (New York: Holmes & Meier, 1980), 58.

2.   "Eliza K. Royle," *SLT*, 11 December 1910, 32.

3.   Howard L. Conrad, ed., *Encyclopedia of the History of Missouri* (New York: Southern History Co., 1901), 4:41.

4.   Eliza Kirtley Royle, "Home Life on the Border before War," in *A Memorial of Sin-*

clair Kirtley and His Family by His Daughters Mary Simpson Turner and Eliza Kirtley Royle* (n.p., 1909), 54, 58–59.

5. North Todd Gentry, *Bench and Bar of Boone County Missouri* (Columbia, Mo.: the author, 1916), 36, 114–15.

6. Eliza Kirtley Royle, "A Sketch of the Life and Character of Captain Sinclair," in *A Memorial of Sinclair*, 1.

7. Ibid., 2–3.

8. Ibid.

9. Mary S. Kirtley Turner, "Eliza Kirtley Royle," in *A Memorial of Sinclair*, 72.

10. John C. Creighton, *The History of Columbia and Boone County* (Columbia, Mo.: Computer Color-Graphics, 1987), 59, 62.

11. Mary S. Kirtley Turner, "A Continuation of a 'Sketch of the Life and Character of Captain Sinclair Kirtley'," in *A Memorial of Sinclair*, 11–12.

12. Ibid., 14–15.

13. Ibid., 11, 14.

14. "Mrs. Eliza Kirtley Royle," *DN*, 10 March 1900, 14.

15. Turner, "A Continuation," 15.

16. Ibid., 15–16.

17. Ibid., 67.

18. Lafayette County, Missouri, Marriage Record, Book D, 297; LDS/FHL, microfilm, no. 959,414.

19. "Death Claims Prominent Man," *SLT*, 7 July 1910, 1.

20. *History of the Bench and Bar of Utah* (SLC: Interstate Press Association, 1913), 105.

21. Turner, "The Present Generation," in *A Memorial of Sinclair*, 68.

22. Thomas J. Noel, Paul F. Mahoney, and Richard E. Stevens, *Historical Atlas of Colorado* (Norman: University of Oklahoma, 1994), 34; Robert L. Brown, *Colorado Ghost Towns—Past and Present* (Caldwell, Idaho: Caxton Printers, 1972), 78–80; Phyllis Flanders Dorset, *The New Eldorado: The Story of Colorado's Gold and Silver Rushes* (New York: Macmillan, 1970), 172.

23. Sandra Dallas, *Colorado Ghost Towns and Mining Camps* (Norman: University of Oklahoma Press, 1985), 47.

24. U.S. Census Bureau, *1870 Census—California: Santa Clara County, San Jose First Ward*, LDS/FHL, microfilm, no. 0,295,388.

25. *Address at the Tenth Anniversary of the First Presbyterian Church of Salt Lake City*, 13 November 1882 (SLC: Utah Printing Company, 1882), 1.

26. "Death Claims Prominent Man."

27. *History of the Bench and Bar*, 105.

28. *Utah, Her Cities, Towns, and Resources* (Chicago: Manly and Litteral, 1891–1892), 149.

29. *Address at the Tenth Anniversary*, 1.

30. Ibid., 2–3.

31. Turner, "Eliza Kirtley Royle," 72–73. While this account contains a number of

factual errors concerning the founding of the Blue Tea and the Ladies Literary Club, it should not be dismissed; it undoubtedly reflects Eliza's thoughts of isolation. Though this book is dated 1909, I am uncertain whether Eliza saw the complete book before her death. The Missouri Historical Society received its copy in 1917 with a note from Mary indicating it was a recent publication.

32. Howe, lyricist of "Battle Hymn of the Republic," was also one of the founders of the women's club movement in the United States.

33. Ora Leigh Traughber, "Reawakened Memoirs in the Annals of Salt Lake Clubdom," *DN*, 24 April 1926, clipping file, SLC Public Library.

34. Blue Tea Minutes, 1876–1885, 19–20, Special Collections, Marriott Library, U of U.

35. Katherine Barrette Parsons, *History of Fifty Years: Ladies Literary Club, Salt Lake City, Utah, 1877–1927* (SLC: Arrow Press, 1927), 24.

36. Patricia Lyn Scott, "Firm in Our Endeavor: The Ladies Literary Club, 1877 to 1927" (paper presented at the Utah Women's History Association Annual Meeting, SLC, 12 March 1983), 2; Parsons, *History of Fifty Years*, 23.

37. Blue Tea Minutes, 29 March 1877, 29.

38. Ibid., 30. The minutes illustrate this action with a membership list showing a line drawn through these names.

39. Blair, 24.

40. Thomas G. Alexander, "Cooperation, Conflict, and Compromise: Women, Men, and the Environment in Salt Lake City, 1890–1930," *Brigham Young University Studies* 35 (January 1995): 9, describes the founders of the Ladies Literary Club as "Mormons, Protestants and Catholics." I have undertaken a study of the early membership of the Ladies Literary Club (1877–1895) to either confirm or deny the commonly held belief that the club's founders were entirely non-Mormon. Initial research has not identified any Mormon members.

41. Scott, "Firm in Our Endeavor," 2. This common understanding was said to exist only for a few years and by the 1890s Mormon women were welcomed as members.

42. Eliza K. Royle, "The Ladies' Literary Club of Salt Lake City," in *Manual of Ladies Literary Club of Salt Lake City for the Columbian Exposition* (SLC: Ladies Literary Club, 1893), 1.

43. Ibid., 2.

44. *SLT*, undated clipping (ca. Feb. 1927). "Snap Shots" (Scrapbook, 1924–27), Ladies Literary Club, SLC.

45. Ibid.

46. Blair, 40.

47. U.S. Bureau of Census, *1880 Census—Utah: Salt Lake County, Salt Lake City, Eleventh Ward*, LDS/FHL, microfilm, no. 1,255,337.

48. Parsons, *History of Fifty Years*, 27.

49. Patricia Lyn Scott, "The Gentile Roots of the Salt Lake City Public Library, 1866–

1898" (paper presented to the Mormon History Association Conference, Provo, Utah, May 1984), 7.

50. "Minutes of the Ladies Literary Club," 21 November 1879, 19; 28 November 1879, 20.

51. Scott, "The Gentile Roots," 9; "Library Honor Due to Women," *SLT*, 20 June [1912], newspaper clipping file, SLC Public Library. The books included authoritative works on science, music, and art and works on educational themes.

52. Scott, "The Gentile Roots," 10.

53. Blair, 71.

54. Scott, "Firm in Our Endeavor," 4.

55. Ibid., 5.

56. "Dedicated Its Home," *SLT*, 8 February 1898, 3.; "The Ladies Literary Club—Home Formally Opened," *SLT*, 8 January 1898, 8.

57. This honorary position was created in 1896. Its first three honorees were "Jennie June" Croly, Julia Ward Howe, and Lucinda Hinsdale Stone. Mary I. Wood, *The History of the General Federation of Women's Clubs: For the First Twenty-two Years of Its Organization* (New York: General Federation of Women's Clubs, 1912), 100–102; Mildred White Wells, *Unity in Diversity: The History of the General Federation of Women's Clubs* (Washington, D.C.: General Federation of Women's Clubs, 1953), 142–43, 488; General Federation of Women's Clubs, *Proceedings of the Fourth Biennial Conference of the General Federation, June 21–27, 1898* (New York: General Federation of Women's Clubs, 1899), 5.

58. Eliza K. Royle, "Letter to Mrs. King, Dated March 29, 1901," Ladies Literary Club, Minutes, 188.

59. Minutes, 21 February 1902, 285; Parsons, *History of Fifty Years*, 99.

60. Minutes, 11 April 1902, 287; Parsons, *History of Fifty Years*, 101.

61. "Death Claims Prominent Man," *SLT*, 7 June 1907, 1; "Passing of Martha Royle, Former Utah Singer," *SLT*, 2 June 1942, newspaper clipping file, USHS, SLC.

62. "Society," *SLT*, 24 April 1907, 5.

63. "Death Claims Prominent Man," 1.

64. SLC Death Records, Book F-1910, 172, LDS/FHL, microfilm, no. 026,555.

65. "Death Claims Prominent Man," 1.

66. Third District Court, SLCo. Probate Case Files, case no. 6112, Utah State Archives, Salt Lake City, Utah.

67. "Elisa Kirtley Royle," *SLT*, 32.

68. Death Records, Book F, 384.

69. "Eliza Kirtley Royle," *SLT*, 32.

70. Scott, "Firm in Our Endeavor," 7.

71. Minutes, 12 September 1902–14 March 1913, 215.

72. "New Clubhouse Is Opened—Handsome Chair Presented," *SLT*, 26 April 1913, 7.

73. Ibid.

74. Ibid.

75. As quoted in Blair, 69.

Chapter 5: Sarah Elizabeth Carmichael

1. Brief accounts of Lizzie's life are found in Ellen L. Jakeman, "Sarah Elizabeth Carmichael Williamson," *Relief Society Magazine* 15 (September 1928): 478–90; Mary M. Root, "Pioneer Poet of Utah: Study of the Life and Work of Sarah Carmichael, One of the State's First Literary Producers," *SLT*, 16 February and 8 March 1936; Edward W. Tullidge, "Carmichael," *Western Galaxy* 1 (May 1888): 334–40; Catherine Hazel Selby, "Sarah Elizabeth Carmichael" (master's thesis, U of U, 1921).

2. Jakeman, 478–79; *DN*, 21 November 1866 and 11 November 1901; *Salt Lake Herald*, 11 November 1901; Brigham H. Roberts, ed., *History of the Church of Jesus Christ of Latter-day Saints* (SLC, 1902–32), 6:175, 7:326, 463; Kate B. Carter, comp., *Heart Throbs of the West* (SLC, 1950), 11:404; Francis W. Kirkham and Harold Lundstrom, eds., *Tales of a Triumphant People: A History of Salt Lake County, Utah, 1847–1900* (SLC, 1947), 24. See also U.S., NA, 1850 Census Schedules, Utah, USHS, SLC, microfilm of holograph, no. A143. The census shows the Carmichaels as Eighth Ward residents and lists four family members: William, joiner, 46; Mary Ann, 42; Mary, 15; Sarah, 13.

3. Kirkham and Lundstrom, *Tales*, 25; Andrew Jenson, *Encyclopedic History of the Church of Jesus Christ of Latter-day Saints* (SLC: Deseret News, 1941), 746; Carter, *Our Pioneer Heritage* (SLC, 1958–71), 2:18.

4. Tullidge, "Carmichael," 335.

5. Jakeman, 489; Root.

6. *Salt Lake Herald*, 11 November 1901.

7. Jakeman, 480–81; Carter, *Our Pioneer Heritage*, 2:18.

8. "To Miss Carmichael, G.S.L. City—," *DN*, 13 April 1859. Eliza R. Snow copied the poem on some unused pages in her Journal and Notebook (1842–44), now in the LDS/CHD.

9. Lizzie's poetry was signed Sarah E. Carmichael, Miss S. E. Carmichael, or S. E. Carmichael. The latter usage led one childhood admirer to assume the writer was a man. See Louisa L. Greene Richards, "Memories of Miss Carmichael's Writings," *Young Woman's Journal* 13 (January 1902): 23–25. Under the editorship of Albert Carrington, the *DN* published many of her poems following her debut with "Truth." Titles and dates of publication through 1859 are as follows: "Perseverance," 19 May 1858; "The World's Wisdom," 2 February 1859; "Pharoah," 30 March 1859; "Wine," 18 May 1859; "What Is There Worth Living For?" 22 June 1859; "The Father's Legacy," 3 August 1859; "Time," 14 September 1859; "Willie's Dream," 21 September 1859; "The Chieftain's Reply," 26 October 1859;

"Thy Mother's Love," 2 November 1859; "History, Romance, and Poetry," 23 November 1859; "Armaund," 14 December 1859.

10. "Brigham Young," *DN*, 17 October 1860.

11. *Poems, Religious, Historical, and Political* (SLC, 1877), 2:1.

12. The handwritten document, undated and untitled, is found in the Susa Young Gates Collection, "Miscellaneous" Box 8, USHS. The writing looks like Susa's; however, since she was not born until 1856, she likely would not have been an eyewitness to the encounter. The document claims that although Lizzie's husband was kind to her, he wanted to commercialize her work. When that failed, the writer continues, he hoped to reap quick profit from an exposé of the Mormon people and their religion which he urged his wife to write. Since Lizzie never wrote a history of the Mormons, one cannot pass judgment on its contents. It is doubtful, nevertheless, that her writing would have fallen into the lurid exposé class.

13. Eliza R. Snow, "Anthem," *DN*, 12 March 1862.

14. John R. Young, *Memoirs of John R. Young, Utah Pioneer, 1847* (SLC, 1920), 117. Prior to Young's mission to the Sandwich Islands in 1864, Lizzie wrote "A Parting Word to My Friend John R. Young," pp. 127–28. It is not clear whether Lizzie was a teacher or a student at the school. One source indicates that she was a "reticent and sensitive public school teacher." See Root.

15. "Programme for the Celebration of the 86th Anniversary of Our National Independence," USHS; *DN*, 9 July and 30 July 1862. The poem and the address are printed in full in the *DN*.

16. Tullidge, "Carmichael," 338.

17. Ibid., 335.

18. "Lucrezia Borgia's Feast," *DN*, 6 May 1863. "The Daughter of Herodias" and "Esau's Petition" appeared in the *DN* on 22 October 1862 and 11 March 1863 respectively. "The Stolen Sunbeam" may be found in Sarah E. Carmichael, *Poems* (San Francisco, 1866), 25–27.

19. William Cullen Bryant, ed. *A Family Library of Poetry and Song. . .*, 2 vols. (New York, 1878), 654–55; May Wentworth, *Poetry of the Pacific: Selections and Original Poems from the Poets of the Pacific States* (San Francisco, 1867), 326–29; Jakeman, 484.

20. Carmichael, *Poems*, 37–41; Richard H. Orton, comp., *Records of California Men in the War of the Rebellion, 1861 to 1867* (Sacramento, 1890), 196; Edward W. Tullidge, *History of Salt Lake City* (SLC, 1886), 281. Orton lists the doctor as "Jonathan M."—not the "Josiah" used by some local writers. Contemporary newspapers used only his initials.

21. Fred B. Rogers, *Soldiers of the Overland* (San Francisco, 1938), 75; *Daily Union Vedette*, 4 July 1864 and 12 August 1866.

22. One writer says the doctor read Lizzie's story of the "Lily of the Valley" and sought her acquaintance. *Salt Lake Herald*, 11 November 1901.

23. Ina Coolbrith, poet laureate of California and a niece of Joseph Smith Jr., vigorously opposed polygamy. Nevertheless, Joseph Fielding Smith said his father, Joseph F. Smith, nephew of Joseph Smith Jr. and president of the LDS Church, regularly corresponded with the Oakland librarian and mentor of Jack London. See Kate Thomas, "Ina Coolibrith," *Relief Society Magazine* 15 (November 1928): 580–85.

24. Brigham H. Roberts, *A Comprehensive History of the Church of Jesus Christ of Latter-day Saints Century 1* (SLC: LDS Church, 1930), 5:72–75; *Daily Union Vedette*, 14 October 1865; *DN*, 19 October 1865. The complete poem is reprinted by Roberts and may also be found in Tullidge, "Carmichael," 337–38, and Carmichael, *Poems*, 21–24.

25. J. H. Beadle, *Polygamy: Or, the Mysteries and Crimes of Mormonism* . . . (Philadelphia, 1882), 320–21; Stanley P. Hirshon, *The Lion of the Lord: A Biography of Brigham Young* (New York, 1969), 293. Hirshon's reference is the New York *World*, 2 October 1870. See also Albert D. Richardson, *Beyond the Mississippi* . . . (Hartford, Conn., 1867), 470–72. Richardson accompanied Schuyler Colfax on his visit to Salt Lake City and the West in 1865.

    The study of Mormon attitudes toward the Civil War goes far beyond the scope of this essay. No doubt opinions on the subject were as widely varied locally as in the East. The *DN* published several of Lizzie's poems which touch on the subject: "Slavery," 20 February 1861; and "Our Country," 25 March 1863. Her poem "Life and Liberty," read at July 4, 1862 ceremonies also speaks to the issue. On the other hand, Eliza R. Snow was critical of the use of poetry to urge support for the war. She asserted that war and famine were inevitable to "avenge the blood/That stains the wall of Carthage jail." See her poem "Response to 'Our Country's Call,' by Wm. C. Bryant" in *DN*, 25 December 1861.

26. Carmichael, *Poems*, v and 28–29.

27. *Daily Union Vedette*, 6, 7, and 12 August 1866. Stein was cashier for Wells, Fargo & Co.'s Overland Express and lived near the Salt Lake Theater on First South. E. L. Sloan, comp., *The Salt Lake City Directory and Business Guide for 1869* (SLC, 1869), 140.

28. *Daily Union Vedette*, 20 November 1866.

29. Accounts of the incident are found in Roberts, *Comprehensive History*, 5:210–12; T. B. H. Stenhouse, *The Rocky Mountain Saints* . . . (SLC, 1904), 618; R. N. Baskin, *Reminiscences of Early Utah* (SLC, 1914), 166–67; and *Daily Union Vedette*, 26 September 1866.

30. *Daily Union Vedette*, 26 October 1866.

31. Ibid., 6 November 1866.

32. Ibid., 18 October 1867.

33. Hubert Howe Bancroft, *History of Nevada, Colorado, and Wyoming, 1540–1888* (San Francisco, 1890), 272; Walter R. Averett, *Directory of Southern Nevada Place Names*, rev. ed. (Las Vegas, 1962), 109.

34.   Evidently Mary Carmichael boarded with the Thomas Gamble family. The 1870 census lists her as an "idiot," age 32, living in the Gamble household between Main and State Streets on Fifth South, around the corner from the old Carmichael home on State. See 1870 Census Schedules, Bear-Weber Counties, Utah, no. A145, and Sloan, *Salt Lake City Directory 1869* . . ., 107. When the Williamsons returned to Salt Lake City, they resumed care of Lizzie's sister. See 1880 Census Schedules, Utah: Salt Lake-Sanpete Counties, no. A148. In 1880 the household consisted of Williamson, physician, 52; Lizzie, 42; Mary, 44; Eliza Jane Elliott, housekeeper, 24; and Richard Whitmore or Whitman, stable man, 17. The Williamsons probably took up residence on or near the Carmichael property, as the 1874 directory lists them in that area. See E. L. Sloan, comp., *Gazeteer of Utah and Salt Lake City Directory* (SLC, 1874), 295 and 321. Selby in "Sarah Elizabeth Carmichael," 7, says Williamson bought a lot next to the old Carmichael home.

35.   Mary Jane Mount Tanner, Journal, 17 May 1874, p. 147, microfilm of holograph, LDS/CHD Archives.

36.   *SLT*, 31 March 1880; Jakeman, 490.

37.   *DN*, 11 November 1901; *Salt Lake Herald*, 11 November 1901; *SLT*, 11 November 1901.

38.   Carmichael, "April Flowers," in *Poems*, 7–8.

Chapter 6: Chipeta

1.   Marshall Sprague, *Massacre: The Tragedy at White River* (Boston: Little, Brown, 1957), p. 306.

2.   Everett Blair, *This Will Be an Empire* (New York: Pageant Press, 1959).

3.   Clifford Duncan, Ute tribal historian, interview by author, SLC, 1994.

4.   George Howe Colt, "Who Was Pocahontas?" *Life*, July 1995, 64.

5.   Duncan interview.

6.   June Lyman and Norma Denver, comp., *Ute People: An Historical Study*, ed. Floyd O'Neil and John Sylvester (SLC: U of U Press, 1970).

7.   Floyd O'Neil, director, American West Center, U of U, interview by the author, 1994.

8.   Roland McCook, telephone interviews by the author, October 1995.

9.   P. David Smith, *Ouray Chief of the Utes* (Ouray, Colo.: Wayfinder Press, 1986).

10.   The conflict was named for both sides of the dispute: White River for that division of the Ute tribe and Meeker for Nathan Meeker, the government agent for the tribe; it appears in the literature under both names. The variant tellings of the massacre are included in several sources: Blair; Dee Brown, *Bury My Heart at Wounded Knee* (New York: Holt, Reinhart, and Winston, 1971); Robert Emmitt, *The Last War Trail* (Norman: University of Oklahoma Press, 1954); Elizabeth Nixon, "The Meeker Massacre" (master's thesis, Colorado State College of Education, 1935);

Smith, 154–68; Sprague; Fred H. Werner, *Meeker: The Story of the Meeker Massacre and Thornburgh Battle September 29, 1879* (Greeley, Colo.: Werner Publications, 1985).

11. Smith, 165.
12. O'Neil interview.
13. "Chipeta's Downfall," *The Denver Republican* (August 1887), typescript copy from the Colorado State Historical Society.
14. Smith. 209.
15. Duncan interview.
16. McCook interviews.
17. Smith, 194.
18. "Chipeta's Downfall."
19. O'Neil interview.
20. Duncan interview.
21. McCook interviews.
22. The Colorado State Historical Society has a collection of photographs of Chipeta.
23. Duncan interview.
24. Lyman and Denver, 93.
25. McCook interviews.
26. Sprague, 207.
27. McCook interviews.
28. Ute Tribal Council Statement of Purpose, 1968.

Chapter 7: Elizabeth Ann Claridge McCune

1. S. C. Dallas, in *Memorial to Elizabeth Claridge McCune, Missionary, Philanthropist, Architect*, ed. Susa Young Gates (SLC: n.p., 1924), 30–41. Unless otherwise specified, all McCune mansion description is from this source.
2. Susa Young Gates, *Memorial to Elizabeth Claridge McCune*, 29.
3. George M. McCune, *Matthew McCune Family History* (SLC: McCune Family Association, 1993), 2AB:364–65.
4. Mary Ellen Love Neff, in *Memorial to Elizabeth Claridge McCune*, 74.
5. Mary Ellen Love Neff, in *Memorial to Elizabeth Claridge McCune*, 74.
6. Elizabeth H. Sparks, in *Memorial to Elizabeth Claridge McCune*, 80–81.
7. Mary Ellen Love Neff, in *Memorial to Elizabeth Claridge McCune*, 75–76.
8. Elizabeth Ann Claridge McCune, autobiography, in *Memorial to Elizabeth Claridge McCune*, 17–18.
9. Elizabeth Claridge McCune, autobiography, 18
10. Elizabeth Claridge McCune, autobiography, 17–18.
11. Juab County Recorder Book, certificate no. 306, p. 306, in George M. McCune, 378.

12. Claudia L. Bushman, *Mormon Sisters: Women in Early Utah* (SLC: Olympus Publishing, 1976), 200.
13. George M. McCune, 387.
14. Ibid., 396–97.
15. Gates, 26-27.
16. George M. McCune, 411.
17. Dallas and Hedges, "Description of McCune Home," LDS/CHD, RS General Board, Susa Young Gates files.
18. Gates, 26.
19. Ibid., 27.
20. George M. McCune, 425–26.
21. Ibid.
22. Gates, 41–44.
23. Ibid., 40.
24. Alfred W. and Elizabeth C. McCune to President Heber J. Grant, 7 October 1920, LDS/CHD, RS General Board, Susa Young Gates files.
25. Susa Young Gates to Alfred W. McCune, 19 October 1920, LDS/CHD, RS General Board, Susa Young Gates files.
26. Elizabeth Claridge McCune to Susa Young Gates, 16 November 1920, Los Angeles, LDS/CHD, RS General Board, Susa Young Gates files.
27. Gates, 71–72.

Chapter 8: Susanna Egera Bransford Emery Holmes Delitch Engalitcheff

1. "Utah's Own Silver Queen Arrives for Summer Visit in Salt Lake City," *SLT*, 12 May 1938, 12; "Susanna Emery-Holmes," *Biographical Record of Salt Lake City and Vicinity* (Chicago: National Historic Record Company, 1902), 211–12. Margaret Godfrey, "The Silver Queen" *Salt Lake City*, September–October 1993, 33–34.
2. Milford Bransford's Bible, courtesy of Dr. Harold Lamb Sr., SLC; John A. Shiver, *Bransford Family History* (Kentucky: McDowell, 1981), 35; see also Sara Cooper's undated will, probated in Lexington, Kentucky, copy in possession of Dr. Lamb Sr.; "Crossing the Plains," a history of the Bransford trip to California. This unpublished account was provided by Stella Enge; it had no author or date. "Milford Bransford," *Park Record*, 25 May 1894; "Milford Bransford Deceased," *Plumas Independent* (California), 26 May 1894.
3. *SLT*, 12 May 1938; John Bransford, Biographical Sketch, courtesy of Vadney Murray, Quincy, California; Susanna Hartman, Susie's niece, interview by the author, Laguna Hills, California, 1993; Jean Murray of Quincy, California, interview by the author, 1993; magazine article from *Elite*, found in Susie's scrapbook at the USHS; entry in Susie's autograph book, 1879–86, from T. M. J. This book is in

the author's possession.

4. Jane Rogers, "Rogers Family History," *Plumas Memories*, #51, Plumas County Historical Society, June 1986, 27; O. N. Malmquist, *The First One Hundred Years: A Story of Salt Lake Tribune* (SLC: USHS, 1971) 211–13; Margaret Lester, *Brigham Street* (SLC: USHS, 1979), 110–20; Raye C. Ringholz, *Diggings and Doings in Park City* (Park City: the author, 1983), 60–64; Raye Ringholz to author, July 1993; "Personal Mention," *Park Record*, 15 November 1884; "Albion Emery," *Tullidge's Quarterly Magazine* (1902): 502–3, USHS; George A. Thompson and Fraser Buck, *Treasure Mountain Home—Park City Revisited* (SLC: Dream Garden Press, 1981), 83.

5. Dr. Harold Lamb, interview by the author, SLC, 1993; Wallace Bransford affidavit, 2, Probate Hearing for Louise Grace Emery Bransford, no. 9027, Third Circuit Court, Third Judicial District, 17 September 1918, Utah State Archives, SLC; Thompson and Buck, 83; "Mrs. Holmes Tells Story of Adoption of Foster Daughter" *DN*, 2 October 1918; Ringholz, 61; "Men and Events Linked with Great Mines of Park City," *Park Record*, 5 June 1931; "Honorable A.B. Emery" (editorial) and "Death of Honorable A.B. Emery," *Park Record*, 16 June 1894; Fraser and Buck, 83–84; *Polk Directory for Salt Lake City 1894*, Salt Lake City Sanborne Maps for 1894, USHS; Albion Emery, Probate Case no. 102, Summit County records; "Brother Albion B. Emery," *Proceedings of the Grand Lodge of Utah 1895* (SLC: Utah Masonic Lodge), 95–98.

6. Emery Probate Records; Fraser and Buck, 79, 84; "For a Fortune," *Park Record*, 22 September 1894; *Park Record*, 5 June 1931; "Chambers vs. Emery," *Pacific Reporter* 45:192–200; unidentified article in Susie's scrapbook; Ringholz, 61; "Receives Title to Millions," *SLT*, 20 month unreadable, 1930.

7. "Susanna Emery-Holmes," *Elite* 21, no. 49 and unidentified clipping, both in Susie's scrapbook; Lester, 111; Bransford affidavit, 3; Hartman interviews; "Mrs. Holmes Again on Witness Stand," *SLT*, 4 October 1918; "Findings of Fact and Conclusions of Law," in Bransford probate records; Lamb interview; Mary Cable, *Top Drawer American High Society from the Gilded Age to the Roaring Twenties* (Hanover: McClelland & Stewart, 1984), 42.

8. Floralee Millsaps, interview with the author, SLC, 1993; Lester, 111; "For Love and Affection," *DN*, 11 October 1899.

9. Joseph Heinerman, "Brigham Young's Grandest Residence, Amelia's Palace," *Montana, the Magazine of Western History* (winter 1979): 58, 62; Millsaps interview; Lester, 112, 114; *Elite* article; Hartman interview; unidentified article in Susie's scrapbook; Sandy Brimhall interview by the author, SLC, 1993.

10. Malmquist, 213; *Biographical Records of Salt Lake City*, 211; "Mrs. Emery-Holmes's Public Reply to Hughes Supporters," *SLT*, 9 September 1916; Hartman interviews; "John Bransford," *SLT*, 24 May 1941; unidentified news clipping in Susie's scrapbook.

11. "Mrs. Holmes Again on Witness Stand;" "Bransford Takes Stand in Court" *SLT*,

11 October 1918; "Bransford Adds to Testimony" *SLT*, 15 October 1918; Grace's wedding announcement, Society Section, *DN*, 6 September 1904 and *SLT*, 7 September 1904; "Husband Weeps As He Testifies in Trial," *DN*, 15 October 1918; "Spectators Barred from Bransford Hearing," *DN*, 11 October 1918; Bransford affidavit.

12. "Mrs. Bransford Dies in California," *SLT*, 25 October 1917; "Actress Testifies Mrs. Bransford Felt Blue," *DN*, 19 October 1918; "Mrs. Holmes May Finish Case Today," *SLT*, 30 October 1918; Hartman Interview; "Florist Testifies in Will Contest," *SLT*, 22 October 1918.

13. "Mrs. Holmes Sues Bransford for $400,000," *SLT*, 21 January 1918; Bransford Probate, Findings of Fact, 18–30; "Mrs. Holmes Loses Suit against Bransford," *DEN*, 25 January 1919; Hartman interview.

14. Brimhall interview; Hartman interview; Lamb interview; "Romantic History Adds Glamour to Eleventh Showcase Design," *Pasadena Star*, 17 April 1975; Pasadena Junior Philharmonic Committee, *Showcase of Interior Design, Notes on El Roble Residence*, undated, courtesy of Pasadena City Library.

15. Cover and cover caption of *California Life*, 21 October 1922; cover and cover article of *California Life*, 21 March 1925; Colonel Holmes probate papers, no. 14129, Utah State Archives; petition to Illinois Court, Holmes Probate from Illinois, in possession of the author; Jack Gallivan of *SLT*, interview with the author, SLC, 1993; "Former Utahn Answers the Call," *Park Record*, 2 October 1925; "Col. Holmes, Once of Salt Lake, Dies East," *SLT*, 2 October 1925; Culver Sherrill, *Crimes without Punishment and Other Tales* (Hicksville, N.Y.: Exposition Press, 1977), 72.

16. Sherrill, 72; "Utah Woman Wed in Paris to Physician," *SLT*, 20 July 1930; unidentified clipping from California newspaper was furnished by Stella Inge; "Prince and Wife Decide to 'Make Up'," *New York Times*, 26 August 1915; "America's 'Silver Queen' Passes through Adelaide," *DN*, 25 August 1930; "Drawing Hidden Fortune from Earth Finest Method, Avers 'Silver Queen'," *Salt Lake Telegram*, 6 September 1932.

17. " 'Silver Queen' Seeks Divorce," *Salt Lake Telegram*, 1 November 1932; Hartman interview; "Utah 'Silver Queen' Plans Visit Here," unidentified SLC newspaper, 6 October 1930; unidentified news clipping from Pasadena Library on Delitch suicide, 5 February 1933.

18. Hartman interview; unidentified Pasadena news clipping, 5 February 1933.

19. Hartman interview; "Palace of 'Silver Queen' Stripped of Treasure," unidentified news clipping (prob. *Pasadena Star*), 5 February 1933.

20. "Utah 'Silver Queen,' 74, Weds 60 Year Old Prince," *SLT*, 20 October 1933; "Prince Weds 'Silver Queen' Second Time," unidentified newspaper clipping courtesy of Dr. Lamb; Ringholz letter to author; "Now the Romantic 'Silver Queen'—Aged 75—May Ditch Her Russian Prince to Marry a Boy!" *San Francisco Chronicle*, 10 February 1935; Hartman interview; "One Time Consul of Czarist Russia in Chicago—Was Officer in Imperial Army," *New York Times*, 28 March

1935; Lester, 119.

21. Hartman interview; Lamb interview; "'Silver Queen' of Utah Closes Famed Career," *Park Record*, 6 August 1942; all of the obituary notices in Utah's papers were essentially the same. "Estate Left by Princess Set at $65,918," *SLT*, 4 June 1943; Ringholz, 64; Susanna B. Engalitcheff's Will, no. 24672, 1, 2, and 5 in probate records, Utah State Archives; Engalitcheff probate records from Los Angeles, California, in the possession of the author; death certificate of Susanna B. Engalitcheff, Vital Statistics Department, Hartford, Connecticut.

22. Hartman interview; "'Silver Queen' Wills Millions to Manager of Estate," *SLT*, 26 August 1942.; Frances Darger, niece of Frank Johnson, Susie's lawyer in SLC, interview with author, 1993; interview with Merna Hansen, LDS Real Estate Department; telephone interview with Angelo Boncaraglio, Taormina, Sicily, 1994; telephone interviews with Lewis Sherrill and Gene Kellog, nephews of Culver Sherrill, 1993. A title search at the SLCo recorder's office revealed that Culver Sherrill received the property from Susie on January 31, 1939. The LDS Church purchased the property on February 25, 1950; Sherrill, *Crimes without Punishment and Other Tales*.

23. Cable, viii, 18, 24, 142; Sherrill, 74; Shiver, 35–135; "Thomas L. Bransford and Col. Colyar's Sketches," article in Susie's scrapbook; Malmquist, 211; Kathryn A. Jacob, "High Society in Washington during the Gilded Age: Three Distinct Aristocracies (Ph.D. diss., Johns Hopkins University, 1986), 266; "A Big Fortune at Stake," *SLT*, 18 December 1894.

24. Cable, vii, 18; Stephen Birmingham, *America's Secret Aristocracy* (Boston: Little, Brown, 1987), 13, 278, 282.

25. Cable, 42, 74; Birmingham, 282; Millsaps interview.

26. Lamb interview; Sherrill, 72; Cable, 20, 22.

27. Boncaraglio interview.

28. Millsaps interview; Mary Dawn Coleman, tour guide of Mt. Olivet Cemetery, interview by the author, 1994; interview with Evans and Early Mortuary staff, 1994; interview with Daniel Lopez, sexton of Mt. Olivet Cemetery, 1994.

Chapter 9: Mother Rachel Urban

1. No collection of Mother Urban stories has been found in the Redd Center (BYU), the Fife Archives (USU), the Marriott Library (U of U), the Park City Historical Society, or the USHS. The stories presented here have been collected by the author from residents of the city and guides for both historical societies. Any available from printed sources are cited when they appear in the text. Many of the stories may be folklore, also told of madams or prostitutes in other towns, but in Park City they are firmly affixed to Mother Urban.

2. Date of birth surmised from her age on the 1910 and 1920 United States' Census records, Utah, Summit County (LDS/FHL).

3. Anne Butler, *Daughters of Joy, Sisters of Misery: Prostitutes in the American West 1865–1869* (Urbana: University of Illinois Press, 1985), 14.
4. Ibid.
5. Timothy J. Gilfoyle, *City of Eros: New York City, Prostitution and the Commercialization of Sex, 1790–1920* (New York: W. W. Norton, 1992), 66, 311.
6. Butler, 15.
7. Colleen Adair Fliedner, *Stories in Stone, Park City, Utah, Miners and Madams, Merchants and Murderers* (Cypress, Calif.: Flair Publishing, 1995), 31.
8. Bureau of Census, Utah, Summit County, 1910, LDS/FHL, microfilm copy.
9. David Fleisher, "The Midnight Angels," *The Lodestar* (summer 1979).
10. Raye C. Ringholz, "The Giddy Girls of Deer Valley Gulch," *Park City* (Ogden, Utah: Meridian International, 1993), 132.
11. Jacqueline Baker Barnhart, *The Fair But Frail: Prostitution in San Francisco 1849–1900* (Reno: University of Nevada, 1986), 34–35.
12. Bancroft quoted in Barnhart, 35–36.
13. Barnhart, 25–26.
14. Ringholz, "Giddy Girls of Deer Valley Gulch," 134.
15. Floralie Millsaps, interview by the author, Salt Lake City, 1995; "A Journey through Time . . . Park City Museum Tour" (Park City Historical Society and Museum, 1994).
16. Raye Ringholz, *Diggings and Doings in Park City* (Park City: the author, 1983), 40.
17. Barnhart, 33.
18. Katherine Reynolds, *Park City* (Park City: Weller Institute for Care of Design, 1984).
19. Summit County Court Records, Box "1915," Park City Public Library.
20. Millsaps interview.
21. Fleisher.
22. Ringholz, "Giddy Girls of Deer Valley Gulch," 134.
23. Noal C. Newbold and Bea Kummer, *Silver and Snow: The Story of Park City* (SLC: Parliament Publishing, 1968), 33–35.
24. Millsaps interview.
25. Newbold and Kummer, 37.
26. Millsaps interview; Fliedner, 32.
27. Millsaps interview; Ringholz, "Giddy Girls of Deer Valley Gulch," 134.
28. Newbold and Kummer, 41–43.

Chapter 10: Mary Teasdel

1. Linda Rose McCage, "Mme. Bougereau, Pathfinder," *New York Times Book Review and Magazine*, 19 February 1922, 16.

2. Ibid.
3. Alice Merrill Horne, *Devotees and Their Shrines: A Handbook of Utah Art* (SLC: Deseret News, 1914), 58.
4. Ibid.
5. Mary Teasdel, "True Art," *Young Woman's Journal*, January 1904: 14.
6. James Haseltine, *100 Years of Utah Art* (SLC: Salt Lake Art Center, 1965), 19.
7. Ibid.
8. James Taylor Harwood, *A Basket of Chips: An Autobiography by James Taylor Harwood* (SLC: Tanner Trust Fund, U of U Library, 1985), 45.
9. Christine Jones Huber, *The Pennsylvania Academy and Its Women* (Philadelphia: Pennsylvania Academy of the Fine Arts, 1973), 21.
10. May Alcott, *Studying Art Abroad and How to Do It Cheaply* (Boston, 1897), 48.
11. Bernard Denvir, ed., *The Impressionists at First Hand* (London: Thames and Hudson, 1987), 37.
12. Marie Bashkirtseff, quoted in Germaine Greer, *The Obstacle Race* (New York: Farrar, Straus, and Giroux, 1979), 317.
13. John Hafen, "Art Student in Paris," *Contributor* (SLC) 15 (1893–94): 487.
14. Horne, 60.
15. Hafen, 487.
16. Horne, 60–61.
17. Cecilia Beaux, *Background with Figures* (Boston: Houghton Mifflin, 1939), 13–27.
18. Martine Herold, *The Academie Julian Is One Hundred Years Old* (n.p., n.d.).
19. Horne, 61.
20. Ibid.
21. Hafen, 487.
22. Linda Nochin, *Women Artists: 1550–1950* (New York: Knopf, 1976), 52.
23. Teasdel, 16.
24. Horne, 64.
25. Ibid., 63.
26. Teasdel, 16.
27. Ibid.
28. Horne, 63.
29. Teasdel, 14–15.
30. Ibid., 14.
31. Ibid.
32. Horne, 47.
33. *DN*, 12 April 1937.

Chapter 11: Maud May Babcock

1. Mary Johnson Webster, in "Tribute to Maud May Babcock," 8 October 1981,

transcript, Box 10, fd 4, Maud May Babcock Collection (MS 83), Special Collections, U of U.

2. Harcourt Peck to Maud May Babcock, 1890, Box 2, fd. 7, Maud May Babcock Collection, U of U.

3. Ronald Quayle Frederickson, "Maud May Babcock and the Department of Elocution at the University of Utah" (master's thesis, U of U, 1965).

4. Ibid., 19–20, 30.

5. Bob Wilson, in "Tribute to Maud May Babcock."

6. Frederickson, 70–71.

7. Ibid., 75.

8. "The Calisthenic Exhibition at the Theater Last Evening," *SLT*, 24 May 1893.

9. Louise Hill Howe Mallone, in "Tribute to Maud May Babcock."

10. Utah Women's Club Tribute to Maud May Babcock, 15 May 1943, transcript, Box 10, fd 5, Maud May Babcock Collection (MS 83), Special Collections, U of U. One of Maud May's many accomplishments listed is the establishment of the first University Dramatics Society (or Club) in the country. But the university paper, *The Utah Chronicle* (30 October 1893), seems to contradict that by complaining that "nearly every college in the U.S. has a Dramatic Society. Why have we not one?" Rather than such an unlikely "first" being credited to Maud May, another source (*Utah Alumnus*, May 1955) in remembrance to the influential teacher states that by the time of Maud May's retirement in 1938 the club had "the longest unbroken record of annual performances of any university dramatic club in North America."

11. "The University Dramatic Club," *The Utah Chronicle*, 14 December 1897.

12. Keith Maurice Engar, "History of Dramatics at the University of Utah from Beginnings until June 1919" (master's thesis, U of U, 1948), 48–49.

13. Ibid., 49.

14. Louise Hill Howe Mallone, in "Tribute to Maud May Babcock."

15. Frederickson, 21.

16. Ibid., 21.

17. Herbert Maw, in "Tribute to Maud May Babcock."

18. Frank Whiting, interview with author, SLC, 3 January 1995.

19. Frederickson, 23.

20. Frank Whiting, in "Tribute to Maud May Babcock."

21. Frederickson, 81.

22. Ibid., 86.

23. Ibid., 94.

24. Ibid., 103–5.

25. Maud May Babcock, "The New Movement in the Theatre," *Young Women's Journal* 29 (September 1918): 492–97.

26. Utah Women's Club Tribute, 8 October 1981.

27. Elva Plummer, interview with author, SLC, 19 January 1995.

28. Babcock's publications include *Handbook for Teachers of Interpretation: A Textbook*

for Teachers and for Prospective Teachers of Oral Expression in High Schools and Colleges (Lincoln, N.Y.: University Publishing Company, 1930); *Interpretive Selections for Colleges. Each with a Basic Purpose* (Chicago: University Publishing Company, 1930); *Interpretive Selections for High Schools: An Aim for Every Selection, Every Selection with an Aim* (Chicago: University Publishing Company, 1930); *Pedagogy of Interpretation: A Textbook for Teachers and Prospective Teachers of Oral Expression in High Schools and Colleges* (n.p., 1930); *Studies in Dialect* (SLC: U of U Press, 1916).

29. While Pioneer Memorial Theatre was still in the planning stages, the decision was made to honor Babcock. When the building was completed in 1962, the student stage was named for her. A plaque there gives her dates of birth and death and itemizes many of her contributions to the school and to drama in the state.

30. Utah Women's Club Tribute.

31. Joseph F. Smith, "Maud May Babcock," *Quarterly Journal of Speech* 41 (April 1955): 211.

Chapter 12: Georgia Lathouris Mageras

1. L. S. Stavrianos, *The Balkans Since 1453* (New York: Holt, Rinehart, and Winston, 1966), 472.
2. Ibid., 467, 468.
3. Ibid., 472.
4. Theodore Saloutos, *The Greeks in the United States* (Cambridge, Mass.: Harvard University Press, 1964), Chapter 2.
5. Thomas Burgess, *Greeks in America* (Boston: Sherman, French, 1913), 165.
6. U.S. Bureau of the Census, *A Report of the Seventeenth Decennial Census of the United States Census of Population: 1950,* vol. 2, *Characteristics of the Population,* part 44, *Utah* (Washington, D.C.: GPO, 1952), 29.
7. *Wyoming Labor Journal* (Cheyenne), 16 June 1922.
8. The biographical notes and quotations by the midwife were obtained from her daughters, Wilma Klekas and Millie M. McMichael, and her Greek town neighbors, including Georgia P. Papanikolas, Thelma Siouris, and Nick and John E. Papanikolas.
9. Maria S. Oikonomidou, *Oi Ellines tis Amerikis Opos Tous Eida* [*The Greeks in America As I Saw Them*] (New York: D. C. Divry, 1916), 85.
10. Helen Uzelac, Annie Sharich, Wilma Klekas, Tony Mageras, Millie McMichael, John Mageras, Eva Gessler.

Chapter 13: Alice Merrill Horne

1. Brief biographical sketches of Alice Merrill Horne are included in Robert S. Olpin, *Dictionary of Utah Art* (SLC: Salt Lake Art Center, 1980), 126–28; Zorah

H. Jeppson, "A Brief Biography of Alice Merrill Horne by Her Daughter," typescript in possession of the writer; Raye Price, "Utah's Leading Ladies of the Arts," *UHQ* 38 (winter 1970): 65–85; Jill C. Mulvay, "Three Mormon Women in the Cultural Arts," *Sunstone* 1 (spring 1976): 29–39; Leah D. Widstoe, "The Story of a Gifted Lady," *Relief Society Magazine* 32 (March 1945): 150–55; and Harriet Horne Arrington and Leonard J. Arrington, "Alice Merrill Horne, Cultural Entrepreneur," in *A Heritage of Faith*, ed. Mary E. Stovall and Carol Cornwall Madsen (SLC: Deseret Book Company, 1988), 121–36.

2. Alice Merrill Horne, "Child of the Frontier," typescript in possession of the writer. This recollection of her early years in Fillmore was written in 1947–48.

3. Ibid.

4. Lola Van Wagenen, "Sister Wives and Suffragists: Polygamy and the Politics of Woman Suffrage in Territorial Utah" (Ph.D. diss., New York University, 1990), 33.

5. Alice Merrill Horne's recollections of her political experiences form several chapters in her typewritten autobiographical history, prepared in 1947–48, copies in the hands of this writer and other family members. The chapters relevant to this essay are entitled "Art Study Ends in Politics," "I Discover the True Meaning of Politics," "Utah the First in the Union to Organize an Art Collection and an Annual Art Exhibition," and "More Bills—Grand Larceny." The following paragraphs are based on "Art Study Ends in Politics," 1–7.

6. Olpin, 8.

7. Jeppson.

8. See note 5.

9. See note 5.

10. Alice Merrill Horne, *Devotees and Their Shrines* (SLC: Deseret News, 1914), 8.

11. Horne, "Utah the First in the Union," 1.

12. See Delila M. Abbott, comp., "Women Legislators of Utah, 1896–1976," (SLC: USHS, typescript).

13. See Ann Gardner Stone, "Dr. Ellen Brooks Ferguson: Nineteenth Century Renaissance Woman," in *Sister Saints*, ed. Vicky Burgess-Olson (Provo, Utah: BYU Press, 1978), 325–39. A talented seamstress, Alice had made herself a beautiful "picture hat" and an Irish linen and lace gown. Evidently she wished to see Ferguson attractively attired as well.

14. Alice Merrill Horne, "Art Study Ends in Politics," 6–7.

15. Ibid.

16. Ibid.

17. See also *SLT*.

18. Horne, "Utah the First in the Union," 1–3.

19. See note 5.

20. Ibid, 4–5.

21. The personalities in the Utah legislature at the time, including Mrs. Horne, are

described in S. A. Kenner, *Utah As It Is* (SLC: Deseret News, 1904). See also *House Journal of the Third Session of the Legislature of Utah* (SLC: Tribune Job Printing, 1899).

22. Ibid. During the 1990 legislative session, the Utah Arts Council repeated this tactic to encourage funding for the arts. It worked that time, too.
23. Horne, "Utah the First in the Union," 5–6.
24. Ibid., 6–7.
25. Ibid.
26. See note 5.
27. The family still has Alice's copy of the original bill with her marginal comments.
28. Horne, "More Bills—Grand Larceny," 1–3.
29. Ibid., 3.
30. Ibid.
31. Ibid.
32. Ibid., 3–5. See also Ralph V. Chamberlin, *The University of Utah: A History of Its First Hundred Years, 1850–1950* (SLC: U of U Press, 1960), 184–85.
33. Alice Merrill Horne, "What Utah Offers the Artists," *The Utah* (SLC, August 1936). Biographical information is taken from the sources mentioned in note 1.
34. BYU, "Alice Merrill Horne," *Dedication of Buildings* (Provo, Utah: BYU, 1954), 50–51.
35. Minerva K. Teichert, Remarks at Funeral of Alice Merrill Horne, 10 October 1948, typescript in possession of the writer.
36. *SLT*, 30 December 1947.
37. Ibid., 19, 20, 21, 22, 23 September 1936.
38. *DN*, 22, 25 September 1936.

Chapter 14: Maude Adams

1. Hugh C. Weir, "Maude Adams," *Human Life*, December 1906, cover; Phyllis Robbins, *Maude Adams: An Intimate Portrait* (New York: G. P. Putnam's Sons, 1956), 119. Robbins was Adams's friend and received her papers after the actress's death. Many of those papers and photos are now in the Marriott Library, U of U.
2. Phyllis Robbins, *The Young Maude Adams* (Francestown, N.H.: Marshall Jones, 1959), 8.
3. James K. Melville, *The Mormon Drama and Maude Adams* (Provo, Utah: BYU Press for Extension Publications, Division of Continuing Education, 1965), 2.
4. Robbins, *The Young Maude Adams*, 31.
5. However, according to the SLC Parks Department, Liberty Park was formed from the farm of Isaac Chase, whose cabin still stands there. Records of both families in the LDS/FHL reveal no relationship between Chase and Adams.
6. Robbins, *The Young Maude Adams*, 33.

7. Melville, 5.
8. Robbins, *The Young Maude Adams*, 62.
9. Ibid., 82.
10. Ibid., 53.
11. Ibid., 107.
12. Anne Seagraves, *Women Who Charmed the West* (Hayden, Idaho: Wesanne Publications, 1991), 69–70.
13. Robbins, *The Young Maude Adams*, 35.
14. Robbins, *Maude Adams: An Intimate Portrait*, 161.
15. Ibid., 3.
16. Ibid., 19.
17. Ibid.
18. Robbins, *The Young Maude Adams*, 116.
19. Robbins, *Maude Adams: An Intimate Portrait*, 194.
20. Ibid., 154.
21. Ibid., 267.
22. Ibid., 288.
23. Ibid., 286.
24. Ibid., 12.
25. Seagraves, 65.
26. Kellene Ricks Adams, "The Incomparable Maude Adams Somewhere in Time," *Pioneer Magazine* (Jan/Feb 1994): 17–19.

Chapter 15: Kuniko Muramatsu Terasawa

1. H. Moriyasu and K. Terasawa. All quotations, unless noted separately, are translations from conversations with Kuniko Terasawa.
2. G. L. Bernstein, ed., *Recreating Japanese Women, 1600–1945* (Berkeley: University of California Press, 1991).
3. W. G. Beasley, *The Meiji Restoration* (Stanford, Calif.: Stanford University Press, 1972).
4. Bernstein.
5. Bernstein.
6. K. Terasawa, "Namida no Naka ni Hiso na Kakugo" ("Among the Tears a Valiant Determination"), trans. Haruko T. Moriyasu, *The Utah Nippo*, 5 May 1939.

Chapter 16: Ivy Baker Priest

1. Interview with Lois Lott, SLC, Utah, 5 January 1995. Lott was a tenant in the apartment building owned by Ivy Baker Priest in Los Angeles in the 1970s and

the two women became good friends. Lott has since moved to SLC and now volunteers for USHS.

2. Josephine Pace, "Kimberly As I Remember Her," *UHQ* 35 (1967): 112–20.
3. Ivy Baker Priest, *Green Grows Ivy* (New York: McGraw Hill, 1958), 31. This candid and charming autobiography takes Ivy's story up to 1957. It is the source of much of the biographical data that follow and, unless otherwise noted, the short quotes as well.
4. *SLT*, 27 November 1952.
5. Priest, 138–49; *SLT*, 26 November 1952; 11 January 1953.
6. Christine Sadler, director of the Washington bureau for *McCall's*, said of the newly sworn treasurer: "Her job is as routine as dishwater, but it has high prestige and frees her for extra-curricular activity . . . her influence in the new administration can be considerable." Quoted in *DN*, 6 April 1953.
7. *SLT*, 4 June 1965.
8. Priest, 230.
9. *SLT*, 4 April and 11 June 1959.
10. *SLT*, 30 June and 7 October 1965; *Ogden Standard-Examiner*, 5 December 1965.
11. *DN*, 16 February 1967; American Mothers Committee, Inc., comp., *Mothers of Achievement in American History, 1776–1976* (Rutland, Vt.: Charles E. Tuttle, 1976), 533; *California Intermountain News*, 21 August 1969.
12. *SLT*, 25 June 1975; *California Intermountain News*, 3 July 1975; Lott interview.

Chapter 17: Esther Rosenblatt Landa

1. School Records, Box 73, Esther Landa Papers, Special Collections, Marriott Library, U of U.
2. Interview with Esther Landa by Robert Goldberg, SLC, 7 November 1994.
3. Ibid.
4. Telephone conversation with Wendell Ashton, 18 December 1994.
5. Interview with Esther Landa by Suki Sandler, 20 April 1982, Box 73, Landa Papers; Landa interview by author.
6. Landa interview by author.
7. Linda Sillitoe, "Esther Landa: Diplomat at Home and Abroad," *DN*, 18 August 1985.
8. Sillitoe.
9. Landa interview by author.
10. "Resumé," Box 73, Landa Papers; Landa interview by author.
11. Landa interview by author.
12. Ibid.
13. "Resumé;" Landa interview by author.
14. Landa interview by author.

15.   "Resumé;" Landa interview by author.
16.   Sillitoe.
17.   "Resumé;" Landa interview by author.
18.   Landa interview by author; "Resumé."
19.   Landa interview by author.
20.   Press release, 23 June 1972, Box 74, Landa Papers.
21.   "Resumé;" biographical materials, Box 74, Landa Papers; Landa interview by author.
22.   Campaign materials, Box 74, Landa Papers.
23.   See Robert A. Goldberg, *Grassroots Resistance: Social Movements in Twentieth Century America* (Belmont, Calif.: Wadsworth Press, 1991), 193–98.
24.   Landa interview by author.
25.   *DN*, 27 April 1976; "Resumé," Box 73, Landa Papers.
26.   "Acceptance Speech," Box 75, Landa Papers; *Council Woman* 37 (March 1975).
27.   Copy of speech in Box 75, Landa Papers.
28.   Ibid.
29.   Landa interview by Sandler.
30.   Betty Friedan, "The Women at Houston," *New Republic*, 10 December 1977; report on the Utah State IWY meeting, Box 76, Landa Papers.
31.   Landa interview by author.
32.   Letty Cottin Pogrebin, *Deborah, Golda, and Me: Being Female and Jewish in America* (New York: Crown, 1991), 154.
33.   Ibid., 156, 160.
34.   Box 75, Landa Papers.
35.   Copy of speech, 18 September 1983, U of U, Box 75, Landa Papers.
36.   Copy of speech, 5 September 1987, Box 75, Landa Papers.
37.   Copy of speech, 2 April 1981, Hinckley Institute, U of U, Box 76, Landa Papers.
38.   Sillitoe, "Esther Landa."
39.   Landa interview by author.
40.   Ibid.
41.   "Private Lives," 22 December 1984, videotaped interview in the author's possession.

Chapter 18: Helen Zeese Papanikolas

1.   Helen Z. Papanikolas, "Growing Up Greek in Helper, Utah," *UHQ* 48 (summer 1980): 244–60 provides keen insights into the author's childhood. I have known Helen for twenty-five years during my tenure on the staff of the *UHQ*. We have had many long conversations about history and literature. Some unattributed quotes in this article are from personal knowledge and remembered conversations. I have tried to mention Helen's major works, but the notes do not contain an exhaustive

bibliography. Focussing on her historical and literary work, I have neglected to mention all the hours she devoted to organizations such as the Children's Service Society, the U of U Library, the USHS (first on the advisory board of editors and later on the board of state history), the Utah Endowment for the Humanities, and church groups. Details of her married life have been minimized in order to focus on her achievements as a writer. She was and is a doting mother and grandmother, cooking special, time-consuming Greek foods for them and producing a beautiful hand-made quilt for each grandchild. I do not consider this brief biography more than a beginning. Hundreds of family, friends, and colleagues need to be interviewed, and, more importantly, she needs to be interviewed at great length to extract from her those telling details she so deftly drew from her parents and hundreds of others.

2. The Zeeses had four daughters: Josephine, Helen, Demetra, and Sophie. A brief biography of George Zeese is found in Wain Sutton, ed., *Utah — A Centennial History* (New York: Lewis Historical Publishing, 1949), 3:207–8. More significant is Helen Z. Papanikolas, *Emily-George* (SLC: U of U Press, 1987).

3. Papanikolas, "Growing Up Greek," 248.

4. Ibid., 249–50.

5. Ibid., 250.

6. Ibid., 251.

7. Ibid.

8. Ibid., 252–53.

9. Ibid., 254.

10. Ibid, 255.

11. Ibid., 255–57.

12. Ibid.

13. Ibid., 257–59.

14. Ibid., 260.

15. Ibid.

16. Papanikolas, *Emily-George*, 45–46, 48.

17. See the University of Utah yearbook, *Utonian*, for the years mentioned.

18. Papanikolas, *Emily-George*, 49–50.

19. Helen Zeese Papanikolas, "The Fortress and the Prison," *Utah Humanities Review* 1 (April 1947): 134–46. Later the journal's name was changed to *Western Humanities Review* to reflect an expanded regional audience.

20. UHQ, Vol. 22, 143–64.

21. UHQ, Vol. 33, 289–315.

22. Page 204. Morgan's monograph *The State of Deseret* was issued as numbers 2, 3, 4 of vol. 8 in 1940. Other complete works published as single issues or volumes of the *UHQ* have been by deceased authors or are edited journals or single-subject, multiauthor works.

23. Helen Zeese Papanikolas, "Magerou, the Greek Midwife," *UHQ* 38 (winter 1970):

50–60, was published in an issue devoted to Utah women that was guest edited by Leonard J. Arrington. See also "Greek Folklore of Carbon County," in *Lore of Faith and Folly*, ed. Thomas E. Cheney (SLC: U of U Press, 1971), 61–77. The third article, "Unionism, Communism, and the Great Depression: The Carbon County Coal Strike of 1933," published in *UHQ* 41 (summer 1973): 254–300, remains remarkable for the sense of immediacy the author was able to create through the use of extensive interviews with participants in the strike. No one who has read it can ever forget the towering figures of the Yugoslav women who marched with their men and even used their bodies to form a shield around the sheriff and escort him to safety.

24.   Among the younger scholars influenced in some way by Helen's work are Philip F. Notarianni, Allan Kent Powell, Ronald G. Coleman, Joseph Stipanovich, Vicente V. Mayer, and Nancy J. Taniguchi.

25.   *Peoples* was published by USHS.

26.   p. x.

27.   See "Wrestling with Death: Greek Immigrant Funeral Customs in Utah," *UHQ* 52 (winter 1984); "Bootlegging in Zion: Making and Selling the 'Good Stuff'," *UHQ* 53 (summer 1985); "Immigrants, Minorities, and the Great War," *UHQ* 58 (fall 1990); and "Ethnicity in Mormondom: A Comparison of Immigrant and Mormon Cultures," in *"Soul-Butter and Hog Wash" and Other Essays on the American West*, ed. Thomas G. Alexander, Charles Redd Monographs in Western History, no. 8 (Provo, Utah: BYU Press, 1978).

28.   Alexander, 91.

29.   The book was published by Swallow Press, a division of Ohio University Press. The review cited is found on page 25 of the press's spring 1995 catalog, quoting *The Greek American*.

Bibliography

Note: While the headquarters of the Family History Library of the Church of Jesus Christ of Latter-day Saints is in Salt Lake City, Utah, all materials in its collection are available at branches world-wide; consequently, no location is given in individual entries in this bibliography.

Abbott, Delila M. "Women Legislators of Utah, 1896–1976." Typescript copy. Utah State Historical Society. Salt Lake City.

Abstracts of Titles. Recorders Office, Salt Lake County, Utah.

"Actress Testifies in Bransford Case." *Salt Lake Tribune*, 19 October 1918.

Adams, Kellene Ricks. "The Incomparable Maude Adams Somewhere in Time." *Pioneer Magazine* (January/February 1994).

Address at the Tenth Anniversary of the First Presbyterian Church of Salt Lake City. 13 November 1882. Salt Lake City: Utah Printing Company, 1882.

"Albion Emery." *Tullidge's Quarterly Magazine* (1902). Utah State Historical Society. Salt Lake City.

Alcott, May. *Studying Art Abroad and How to Do It Cheaply*. Boston, 1879.

Alexander, Thomas G. "Cooperation, Conflict, and Compromise: Women, Men, and the Environment in Salt Lake City, 1890–1930." *Brigham Young University Studies* 35 (January 1995).

———, ed. *"Soul-Butter and Hog Wash" and Other Essays on the American West*. Provo, Utah: Brigham Young University Press, 1978.

Alter, J. Cecil. *Early Utah Journalism*. Salt Lake City: Utah State Historical Society, 1938.

American Mothers Committee, Inc., comp. *Mothers of Achievement in American History, 1776–1976*. Rutland, Vt.: Charles E. Tuttle, 1976.

"America's 'Silver Queen' Passes Through Adelaide." *Salt Lake Tribune*, 25 August 1930.

Anderson, Sister M. Augusta. Letters. Archives, St. Mary's. Notre Dame, Indiana.

Arrington, Harriet Horne. "Alice Merrill Horne: Art Promoter and Early Utah Legislator." *Utah Historical Quarterly* 58 (summer 1990).

Arrington, Leonard J. *Great Basin Kingdom: An Economic History of the Latter-day Saints 1850–1900*. Cambridge: Harvard University Press, 1958.

Averett, Walter R. *Directory of Southern Nevada Place Names*. Rev. ed. Las Vegas, 1962.

Babcock, Maud May. Collection MS83. Special Collections, Marriott Library, University of Utah. Salt Lake City.

————. *Handbook for Teachers of Interpretation: A Textbook for Teachers and for Prospective Teachers of Oral Expression in High Schools and Colleges*. Lincoln, N. Y.: University Publishing Company, 1930.

————. *Interpretive Selections for Colleges, Each with a Basic Purpose*. Chicago: University Publishing Company, 1930.

————. *Interpretive Selections for High Schools: An Aim for Every Selection, Every Selection with an Aim*. Chicago: University Publishing Company, 1930.

————. "The New Movement in the Theatre." *Young Women's Journal* 29 (1918).

————. *Pedagogy of Interpretation: A Textbook for Teachers and Prospective Teachers of Oral Expression in High Schools and Colleges*. N.p., 1930.

————. *Studies in Dialect*. Salt Lake City: University of Utah Press, 1916.

Bancroft, Hubert Howe. *History of Nevada, Colorado, and Wyoming, 1540–1888*. San Francisco, 1890.

Barnhart, Jacqueline Baker. *The Fair But Frail: Prostitution in San Francisco 1849–1900*. Reno: University of Nevada, 1986.

Baskin, R. N. *Reminiscences of Early Utah*. Salt Lake City, 1904.

Beadle, J. H. *Polygamy; Or, The Mysteries and Crimes of Mormonism. . . .* Philadelphia, 1882.

Beasley, W. G. *The Meiji Restoration*. Stanford, Calif.: Stanford University Press, 1972.

Beaux, Cecilia. *Background with Figures*. Boston: Houghton Mifflin, 1939.

Bernstein, G. L., ed. *Recreating Japanese Women, 1600–1945*. Berkeley: University of California Press, 1991.

Biographical Records of Salt Lake City and Vicinity. Chicago: National Historic Record Company, 1902.

Birmingham, Stephen. *America's Secret Aristocracy*. Boston: Little Brown, 1987.

Blair, Everett. *This Will Be an Empire*. New York: Pagent Press, 1959.

Blair, Karen J. *The Clubwoman as Feminist: True Womanhood Redefined, 1868–1914*. New York: Holmes & Meier, 1980.

Bletter, Diana, and Lori Grinker. *The Invisible Thread: A Portrait of American Jewish Women*. New York: Jewish Publication Society, 1989.

Bluemel, Elinor. *One Hundred Years of Colorado Women*. N.p., 1973.

Blue Tea Minutes, 1876–1885. Special Collections, Marriott Library, University of Utah. Salt Lake City.

Books of the Dead. Salt Lake City Cemetery.

Bradley, Martha S. "Mary Teasdel: Yet Another American in Paris." *Utah Historical Quarterly* 58 (summer 1990).

"Bransford Adds to Testimony." *Salt Lake Tribune*, 15 October 1918.

Bransford Family Bible in possession of Dr. Harold Lamb. Salt Lake City, Utah.

Bransford File. Plumas County Museum. Quincy, California.

"Bransford Takes Stand in Court." *Salt Lake Tribune*, 11 October 1918.

"Bransford Wins Suit for Estate." *Salt Lake Tribune*, 26 January 1919.

Brigham Young University. "Alice Merrill Horne." *Dedication of Buildings*. Provo, Utah, 1954.

Bringhurst, Newell G. *Saints, Slaves and Blacks: The Changing Place of Black People Within Mormonism*. Westport, Conn.: Greenwood Press, 1981.

Brooks, Juanita. *The History of the Jews in Utah and Idaho*. Salt Lake City, 1973.

"Brother Albion B. Emery." *Proceedings of the Grand Lodge of Utah 1895*. Salt Lake City: Utah Masonic Lodge.

Brown, Dee. *Bury My Heart At Wounded Knee*. New York: Holt, Reinhart and Winston, 1971.

Brown, Robert L. *Colorado Ghost Towns — Past and Present*. Caldwell, Idaho: Caxton Printers, 1972.

Bryant, William Cullen, ed. *A Family Library of Poetry and Song*. . . . 2 vols. New York, 1878.

Bureau of the Census. *Federal Census Schedules*. San Jose First Ward, Santa Clara County, California, 1870. Microfilm copy. LDS Family History Library.

———. Salt Lake County. 1820, 1840, 1850, 1870, 1880, 1890, 1910, 1920, 1950. Microfilm Copy. LDS Family History Library and Utah State Historical Society. Salt Lake City.

———. Summit County, Utah. 1910, 1920. Microfilm copy. LDS Family History Library.

Burgess, Thomas. *Greeks in America*. Boston: Sherman, French, 1913.

Bush, Lester E., Jr. "Mormonism's Negro Doctrine: An Historical Overview." *Dialogue* 7 (spring 1973).

Butler, Anne. *Daughters of Joy, Sisters of Misery: Prostitutes in the American West 1865–1869*. Urbana: University of Illinois Press, 1985.

Cable, Mary. *Top Drawer American High Society from the Gilded Age to the Roaring Twenties*. Hanover: McClelland & Stewart, 1984.

California Life, 21 Oct. 1922 and 21 March 1925.

"The Calisthenic Exhibition at the Theater Last Evening." *Salt Lake Tribune*, 24 May 1893.

Cannon, Angus M. *Letterpress Copybooks*. Salt Lake City: LDS Church Historical Department.

Carmichael, Sarah E. *Poems*. San Francisco, 1866.

Carter, Kate B., comp. *Heart Throbs of the West*. Vol. 11. Salt Lake City, 1950.

———. *Our Pioneer Heritage*. Vol. 2. Salt Lake City, 1959.

———. *The Story of the Negro Pioneer*. Salt Lake City: Utah Printing Company for the Daughters of the Utah Pioneers, ca. 1965.

Centenary Chronicles of the Sisters of the Holy Cross. Vol. 5, *Our Western Province*. Privately printed, n.d.

Chamberlain, Ralph V. *The University of Utah: A History of Its First Hundred Years, 1850–1950.* Salt Lake City: University of Utah Press, 1960.

"Chambers vs. Emery." *Pacific Reporter* 45. Utah State Law Library. Salt Lake City.

Cheney, Thomas E., ed. *Lore of Faith and Folly.* Salt Lake City: University of Utah Press, 1971.

"Chipeta's Downfall." *The Denver Republican,* August 1887.

Clark, James R., ed. *Messages of the First Presidency.* Salt Lake City: Bookcraft, 1966.

"Col. Holmes, Once of Salt Lake, Dies East." *Salt Lake Tribune,* 2 October 1925.

Colt, George Howe. "Who Was Pocahontas?" *Life,* July 1995.

Conrad, Howard L., ed. *Encyclopedia of the History of Missouri.* Vol. 4. New York: Southern History Co., 1901.

Cooper, Sara. Will. Copy in possession of Judy Dykman.

Creighton, John C. *The History of Columbia and Boone County.* Columbia, Mo.: Computer Color-Graphics, 1987.

"Crossing the Plains." Unpublished history of the Bransford family trip to California, n.d. Copy in possession of Judy Dykman.

Dallas, Sandra. *Colorado Ghost Towns and Mining Camps.* Norman: University of Oklahoma Press, 1985.

Daughters of the Utah Pioneers. *Builders of Uintah, A Centennial History of Uintah County 1872 to 1947.* Springville, Utah: Art City Publishing, 1947.

"Death Claims Prominent Man." *Salt Lake Tribune,* 7 July 1910.

"Death Comes to Utah's 'Silver Queen.'" *Salt Lake Tribune,* 5 August 1942.

"Death of Honorable A. B. Emery." *Park Record,* 16 June 1894.

"Dedicated Its Home." *Salt Lake Tribune,* 8 Feburary 1898.

Denvir, Bernard, ed. *The Impressionists at First Hand.* London: Thames and Hudson, 1987.

Dorset, Phyllis Flanders. *The New Eldorado: The Story of Colorado's Gold and Silver Rushes.* New York: Macmillan, 1970.

"Drawing Hidden Fortune from Earth Finest Method, Avers 'Silver Queen.'" *Salt Lake Telegram,* 6 September 1932.

Dykman, Judy. "Utah's Silver Queen and the 'Era of the Great Splurge.'" *Utah Historical Quarterly* 64 (winter 1996).

Early Church Information File. LDS Family History Library.

Eighth Ward Relief Society Minute Books, 1867–77, 1879–85, 1882, 1892, 1894–1902, 1905–13; Record of Disbursements, 1908-11. LDS Family History Library.

"Eliza K. Royle." *Salt Lake Tribune,* 11 December 1910.

Emery-Holmes, Susanna file. Public Library. Pasadena, California.

Emery-Holmes, Susanna. Scrapbook. Utah State Historical Society. Salt Lake City.

Emigration. Vol. 1, 1831-1848. LDS Church Historical Department. Salt Lake City.

Emmitt, Robert. *The Last War Trail.* Norman: University of Oklahoma Press, 1954.

Engalitcheff, Susanna B. Death certificate. Department of Vital Statistics. Hartford, Connecticut.

Engar, Keith Maurice. "History of Dramatics at the University of Utah from Beginnings until June 1919." Master's thesis, University of Utah, 1948.

"Estate Left by Princess Set at $65,918." *Salt Lake Tribune*, 4 June 1943.

Fleisher, David. "The Midnight Angels." *The Lodestar* (summer 1979).

Fliedner, Colleen Adair. *Stories in Stone, Park City, Utah, Miners and Madams, Merchants and Murderers.* Cypress, Calif.: Flair Publishing, 1995.

"Florist Testifies in Will Contest." *Salt Lake Tribune*, 22 October 1918.

"For a Fortune." *Park Record*, 22 September 1894.

"Former Utahn Answers the Call." *Park Record*, 2 October 1925.

Foy, Leslie T. *The City Bountiful.* Bountiful, Utah: Horizon, 1975.

Frederickson, Ronald Quayle. "Maud May Babcock and the Department of Elocution at the University of Utah." Master's thesis, University of Utah, 1965.

Friedan, Betty. "The Women at Houston." *New Republic*, 10 December 1977.

Gates, Susa Young. Files. Relief Society General Board. LDS Church Historical Department. Salt Lake City.

————, ed. *Memorial to Elizabeth Claridge McCune, Missionary, Philanthropist, Architect.* Salt Lake City, 1924.

General Federation of Women's Clubs. *Proceedings of the Fourth Biennial Conference of the General Federation, June 21–27, 1898.* New York: General Federation of Women's Clubs, 1899.

Gentry, North Todd. *Bench and Bar of Boone County Missouri.* Columbia, Mo.: the author, 1916.

Gilfoyle, Timothy J. *City of Eros: New York City, Prostitution and the Commercialization of Sex, 1790–1920.* New York: W. W. Norton, 1992.

Godfrey, Margaret. "The Silver Queen." *Salt Lake City*, September-October 1993.

Goldberg, Robert A. *Back to the Soil: The Jewish Farmers of Clarion, Utah, and Their World.* Salt Lake City: University of Utah Press, 1986.

————. *Barry Goldwater.* New Haven, Conn.: Yale University Press, 1995.

————. *Grassroots Resistance: Social Movements in Twentieth Century America.* Belmont, Calif.: Wadsworth Press, 1991.

————. *Hooded Empire: The Ku Klux Klan in Colorado.* Urbana: University of Illinois, 1981.

Greer, Germaine. *The Obstacle Race.* New York: Farrar Straus Giroux, 1979.

Hafen, John. "Art Student in Paris." *Contributor* 15 (1893-94).

Hamilton, Patricia A. *Health Care Consumerism.* St. Louis: C.V. Mosby, 1982.

Harwood, James Taylor. *A Basket of Chips: An Autobiography by James Taylor Harwood.* Salt Lake City: Tanner Trust Fund, University of Utah Library, 1985.

Haseltine, James. *100 Years of Utah Art.* Salt Lake City: Salt Lake Art Center, 1965.

Heinerman, Joseph. "Brigham Young's Grandest Residence, Amelia's Palace." *Montana, the Magazine of Western History* (winter 1979).

Herold, Martine. *The Academie Julian Is One Hundred Years Old.* N.d.

Hirshon, Stanley P. *The Lion of the Lord: A Biography of Brigham Young.* New York: Knopf, 1969.

Historical Record, 1856-75. Salt Lake City: LDS Church Historical Department.

History of the Bench and Bar of Utah. Salt Lake City: Interstate Press Association, 1913.

Holloway, John. "A Famous Squaw." *The Colorado Graphic* 3, 4 (24 September 1887). Typescript copy. Colorado State Historical Society. Denver.

"Honorable A. B. Emery." *Park Record*, 16 June 1894.

Horne, Alice Merrill. "Child of the Frontier." Unpublished autobiography in possession of Harriet Horne Arrington. Salt Lake City.

————. *Devotees and Their Shrines: A Handbook of Utah Art.* Salt Lake City: Deseret News, 1914.

————. "What Utah Offers the Artists." *The Utah*, August 1936.

House Journal of the Third Session of the Legislature of Utah. Salt Lake City: Tribune Job Printing, 1899.

Huber, Christine Jones. *The Pennsylvania Academy and Its Women.* Philadelphia: Pennsylvania Academy of the Fine Arts, 1973.

"Husband Weeps As He Testifies in Trial." *Deseret News*, 15 October 1918.

Jacob, Kathryn A. "High Society in Washington during the Gilded Age: Three Distinct Aristocracies." Ph.D. diss., Johns Hopkins University, 1986.

Jakeman, Ellen L. "Sarah Elizabeth Carmichael Williamson." *Relief Society Magazine* 15 (September 1928).

James, Jane Elizabeth. "Life Sketch of Jane Elizabeth Manning James." LDS Church Historical Department. Salt Lake City.

————. "A Reminiscence of Joseph Smith." *Dialogue* 5 (summer 1970).

Jenson, Andrew. *Encyclopedic History of the Church of Jesus Christ of Latter-day Saints.* Salt Lake City: Deseret News Publishing Company, 1941.

Jeppson, Zorah H. "A Brief Biography of Alice Merrill Horne by Her Daughter." Unpublished manuscript.

"John Bransford," *Salt Lake Tribune*, 24 May 1941.

Journal History. Manuscript. LDS Church Archives. Salt Lake City.

"A Journey through Time . . . Park City Museum Tour." Park City Historical Society and Museum, 1994.

Kenner, S. A. *Utah As It Is.* Salt Lake City: Deseret News, 1904.

Kirkham, Francis W., and Harold Lundstrom, eds. *Tales of a Triumphant People: A History of Salt Lake County, Utah, 1847–1900.* Salt Lake City, 1947.

Kiskadden, Annie Adams. "The Life Story of Maude." *Green Book Magazine*, June 1914.

————. "The Sweetest Story Ever Told." *Green Book Magazine*, September 1914.

"The Ladies Literary Club-Home Formally Opened." *Salt Lake Tribune*, 8 January 1898.

Ladies Literary Club Minutes. Ladies Literary Club. Salt Lake City.

Lafayette County, Missouri. Marriage Record, Book D, 297. LDS Family History Library.

Landa, Esther. Papers. Special Collections, Marriott Library, University of Utah. Salt Lake City.

Lester, Margaret. *Brigham Street.* Salt Lake City: Utah Historical Society, 1979.

Litwack, Leon F. *North of Slavery.* Chicago: University of Chicago Press, 1961.

Lowes, John Livingston. *The Road to Xanadu*. Boston: Houghton Mifflin, 1964.

Lyman, June, and Norma Denver, comp. *Ute People: an Historical Study*. Ed. Floyd A. O'Neil and John Sylvester. Salt Lake City: University of Utah Press, 1970.

Lythgoe, Dennis L. "Negro Slavery and Mormon Doctrine." *Western Humanities Review* 21 (autumn 1967).

Maag, Margaret Judy. "Discrimination against the Negro and Insitituional Efforts to Eliminate It." Master's thesis, University of Utah, 1970.

Malmquist, O. N. *The First One Hundred Years: A Story of the Salt Lake Tribune*. Salt Lake City: Utah State Historical Society, 1971.

Marcus, Jacob Rader. *The American Jewish Woman, 1654-1980*. New York, 1981.

McCage, Linda Rose. "Mme. Bougereau, Pathfinder." *New York Times Book Review and Magazine*, 19 February 1922.

McCune, George M. *Matthew McCune Family History*. Vol. 2AB. Salt Lake City: McCune Family Association, 1993.

Melville, James K. "The Mormon Drama and Maude Adams." Provo, Utah: BYU Press for Extension Publications, Division of Continuing Education, 1965.

"Men and Events Linked with Great Mines of Park City." *Park Record*, 5 June 1931.

Merrill, Clarence. "History of Albert Merrill with Some Information and Dates of His Ancestors. . . ." LDS Church Historical Department. Salt Lake City.

"Milford Bransford Deceased." *Plumas (California) Independent*, 26 May 1894.

"Milford Bransford." *Park Record*, 25 May 1894.

Minutes of the meetings of the Council of the Sisters of the Holy Cross. Archives, St. Mary's. Notre Dame, Ind.

Mooney, Bernice Maher. *The Salt of the Earth: The History of the Catholic Church in Utah, 1776-1987*. Salt Lake City: The Catholic Diocese of Salt Lake City, 1987.

"Mrs. Bransford Dies in California." *Salt Lake Tribune*, 25 October 1917.

"Mrs. Eliza Kirtley Royle." *Deseret News*, 10 March 1900.

"Mrs. Emery-Holmes Is Bride of Physician at 71." *Salt Lake Telegram*, 19 July 1930.

"Mrs. Emery-Holmes Public Reply to Hughes Supporters." *Salt Lake Tribune*, 9 September 1916.

"Mrs. Holmes Again on Witness Stand." *Salt Lake Tribune*, 4 October 1918.

"Mrs. Holmes Loses Suit Against Bransford." *Deseret Evening News*, 25 January 1919.

"Mrs. Holmes May Finish Case Today." *Salt Lake Tribune*, 30 October 1918.

"Mrs. Holmes Sues Bransford for $400,000." *Salt Lake Tribune*, 21 January 1918.

"Mrs. Holmes Takes Stand As Witness." *Salt Lake Tribune*, 3 October 1918.

"Mrs. Holmes Tells Story of Adoption of Foster Daughter." *Deseret News*, 2 October 1918.

Mulder, William T. "The Mormons in American History." Reynolds Lecture. Salt Lake City: University of Utah, 15 January 1957.

Mulvay, Jill C. "Three Mormon Women in the Cultural Arts." *Sunstone* 1 (spring 1976).

Murphy, Miriam B. "Sarah Elizabeth Carmichael: Poetic Genius of Pioneer Utah." *Utah Historical Quarterly* 43 (winter 1975).

Murray, Vadney. Brief biography of John Bransford. Copy in possession of Judy Dykman.

Salt Lake City.

Newbold, Noal C., and Bea Kummer. *Silver and Snow: The Story of Park City*. Salt Lake City: Parliament Publishing, 1968.

"New Clubhouse Is Opened—Handsome Chair Presented." *Salt Lake Tribune*, 26 April 1913.

Nixon, Elizabeth. "The Meeker Massacre." Master's thesis, Colorado State College of Education, 1935.

Nochin, Linda. *Women Artists 1550–1950*. New York: Knopf, 1976.

Noel, Thomas J., Paul F. Mahoney, and Richard E. Stevens. *Historical Atlas of Colorado*. Norman: University of Oklahoma, 1994.

Nowlan, Sister M. Emerentiana. Unpublished chronicles. Archives, St. Mary's. Notre Dame, Ind.

"Now the Romantic 'Silver Queen'—Aged 75—May Ditch Her Russian Prince to Marry a Boy." *San Francisco Chronicle*, 10 February 1935.

Oikonomidou, Maria S. *Oi Ellines tis Amerikis Opos Tous Eida [The Greeks in America as I Saw Them]*. New York: C. C. Divry, 1916.

Olpin, Robert S. *Dictionary of Utah Art*. Salt Lake City: Salt Lake Art Center, 1980.

Olsen, Vicky Burgess, ed. *Sister Saints*. Provo, Utah: Brigham Young University Press, 1978.

"One Time Counsul of Czarist Russia in Chicago—Was Officer in Imperial Army." *New York Times*, 28 March 1935.

Orton, Richard H., comp. *Records of California Men in the War of the Rebellion, 1861 to 1867*. Sacramento, 1890.

Pace, Josephine. "Kimberly As I Remember Her." *Utah Historical Quarterly* 35 (1967).

Papanikolas, Helen Z. *Emily-George*. Salt Lake City: University of Utah Press, 1987.

———. "The Fortress and the Prison." *Utah Humanities Review* 1 (April 1947).

———. "Growing Up Greek in Helper, Utah." *Utah Historical Quarterly* 48 (summer 1980).

———. "Magerou, the Greek Midwife." *Utah Historical Quarterly* 38 (winter 1970).

———, ed. *The Peoples of Utah*. Salt Lake City: Utah State Historical Society, 1976.

———. *Small Bird, Tell Me*. Athens: Ohio University Press, 1993.

———. "Unionism, Communism, and the Great Depression: The Carbon County Coal Strike of 1933." *Utah Historical Quarterly* 41 (summer 1973).

Parsons, Katherine Barrette. *History of Fifty Years: Ladies Literary Club, Salt Lake City, Utah, 1877–1927*. Salt Lake City: Arrow Press, 1927.

"Passing of Martha Royle, Former Utah Singer." *Salt Lake Tribune*, 2 June 1942.

Patriarchial Blessing File, LDS Family History Library.

Patterson, Ada. *Maude Adams: A Biography*. New York: Meyer Bros., 1907.

"Patty Sessions." *Woman's Exponent* 13, nos. 7, 8, 11, 12, 17, 19; 14, nos. 1, 12 (1884–85). LDS Church Historical Department. Salt Lake City.

"Personal Mention." *Park Record*, 15 November 1884.

Poems, Religious, Historical, and Political. Vol. 2. Salt Lake City, 1877.

Pogrebin, Letty Cottin. *Deborah, Golda, and Me: Being Female and Jewish in America.* New York: Crown, 1991.

Polk Directory for Salt Lake City, 1894.

Price, Raye. "Utah's Leading Ladies of the Arts." *Utah Historical Quarterly* 38 (winter 1970).

Priest, Ivy Baker. *Green Grows Ivy.* New York: McGraw Hill, 1958.

"Prince & Wife Decide to 'Make Up.'" *New York Times*, 26 August 1915.

"Private Lives." Video taped interview with Esther Landa, 22 December 1984. In the possession of Robert A. Goldberg. Salt Lake City.

Probate Case Files, Third District Court for Salt Lake County. Utah State Archives. Salt Lake City.

Probate records. Kane County, Illinois.

Probate records. Los Angeles County Records. Los Angeles.

Probate records. Summit County Records. Coalville, Utah.

"Receives Title to Millions." *Salt Lake Tribune*, 20 month unknown 1930.

"Record of Orders, Returns and Courts Martial &c. of 2nd Brigade, 1st Division, Nauvoo Legion." Typescript copy. LDS Family History Library.

Records of Members. LDS Family History Library.

Revolutionary War Pension and Bounty-land Application Film, National Archives Microcopy 804, roll 2411.

Reynolds, Katherine. *Park City.* Park City: Weller Insititute for Care of Design, 1984.

Richards, Louisa L. Greene. "Memories of Miss Carmichael's Writings." *Young Woman's Journal* 13 (January 1902).

Richardson, Albert D. *Beyond the Mississippi.* . . . Hartford, Conn., 1867.

Ringholz, Raye C. *Diggings and Doings in Park City.* Park City: the author, 1983.

———. "The Giddy Girls of Deer Valley Gulch." *Park City.* Ogden, Utah: Meridian International, 1993.

Robbins, Phyllis. *Maude Adams: An Intimate Portrait.* New York: G. P. Putnam's Sons, 1956.

———. *The Young Maude Adams.* Francestown, N. H.: Marshall Jones, 1959.

Roberts, Brigham H. *A Comprehensive History of the Church of Jesus Christ of Latter-day Saints. Century 1.* Salt Lake City: Church of Jesus Christ of Latter-day Saints, 1930.

———. ed. *History of the Church of Jesus Christ of Latter-day Saints.* Salt Lake City, 1902–32.

Rogers, Fred B. *Soldiers of the Overland.* San Francisco, 1938.

Rogers, Jane. "Rogers Family History." *Plumas Memories* 51 (June 1986).

"Romantic History Adds Glamour to Eleventh Showcase Design." *Pasadena Star*, 17 April 1975.

Root, Mary M. "Pioneer Poet of Utah: Study of the Life and Work of Sarah Carmichael, One of the State's First Literary Producers." *Salt Lake Tribune*, 16 February and 8 March 1936.

Royle, Eliza Kirtley. "The Ladies' Literary Club of Salt Lake City." In *Manual of Ladies*

Literary Club of Salt Lake City for the Columbian Exposition. Salt Lake City: Ladies Literary Club, 1893.

Royle, Eliza Kirtley, and Mary Simpson Turner. *A Memorial of Sinclair Kirtley and His Family by his daughters Mary Simpson Turner and Eliza Kirtley Royle.* N.p., 1909.

Saloutos, Theodore. *The Greeks in the United States.* Cambridge, Mass.: Harvard University Press, 1964.

Salt Lake City Assessment Rolls. Salt Lake County Recorders Office.

Salt Lake City Death Records, Book F-1910, 172. LDS Family History Library.

Salt Lake City Directory, 1869, 1889. New York: U. S. Directory Publishing Co.

Salt Lake City Directory, 1891–92, 1893, 1894–95. Salt Lake City: R. J. Polk and Company.

Salt Lake City, Sanborne Maps, 1894. Utah State Historical Society. Salt Lake City.

Schneider, Susan Weidman. *Jewish and Female: Choices and Changes in Our Lives Today.* New York: Simon & Schuster, 1984.

Scott, Patricia Lyn. "Firm in Our Endeavor: The Ladies Literary Club, 1877 to 1927." Unpublished paper presented at the Utah Women's History Association Annual Meeting, Salt Lake City, 12 March 1983.

―――. "The Gentile Roots of the Salt Lake City Public Library, 1866-1898." Unpublished paper presented at the Mormon History Association conference, Provo, Utah, May 1984.

Seagraves, Anne. *Women Who Charmed the West.* Hayden: Idaho: Wesanne Publications, 1991.

Selby, Catherine Hazel. "Sarah Elizabeth Carmichael." Master's thesis, University of Utah, 1921.

Sessions, Patty Bartlett. Diaries and Account Book. Access no. 18362-ARCH-88. LDS Church Archives. Salt Lake City.

Sessions, Perrigrine. Reminiscences and Diaries, 1839–1886. Access no. 35927-ARCH-88. LDS Church Archives. Salt Lake City.

Sherrill, Culver. *Crimes without Punishment and Other Stories.* Hicksville, New York: Exposition Press, 1977.

Shiver, John A. *Bransford Family History.* Kentucky: McDowell, 1981.

Showcase of Interior Design, Notes on El Roble Residence. Pasadena, California: Pasadena Junior Philharmonic Committee. N.d.

Sillitoe, Linda. "Esther Landa: Diplomat at Home and Abroad." *Deseret News,* 18 August 1985.

" 'Silver Queen' of Utah Closes Famed Career." *Park Record,* 6 August 1942.

" 'Silver Queen' Seeks Divorce" *Salt Lake Telegram,* 1 November 1932.

" 'Silver Queen' Wills Millions to Manager of Estate." *Salt Lake Tribune,* 26 August 1942.

Sloan, E. L., comp. *Gazeteer of Utah and Salt Lake City Directory.* Salt Lake City, 1874.

―――. *Salt Lake City Directory and Business Guide for Salt Lake City, 1869.* Salt Lake City.

Sloan, Robert W., ed. *Utah Gazetteer and Dictionary, 1884.* Salt Lake City: Herald Printing and Publishing Company.

Smith, David. *Ouray Chief of the Utes*. Ouray, Colo.: Wayfinder Press, 1986.

Smith, George Albert. Papers. Special Collections, Marriott Library, University of Utah. Salt Lake City.

Smith, Joseph F. "Maud May Babcock." *Quarterly Journal of Speech* 41 (April 1955).

———. Papers. LDS Church Historical Department. Salt Lake City.

"Snap Shots [Scrapbook, 1924-27]." Ladies Literary Club. Salt Lake City.

Snow, Eliza. "Anthem." *Deseret News*, 12 March 1862.

Somers, Herman Miles, and Anne Ramsay Somers. *Doctors, Patients, and Health Insurance: The Organization and Financing of Medical Care*. Washington, D.C.: Brookings Institution, 1961.

"Spectators Barred from Bransford Hearing." *Deseret News*, 11 October 1918.

Sprague, Marshall. *Massacre: The Tragedy at White River*. Boston: Little, Brown, 1957.

Stavrianos, L. S. *The Balkans Since 1453*. New York: Holt, Rinehart, and Winston, 1966.

Stenhouse, Lorenzo, ed. *Utah Gazetteer and Directory, 1888*. N.p.

Stenhouse, T. B. H. *The Rocky Mountain Saints*. Salt Lake City, 1904.

Stovall, Mary E., and Carol Cornwall Madsen, eds. *A Heritage of Faith*. Salt Lake City: Deseret Book Company, 1988.

Summit County Court Records, Box "1915." Park City Public Library.

Sutton, Wain, ed. *Utah: A Centennial History*. 3 vols. New York: Lewis Historical Publishing, 1949.

Taggart, Stephen G. *Mormonism's Negro Policy: Social and Historical Origins*. Salt Lake City: University of Utah Press, 1970.

Tanner, Mary Jane Mount. Journal. Microfilm of holograph. LDS Church Archives. Salt Lake City.

Tax Records, 1879–86, Plumas County, California.

Taylor, John. Papers. LDS Church Historical Department. Salt Lake City.

Taylor, Joseph E. Papers. LDS Church Historical Department. Salt Lake City.

Teasdel, Mary. "True Art." *Young Woman's Journal*, January 1904.

Teichert, Minerva K. Remarks at the Funeral of Alice Merrill Horne, 10 October 1948. Typescript.

Terasawa, Kuniko. "Namida no Naka ni Hiso no Kakugo" ("Among the Tears a Valiant Determination"). Trans. Haruko T. Moriyasu. *The Utah Nippo*, 5 May 1939.

Thomas, Kate. "Ina Coolbrith." *Relief Society Magazine* 15 (November 1928).

Thompson, George A., and Fraser Buck. *Treasure Mountain Home: Park City Revisited*. Salt Lake City: Dream Garden Press, 1981.

Traughber, Ora Leigh. "Reawakened Memoirs in the Annals of Salt Lake Clubdom," *Deseret News*, 24 April 1926, clipping file, Salt Lake City Public Library.

Tullidge, Edward W. "Carmichael," *Western Galaxy* 1 (May 1888).

———. *History of Salt Lake City*. Salt Lake City, 1886.

"The University Dramatic Club." *The Utah Chronicle*, 14 December 1897.

Utah, Her Cities, Towns and Resources. Chicago: Manly and Litteral, 1891.

"UTAH: Salt Lake City" Box. Archives, St. Mary's. Notre Dame, Ind.

"Utah 'Silver Queen' Plans Visit Here." Unidentified Salt Lake newspaper, 6 October 1930.

"Utah 'Silver Queen,' 74, Weds 60 Year Old Prince." *Salt Lake Tribune*, 20 October 1933.

"Utah's Own Silver Queen Arrives for Summer Visit in S.L.C." *Salt Lake Tribune*, 12 May 1938.

"Utah Woman Wed in Paris to Physician." *Salt Lake Tribune*, 20 July 1930.

Van Hoosear, David Hermon. "Annals of Wilton." *Wilton (Connecticut) Bulletin*, 23 March 1939.

Van Wagenen, Lola. "Sister Wives and Suffragists: Polygamy and the Politics of Woman Suffrage in Territorial Utah." Ph.D. diss., New York University, 1990.

Warner, Mrs. Vilate. Obituary. *Deseret Evening News*, 4 March 1897.

Weir, Hugh C. "Maude Adams." *Human Life*, December 1906.

Wells, Mildred White. *Unity in Diversity: The History of the General Federation of Women's Clubs*. Washington, D.C.: General Federation of Women's Clubs, 1953.

Wentworth, May. *Poetry of the Pacific: Selections and Original Poems from the Poets of the Pacific States*. San Francisco, 1867.

Werner, Fred H. *Meeker: The Story of the Meeker Massacre and Thornburgh Battle, September 29, 1879*. Greeley, Colo.: Werner Publications, 1985.

Widtsoe, Leah D. "The Story of a Gifted Lady." *Relief Society Magazine* 32 (March 1945).

Wolfinger, Henry J. "Jane Manning James: A Test of Faith." *Social Accommodation in Utah*. Ed. by Clark S. Knowlton. Salt Lake City: University of Utah, American West Center, 1975.

Wood, Mary I. *The History of the General Federation of Women's Clubs: For the First Twenty-two Years of its Organization*. New York: General Federation of Women's Clubs, 1912.

Woodruff, Wilford. Journals. LDS Church Historical Department. Salt Lake City.

Works Progress Administration. Biographical Sketches. Utah State Historical Society. Salt Lake City.

Young, John R. *Memoirs of John R. Young, Utah Pioneer, 1847*. Salt Lake City, 1920.

Young, Zina D. H. Papers. LDS Church Historical Department. Salt Lake City.

Zabriski, George Olin. "Compilation of the Black Population from the 1860 Federal Census for Utah." Subject file "Negroes." Utah State Historical Society. Salt Lake City.